Secularism in India: Concept and Practice

Secularism in India: Concept and Practice

Editors

Uday Mehta

Ram Puniyani

Foreword

Irfan Engineer

KALPAZ

ISBN: 978-93-5128-230-3

Price: ₹ 1150

First Published, 2017

Published by

Kalpaz Publications
C-30, Satyawati Nagar,
Delhi – 110052
E-mail: kalpaz@hotmail.com
Ph.: 9212142040

Printed at: G. Print Process, Delhi

Cataloging in Publication Data—DK
Courtesy: D.K. Agencies (P) Ltd. <docinfo@dkagencies.com>

Secularism in India : concept and practice / editors, Uday Mehta, Ram Puniyani.
pages cm
Contributed articles.
Includes bibliographical references.
ISBN 9789351282303

1. Secularism—India. 2. Religion and politics—India. I. Mehta, Uday, editor. II. Puniyani, Ram, editor.

BL2765.I5S43 2016 DDC 322.10954 23

Contents

Section - C

Globalisation and Challenges to Secularism

Section - D

Nehru and Practice of Indian Secularism

Dedication

We dedicate this book to the memory of Dr Asghar Ali Engineer, the founder Chairman of Centre for Study of Society and Secularism, the activist-scholar of highest calibre and express our gratitude to his role in shaping the work of CSSS and for laying the foundations for social interventions to preserve communal harmony, peace and justice in the society.

Acknowledgement

We sincerely thank the authors who have contributed to this volume. We are also thankful to Irfan Engineer, Neha Dabhade and Kumar for their valuable help in bringing out this volume. Some of the essays included in this volume are from Indian Journal of Secularism; we thank the journal for the same.

Editors

Professor Uday Mehta is sociologists with broad interdisciplinary background. He received his SSA and Ph. D. from TISS and Mumbai University respectively. He has made immense contribution to the field of sociology through many of his books, such as Agrarian Strategies in India, State Secularism and Religion: Western and Indian Experience (co-editor: Asghari Ali Engineer), and Modern God Men in India. He has also contributed articles in various anthologies movements like Housing Rights and Preservation of Secular Values in the country. His one of the most recent publication is Sectarianism Politics and Development.

Professor Ram Puniyani (Former Professor IIT Mumbai) is associated with various secular initiatives and has been part of various investigation reports on violation of human rights of minorities.

Has been part of **people's tribunals** which investigated the violation of rights of minorities in Orissa and Madhya Pradesh. Has written Communal Politics: Facts Versus Myths, Second Assassination of Gandhi, Deconstructing Terrorist Violence, Dalits Social Justice, and edited, Religion, Power and Violence, Mumbai: Post 27/11: Alternative Perspective, **Recipient of Indira Gandhi National Integration Awards 2006, National Communal Harmony Award 2007, Mukundan C. Menon Human Rights Award 2015.**

Authors

Professor Romila Thapar, one of the world's leading experts on the history of early India, is currently Professor Emeritus in History at Jawaharlal Nehru University, New Delhi. She was awarded the prestigious Kluge Award for Lifetime Achievement in the Study of Humanity in 2008. Her immense contribution to the study of early India has been internationally recognised, and she has received honorary degrees from universities across the world. She is the author of *Asoka and the Decline of the Mauryas (1961), A History of India (1966), Ancient Indian Social History: Some Interpretations (1978)* among many other of her well known works.

Dr Asghar Ali Engineer (10 March 1939 – 14 May 2013) was an Indian reformist- writer and social activist. Internationally known for his work on liberation theology in Islam, he led the Progressive Dawoodi Bohra movement. The focus of his work was on communalism and communal and ethnic violence in India and South Asia. Engineer also served as head of the Institute of Islamic Studies and the Centre for Study of Society and Secularism, both of which he founded in 1980 and 1993 respectively. He also made contributions to *The God Contention*, a website comparing and contrasting various worldviews. Engineer was given several awards during his lifetime, including the Communal Harmony Award in 1997 and the Right Livelihood Award in 2004 for his "strong commitment to promote values of co-existence and tolerance.

Rudolf C. Heredia

Rudolf C. Heredia, (Ph.D. University of Chicago, 1979), taught sociology at St. Xavier's College, Mumbai. At the Indian Social Institute, Delhi, he was director of research, editor of the institute's journal, *Social Action* and more recently a research fellow there. Among his more recent publications are: *Changing Gods: Rethinking Conversion in India*, Penguin, 2007; *Taking Sides, Reservations Quotas and Minority Rights in India*, Penguin, 2012. He has published in journals like the *Economic and Political Weekly*. He is now an independent researcher, based in Mumbai. At present he is working on collective violence in India.

Michel Boivin

Michel Boivin is a French historian and anthropologist who specialises in the Muslim world. Trained in contemporary history, Islamic studies and ethnology, he is currently Senior Research Fellow at the Centre national de la recherche scientifique (CNRS: French National Center for Scientific Research) and a member of the CEIAS (Center for South Asian Studies) at the School for Advanced Studies in the Social Sciences (EHESS). His works include "History and Anthropology of the Muslim Societies of South Asia" and "Authority and Politics in the Sufism of South and Central Asia." In addition, he contributes to the organisation of two CEIAS research groups: "Vernacular Cultures and New Muslim Elites," with Julien Levesque, and "Gujarati and Sindhi Studies: Societies, Languages and Cultures," with Pierre Lachaie

Dr Ashok S. Chousalkar

Dr Ashok Chousalkar (Born 1950) after obtaining his M.A. and Ph.D. Degree from University of Bombay in 1973 and 1979 respectively joined the Department of Politics, Shivaji University, Kolhapur as a lecturer. Dr Chousalkar has many articles and research papers to his credit in English and Marathi. His publications and researches are concerned with ancient Indian political thought, modern Indian political thoughts, comparative political theory and politics in Maharashtra. Recently, he completed a monograph on the concept of rebellion as enunciated in Kautilya's *Arthashastra* and Aristotle's *Politics.*

Dr Madhavi Yasin

A renowned Historian and Scholar, Author of Numerous Books on History, like EMERGENCE OF NATIONALISM, CONGRESS AND SEPARATISM, INDIA'S FOREIGN POLICY AND DUFFERIN YEARS, BRITISH PARAMOUNTCY IN KASHMIR. She was born in Lucknow where from she did her post graduation and later Ph.D. in History. She along with her Husband and reputed Historian Dr Mohd Yasin came to Kashmir in 1965. They established the Department of History in Kashmir University from a Scratch. Dr Yasin did some pioneering work and compiled some great Texts on History.

Justice H Suresh

Hosbet Suresh is a former judge of the Bombay High Court who has led a number of commissions that investigated violations of human rights. He obtained his L.L.M. from Bombay University. From 1967 to 1968 Suresh was Assistant Government Pleader in the Bombay City Civil and Sessions Court. On 29 November 1968 he was appointed a judge of the Bombay City Court and Additional Sessions Judge, Greater Bombay. On 12 June 1987 was appointed permanent Judge of the Bombay High Court. He retired from the High Court on 19 July 1991.

Rohini Hensman is a writer, researcher and activist working on feminism and women's rights, labour rights, minority rights, and the economic and political impact of globalisation. She has published books as well as numerous articles and book chapters on these issues, including *Workers, Unions, and Global Capitalism: Lessons from Bombay*. She has also written two political novels: *To Do Something Beautiful*, set in Bombay, and *Playing Lions and Tigers*, set in Sri Lanka.

Foreword

The debate regarding desirability of secularism and how it should be defined is not going to be concluded any soon. There many perspectives on secularism. These perspectives have been debated through ages, particularly since nineteenth century. In India, the term gained currency during the colonial period. On one hand the British government declared that they would not interfere in religious affairs of Indian subjects – a promise not honestly kept. On the other hand, the freedom movement mobilised the people with the vision of a democratic state that would not favour any religion. Religious idioms were freely employed to mobilise the people in the freedom movement. Staunch secularists feel using religious idiom to mobilise people compromised the ideals of secularism whereas pragmatic secularists feel that it would not have been possible to broad base the movement without employing such idioms and moreover, the principle of secularism – viz. religious identity of citizen being irrelevant for governance – was in any case not compromised. The term secularism was not deployed to signify being anti-religious or even irreligious in South Asia, but to signify that governance would not be based on the religion of the citizens. "Secularism" was not apposed against religion but against communal or cultural nationalism. Communal nationalists defined citizens based on culture and religion and wanted rights and privileges of citizens to be based on the religion they were born into.

The debates about secularism were carried into Constituent Assembly. The issue of contours of religious freedom of all persons; ban on cow slaughter; conversions; use of the term 'secularism' in the preamble of the Constitution; rights of religious denominations to establish and administer places for religious worship and undertake charitable activities; rights of minorities to establish and administer educational institutions; prohibition on spending tax payers money for promotion or maintenance of any particular religious denomination were intensely debated in the Constituent Assembly. The general sense was that the state would not be irreligious, but would imbibe reformatory zeal particularly pertaining to caste system within Hindus which included opening up public temples for entry of all Hindus, etc.; that the state would be an impartial umpire in conflicts between followers of two or more religious communities and that citizens would have freedom to profess, practice and even propagate their religion. The citizens were expected to respect all religions and live with "others" in spirit of harmony and the state would not permit hate speeches against followers of 'other' religions. The state would facilitate interreligious marriages by enacting Special Marriages Act. This was summed up as "*sarva dharma samabhav*".

The right wing religious and communal nationalists influenced the state to adopt practices and policies that were against the social contract as represented in the Constitution. The left and liberals criticised secularism as practiced in India. The anti-cow slaughter legislations and anti-conversion legislations in the 1960s, partial behaviour of the state in communal riots, the thrust of nationalism and school textbooks that uncritically represented the attitudes, values, culture and perspective of upper-caste from majority community are instances of the disproportionate influence right wing communal nationalists on the State. Dr B R Ambedkar's efforts to ensure equal rights and dignity to women were defeated and Hindu Code Bill was withdrawn.

The left and liberals on the other hand mounted criticism of secularism as practiced by the Indian state. They felt that the state was not irreligious enough. Going through the proceedings of a seminar on secularism in 1970s gives insights into the left and liberal view of secularism. The speakers in the seminar criticised the Indian State for using Hindu religious symbols freely in inaugural functions, allowing religious symbols to be installed in police stations and state transport buses, broadcasting religious bhajans through the state media like the All India Radio and Doordarshan. The left and liberals also demanded legislation of uniform civil code.

The Indian National Congress in 1970s used the slogan of secularism to rally the Muslim community politically behind it.

However, for the Congress led by Mrs Indira Gandhi (and later Rajiv Gandhi), secularism neither signified ensuring irreligious state, nor ensuring impartiality of state in mediation of conflicts between followers of different religious communities nor ensuring that citizens have freedom to profess, practice and propagate religion of their choice. The state was a silent spectator to idols of Lord Ram smuggled inside Babri Masjid. The state did not ensure that those who planned and executed communal violence were brought to justice. On the contrary, excessive force was used on minorities during communal violence who were actually victims of majority violence. The state did nothing to bring the guilty officials to the book. Minorities were discriminated in educational institutions, jobs and livelihoods, extending benefits of welfare schemes of the state and providing infrastructure like roads, water, electricity and schools in minority concentrated areas. This resulted in socio-economic and educational backwardness among minorities. Congress did not take any action against those who stigmatised the minorities to be anti-nationals, foreigners, agents of Pakistan working to ultimately overwhelm Hindu population in "their homeland". Later they were also stigmatised as terrorists and targeted by security forces. Christians were stigmatised as being on conversion spree.

Secularism to Congress signified that religious communities were free to follow their religion prescribed codes in matter of family laws pertaining to marriage, divorce, custody of children, inheritance, maintenance, adoption etc., even disregarding the Constitutional mandate of gender equality. The religious codes were determined by the conservative, orthodox and fundamentalist sections of the communities. Congress' secularism ensured hegemony of fundamentalists and conservative sections over the entire community on one hand and the fundamentalist-conservative sections would in return ensure political support of the community to the Congress.

Right wing Hindu nationalists sharply attacked the Congress's version of secularism as appeasement of minorities. They stood for forcible assimilation of minorities into Hindu nationalist identity and indeed in their schemes of all citizens of the country could only have one identity – nationalists and nationalism must draw from ancient Hindu upper caste traditions. They declared Hindus to be a nation from times immemorial. Minorities being allowed to follow their own separate family laws encouraged within them a separatist mentality. While the Hindu nationalists were silent on the backwardness of the minorities, they would oppose most insubstantial affirmative action to ensure that minorities would be at par with others as instance of pseudo-secularism. The concept of secularism of other regional parties which vied for political and electoral support of the Minorities too was much like Congress ensuring the number and intensity of communal violence was kept in check but did not ensure non-discrimination of minorities in education, jobs, livelihoods, and in distribution of other state largess. Minorities would have a choice on whom to trust more for their security – Congress or regional parties like the ones led by Mulayam Singh and Laloo Prasad in their respective states. Sadly, the ideological clarity of the leadership of the Parliamentary left parties on the issue of secularism did not translate into practice in the states where they were in power. Minorities were as backward and discriminated in left ruled state as in other states, although the left, like other regional parties was successful in preventing outbreaks of communal riots.

After the 1980s, the country went through a series of turmoils and communal violence. In the year 1986, the Apex Court held that divorced Muslim women were entitled to maintenance from her ex-husband under Criminal Procedure Code which was applicable to all irrespective of religion they followed. The Muslim leadership mobilised the community to demand a legislation to exclude divorced Muslim women from the applicability of S. 125 of Cr.P.C. from being entitled to maintenance as under the Muslim family code Muslim male was responsible for maintenance of divorced wife only during iddat period of four months when she could not re-marry. The Congress Party annulled the Supreme Court judgment in the Shahbano case to pacify the agitated Muslim fundamentalists. In response, the Hindu nationalists mobilised aggressively to assert their hegemony and demanded opening of the gates of Ramjanmabhoomi temple for *darshan* and worship of all Hindus inside the Babri Masjid. Their mobilisation was accompanied by series of communal violence in 1980s. In 1992, the Babri Masjid was demolished which led to major riots in Mumbai, Surat, and many other cities and towns in the country.

The debate around secularism changed after 1992. The anti-religion thrust of proponents of left liberal secularism toned down.

A section rejected all traditions on the ground that their source was religion and therefore unscientific. Some of them now started looking for liberative and egalitarian traditions to oppose orthodoxy and hegemonic traditions. The left liberals gave up the demand of Uniform Civil Code as they feared that the Hindu nationalists had gained considerable clout and would impose Hindu laws on the minorities rather than ensure gender just laws. A section of post-modernists attacked the concept of secularism as hegemonic and modern concept that was uncomfortable with religion in public space. Anti-secularists demanded that dichotomy of religion and public space be done away with and recover values of tolerance and traditions of living together with differences. They distinguished *religion as faith* that was inseparable part of community lives from *religion as ideology* that was used religion as an instrument of power and hegemony. While rejecting the latter, religion need not be discarded or banished from public space.

The cry for secularism became cry for pluralism, multiculturalism and inter-culturalism. Religious practices and traditions of subaltern classes were written about. The religio-cultural traditions of subaltern communities and their practices of living in harmony with nature and with other human beings were studied. Search began for religio-cultural traditions that could be part solution. Need for space in public arena for collective identities was felt.

Centre for Study of Society and Secularism (CSSS) established in 1993 by Dr Asghar Ali Engineer advocated for secularising the society, looked at nuanced role of religion in individual lives, society and its interrelation with the state. CSSS published many seminars on the issue and published journal initially called *"Towards Secular India"* which was later registered as *"Indian Journal of Secularism"*. The Journal was published in 1993 and many scholars and prominent national and international scholars contributed their research papers. The pages of the Journal are wealth of information on the issues of secularism, religion, sociological studies, religious conflicts, ethnic conflicts, gender issues etc. The editors of this volume have compiled some of the best articles on secularism published in IJS and also invited fresh articles to fill up some gaps that were identified by the editors. The result is this rich compilation which is before the readers now.

CSSS thanks the editors and the contributors to the volume without whose hard work the volume would not have seen the light of the day. CSSS also thanks Kalpaz Publications for agreeing to publish the book.

24-06-2016 **Irfan Engineer**

Introduction

I

Since Independence, even earlier Secularism has been a much debated word in India for various reasons. Some political streams have criticised this concept all through. More so since last three decades; since the time of Ram Temple movement; the term secularism has come under more sever attack. The debate on the issue keeps resurfacing and it did come up again when it was decided to start celebration of Constitution day on 26 November 2015.

On this occasion it was said that the perverse use of the term secularism is causing the social tensions. It was said that it is the most misused term in the country and this misuse is causing social tensions. It was reasserted that this term has Western roots and stands for separation between religion and state. In India, since India's religion itself is secular such a concept is not needed here.

Yet again it had come to fore when on the occasion of Republic day 2015 the words Secular and Socialist were dropped from the government advertisements. The facsimile of Indian Constitution's preamble which was used for advertisement did not have these words. When it was questioned how come these words are missing, which are part of the preamble, it was said that this is the 'original' Constitutions' preface. Officials retorted that Nehru and Ambedkar were no less secular; still these words were not put in the preamble of Constitution in 1950. At that time Nehru was Prime Minister and Ambedkar was the Chief of the drafting committee. Some political streams said that these words should be deleted for good as we are neither socialist nor secular. Some leaders bluntly stated that we are a Hindu nation so why these words should be there in the preamble of our Constitution.

Earlier to that in the aftermath of the 2014 elections Congress, Communist parties, Samajvadi and many other parties on the secular side, parites which can be called secular in some sense; bit the dust. In the review of defeat the major opposition party Congress, which has been in power for maximum number of years, planned a review of election results. One major opinion from its top leader came forth to say that the secularism practiced by Congress was seen more as an appeasement of minorities (read Muslims) and so the large sections turned against it emasculating the party to a mere 19 per cent votes with 44 seats in Lok Sabha. In a free for all; different opinions on secularism; and failure of Congress are coming forth.

BJP, another major electoral party, in response to the observations of Congress party stated that "We (BJP) have always said secularism should mean justice for all, appeasement of none, discrimination against none." Ironically this assertion, which negates the very concept of a democratic and secular society, has come to be perceived by many as 'the secularism'.

At the time of Independence critics went on to say that state is not curbing religious practices in official places and called it an erosion of secularism. What we see today in most public places, the pantheon of Hindu deities adorning the government offices and vehicles, and is passé' was criticised by many. Hindu practices like Bhumi Pujan (worshipping land) before construction of government buildings became part of 'normal practice'. Sarswati Puja, Surya Namaskar in some government outfits by now is becoming a matter of routine. When Nehru was asked by Andre Malraux about such religious practices going around, Nehru did confess that we have a secular constitution but the society is in the grip of religiosity. Nehru had refused to let India's first President Rajendra Prasad inaugurate Somnath Temple in official capacity. On the contrary today the Prime Minister performs Ganga Aarti as a part of the official programme. It has been a journey of sorts.

II

In Europe secularism begins with the rise of industrial society. It was the struggle of rising classes of Industrialists and modern educated sections against the kingdom and the organised Church. In India, due to prevalence of colonial society the beginning of secular values and practices has been very different. While in the Kingdoms the feudal lords were ruling in close alliance with religious clergy, the process of secularisation in India began with the coming of industrialisation and modern education during the British period. With the rise of newer classes, the industrialists, workers and modern educated classes, the concept of India, 'India as a nation in the making' started coming up. The kings and feudal lords, who were later joined in by a section of elite upper caste/educated section of society came up with communal outfits, Muslim League and Hindu Mahasabha-RSS. As such these sections were disturbed as now new power equations in society were emerging and their 'divine rights to rule' were under threat. They presented the new political situation as a threat to their religion while it was a threat to their social hierarchy. While the rising classes were all inclusive, incorporating people of all religions, the latter declining sections-communal formations were restricted to Muslims or Hindu elite respectively.

The rising classes were talking about secular democratic India while the communal organisations floated Religious nationalism i.e. Muslim Nationalism or Hindu Nationalism respectively and were opposed to secularism. They have been total obstacle to the process of secularisation. The triangle of British policy of divide and rule on one hand and Muslim and Hindu communalists on the other led to the formation of Pakistan in the name of Islam and 'India that is Bharat' on the basis of plural, secular values. Pakistan went through a painfully long trajectory where after the demise of Quaid-e-Azam Jinnah, a leader with secular soul in the communal body of Muslim League, led to the blunt and assertive upsurge of communalism, Islamic Fundamentalism, dominated by Mullahs and Military in the driving seat. It went through different ups and downs; its situation worsened by the US intervention which went on strengthening the communal elements there. Lately, the secular elements in Pakistan are trying to come up from the stranglehold of the domination of Islamic fundamentalism and army alliance.

In India, the trajectory had been very different. After Independence Muslim League became weaker with major leaders leaving for Pakistan. The remaining part was weak and many small Muslim communal parties did come up in due course. The communal outfit Hindu Mahasabha soon went into oblivion; while the progenitor of Hindu nationalism, RSS went on to float different organisations to achieve its goal of Hindu Rashtra. Initially it helped to form Bhartiya Jansangh with elements drawn from Hindu Mahasabha. Later RSS was in total command and though it was not in the forefront in electoral arena, it kept spreading 'adverse common sense' against Muslims in the beginning and later against Christians. The communal version of history was made popular, 'Muslims are more loyal to Pakistan', and the atrocities of Muslim kings became the cannon fodder of painting the negative image of today's Muslim minority.

In this scenario three factors shaped the nature of things to come. One, the wide prevalence of adverse 'social common sense' against Muslims became part of social thinking. Two, the communal violence in which; majority of the victims have been Muslims; shook the deeper psyche of the community. This in turn led to strengthening of orthodox elements and dominance of Mullahs and communal politics within Muslim community. The third factor was the marginalisation of Muslim community in the economic and social sphere. It is in this backdrop that Congress tried to walk the talk of secularism and faced severe obstacles. It was not up to facing the issue of communalism and at times it also kept hand in glove with communal forces. It failed to curb the menace of this violence and many major acts of violence took place during Congress rule. Despite its basic allegiance to secular values its practice was riddled with opportunism leading to the violence. Congress itself had many communal elements within and the leadership at times played an negative role by compromising with communalism on regular basis.

So Congress did little to curb this menace. In a democratic society a secular dispensation should be doing all to uphold the principles of secularism. In the matters of prevention of communal violence against Muslims-Christians and in the matters of economic issues, its attempts were half hearted due to many factors. As an umbrella party with secular ideology and plethora of communal opportunist elements within, it could not go far in taking the affirmative action for the community so instead it went on appeasing the orthodox elements within the community, as was most visible in Shah Bano case. The community as a whole remained a victim of violence on one side and suffered discrimination on the other. The statistics about violence data and reports like Gopal Singh Commission, Sachar Committee and Rangnath Mishra Commission tell the story not only of the Muslim community but also of the travails through which our democracy had to pass, where a big chunk of population remained neglected.

While all this was on, the reach of communal politics kept enlarging and already in 1980s the Ram Temple movement became the spring board for their ascendance into electoral arena. The intensity of communal violence went on worsening leading to polarisation of society along religious lines and ghettoisation of Muslim minorities. The anti-Christian violence began in late 1990s and added to the worsening scenario. Communal politics kept taking up identity issues on regular basis, Ram Temple issue being the first major one. Later gradually issue of Love Jihad, Ghar Wapasi and Beef ban came up in the social arena. The perception that Congress is appeasing Muslims ran parallel to increasing marginalisation and insecurity of the community. As a matter of fact, Congress policies have not benefitted the Muslim community in any significant way. The words, pronouncements and intentions of Congress fell on the hard rock of communalised polity.

Making the statements like 'They have a first right on national resources' (Manmohan Singh) was used to show the affirmative action of Congress. As a matter of fact seen in the context of a caring state, to say that weaker sections have first right on national resources should be the sign of a state committed to welfare of all. So Congress dilemma of wanting to implement secular policies, protection of minorities and affirmative action for them, fell flat. At the same time it did give a handle to the communal opponents to project as if Congress is there only for Muslims. The UPA I and II showed that the caring affirmative action was targeted not only for Muslims but also for other different disadvantaged sections of society as well. Same way the attempt to bring Communal violence prevention bill was nullified through a vicious propaganda.

Appeasement of minorities has been one of the propaganda slogans. The problem is much deeper. The problem relates to the semi-secularised society, the ascendance of communal politics, majority and minority both, and so finally landing up to mere electoral arithmetic of talking (not implementing) of schemes to win over the minority votes. Problem relates to opportunism where the practice of secularism has been faltering. There is a serious need for introspection, as to what does the practice of secularism means in an uneven society. As the matters stand today the very concept of secularism is being questioned lock stock and barrel. The issue of caste phenomenon is not spelt adequately in the debate. The caste issue has the close linkage to the process of secularisation and with the very process being pushed back the issue of social justice is taking a back seat.

III

Secularism as a concept and policy had a good run in the World with the coming up of industrial society. The unevenness of the World has affected the concept in a deeper way. While the European countries witnessed the rise of secularism as the state policies, the colonies had a different trajectory. The colonial powers, in order to control the trade and markets spread all over and colonised a large mass of humanity, the vast chunks of countries around. Many of these countries were having feudal system of organisation, a rudimentary authoritarian-military-feudal state. With colonisation the processes of industrialisation-modern education and rise of nascent industrialists, working classes and modern educated classes did come up. These 'rising classes came up in various digress in different countries. The tragedy was despite the coming up of new classes and the newer values oriented towards democracy; the older values and relations continued to survive. The problem has been that total spread of these values was not there and so the older classes of landlords in conjunction with the clerical elements also continued. The struggle between the newer rising classes; foundation of modern democratic society, and the declining classes of landlords in association with clergy also continued. The latter also continued to survive and they threw up politics in the name of religion. The rising classes had inherent secular values while the declining classes hid their socio-economic interests in the garb of religion.

Even the foundation of many of these post-colonial states was mired in the web of feudal values of hierarchy of cast and gender. These classes harped on the glories of the past and eulogised some icon from the feudal times as their role model. In many countries even the modern constitutions were there in theory soon to be replaced by provisions for values of hierarchy and dominance of feudal classes. These classes were/are in close alliance with the organised clergy (Pakistan, Myanmar) and rule in close alliance with the army. In South Asian countries these struggles between rising and declining classes is ruling the roost and see saw battles are visible all around.

While the decades of 1940s -1950 saw the rise of anti-colonial nationalisms, generally inspired by progressive ideologies, the decades from 1980 and 1990s are witnessing a retrograde movement all around. Talking globally many European nations have regressed due to rise of sectarian nationalisms and global Islamophobia. In South Asia the Mynmar and Pakistan saw an alliance of Clergy (Mullah or Sangha) and army with the Imperialism and trying to suppress the secular-democratic spirits. Sri Lanka saw the massive state sponsored anti-Tamil massacre. It is during this phase that secularism has been questioned and opposed in India more than before.

IV

This book tries to locate the debate on secularism mainly in India in contemporary times. The essays incorporated here deal with diverse aspects of the issue involved.

Romila Thapar in her "Indian Society and the Secular" takes a broad view of the debate around the issue and locates the obstacles to the process of secularisation. The central aspect of the problem as per her is rooted in the issue of caste. She explains as to what she means by the terms secular, secularism, and secularising. Secular as per her is that which relates to the world but is distinct from the religions. She points out "Secularism involves questioning the control that religious organisations have over social institutions. It does not deny the presence of religion in society but demarcates the social institutions over which religion can or cannot exercise control. This distinction is important. Secularising is the process by which society changes and recognises the distinction."

She further adds that a change of mind set is needed for secular society and the citizens have to cease to think of as identified primarily by religion, caste, or language, and start thinking of primarily as equal citizens of one nation, both in theory and in practice. And this in turn involves mutual obligations between the state and the citizen applicable to all. She states "The relationship of other identities such as religion, caste, language and region, will inevitably become secondary. These latter have to be adjusted so as to ensure that the rights of citizenship together with what they entail, remain primary. Eventually the state will not be expected to provide patronage to any religion or to support any religious organisation."

"Secularism in India" by Asghar Ali Engineer grapples with the issue in a historical context linking with contemporary issues. As per him the rise of communalism was "...not religious but political and a result of struggle for political power between the educated middle and upper classes of both the communities. Had it been a religious problem, the religious leaders would have led it. But the two-nation theory was propounded by Jinnah, a Barrister at Law, who was almost an irreligious person and was, more or less, unaware of the teachings of Islam. Profoundly religious scholars like Maulana Abul Kalam Azad and the organisation of Islamic theologians, the *Jami'at al-Ulama-i-Hind* vehemently opposed partition and supported composite nationalism on religious grounds."

His understanding is that the Indian National Congress, however, was committed to a secular democratic State despite the communal problem and redeemed its promise on 26th January 1950 by promulgating the Constitution. It indeed was a milestone for multi-religious India.

Further commenting on today's situation he says "There is no doubt that today minorities like Muslims and Christians feel much more insecure than during the decades following independence. Nehru had hoped that with greater education in the country there will be more and more secularisation of society but unfortunately, just the opposite has happened. There is more and more communalisation instead."

On similar note Ram Puniyani in his "Secularism: Concept and Scenario" lays down the historical perspective of the rise of secularism in India. For him the core understanding of the issue is located in the nature of industrialisation process. As per him with onset of industrialisation process, the earlier ideological chains proved to be an obstacle to the emerging industrial society. It is in this realm that one has to understand the loosening hold of clergy and some religious traditions on the totality of social life. One has to understand the social norms developing around modern rationality, ideas from science i.e. the beginning of 'age of reason', in contrast to 'age of faith'. The farmer having its roots in science and technology and later in the clergy's interpretation of the word of God, clergy's imposition of ideologies in the name of religion, clergy's use of emotions of people for smoothening the exploitative social system of feudalism.

Uday Mehta takes up the task of going to the roots and genesis of the concept in *"Secularism, Secularisation and Modernity: A Sociological Perspective of the Western Model"*. He gives the detailed outline of the concept and in his essay the first section deals with the Protestant Reformation in Europe and specifically with the Reformation in Germany. He points out "We have done detailed appraisal of the Reformation in Germany, keeping in view the peculiar features of the Germans economy, its feudal structure and quality. In spite of its backward economy and weak political structure, the Reformation made the first initial dent in Germany. Secondly, revolutionary, insurrectionary movement found the most powerful and militant expression in Germany, despite or because of its backward economy and weak polity. Marx and Engels' appraisal of the German situation and peasant wars, even today, sound so refreshing and revealing. Engels particularly, has given considerable weightage to radical role of the religion, especially the early Christianity in inspiring revolutionary movement in Europe. As noted earlier, till the advent of the capitalism, religion probably provided the only effective and easily accessible mechanism to ventilate the aspirations, as well as the protest of the oppressed strata. Even after the advent of the capitalism, its significance as the "weapon of weak" should not be minimised. Keeping this consideration in view, we have dealt with the Reformation in Germany more exhaustively. Second section provides with appraisal of the Reformation in England and also deals with the impact of Industrial Revolution in UK. Third section deals with the French Revolution and Reformation in France. We have gone into causes and consequences of the French Revolution and their impact on secularisation process, religious institutions and practices. This survey of the French Revolution, we thought, is relevant in the context of understanding distinct features of the secularisation process, secular state and religious institutions and practices in Europe. The Fourth section focuses on the recent studies on popular religious and the revival movements in Europe and specifically in France. The emergence of new studies of religion in Europe in last over a decade has significantly altered our understanding of rise and decline in religious influence in the west, since the French and Industrial Revolution."

He takes up recent studies on "feminisation of religion" in terms of changes in devotional practices in Catholic Europe especially in

France that led to increasing involvement of women in religious practices which are quite revealing. These studies also bring out as to how religious institutions have become instrumental in empowerment of women and religion being used as an effective "weapon of weak" by women in large numbers in France during the nineteenth century. The last section of this essay deals with the emergence of numerous radical, militant religious sects in England since the advent of the Industrial Revolution. It also deals with their decline and cooption with the established religious or social institutional structure over a period of time in UK.

Rudolf Heredia engages with secularism-Nation building, confiscation of Church property, elements of whole human life cease to be controlled by clergy in his "*Secularism and Secularisation: Nation building in a Multi-religious society*". As per him with the process of secularisation there is a change in the relationship of religion and society. There are shades of secularism like positive secularism as claimed by BJP, the proponent of Hindutva politics while same tendency asserts that people like Gandhi and Nehru are pseudo secularists. In this case what is being presented as Positive secularism is communalism as such. Nehru and Gandhi are accused of appeasing the minorities so they are dubbed as pseudo secularists. As such the movements led by Phule and Ambedkar have deep secular potential.

In 'On the roots of Secularism" Andreas D'Souza outlines as to how the process of rooting of secularism is also a conscious rejection of all forms of supernatural and sacred. It means freedom of individual and the authority of religion is challenged. Locating the changing backdrop of secularism Uday Mehta in his 'Religion and Globalisation' makes a point that "It is not only in India but even in Western countries particularly in industrially advanced nations such as the United States of America (USA) that, new along with traditional religious movements have gained an unprecedented momentum in recent years. The growing influence of religion in USA and China has been widely reported. The powerful influence of Church in Polish solidarity movement and Buddhist impact of Vietnamese liberation struggle has also been widely acknowledged. The dominant role of the Monastery in overthrow of the recent reactionary political upheaval in Sri Lanka could not be overstressed. The decisive influence of Islamic fundamentalism in Iranian revolution and several other Muslim countries has been sufficiently highlighted, while the emergence and significance of the liberation theology in Latin America would call for an independent appraisal."

The appeal of religion has changed it forms in the era of globalisation. Still "Nevertheless for the overwhelming majority of the toiling population all over the world working hard for survival, the religion probably continues to be sigh of the oppressed, or the soul of the soulless world." As a global phenomenon one can discern that fundamentalism is there in all the religions. In India, modern gurus are expression of this in a glaring form. Michael Boivin takes up a particular case of veil in France in his "National Education versus Veil: Secularism and Islam in France". The policy of state *vis-à-vis* individual's choice, public versus private space is discussed in this essay.

Ashok Chusalkar in a very relevant theme takes up Nehru's policies in the arena of state and religion in his "Pandit Nehru on Communalism and Nationalism in India." Nehru has been criticised by many for his upright stance on the issue of secularism in a society gripped in religiosity. His contribution has been basic in laying the practical foundations of separating the state from religion. This essay points out that Nehru had a deep sense of history and he opposed religious nationalism. Madhvi Yasin, in her "Nehruvian Secularism and the minority problem" argues that Nehru was very much rooted in the diversity of the country and had reflected deeply on the toleration as propounded by Emperor Asoka. S.H. Patil in "Manav Dharma and Pt. Nehru's Concept of Secularism" points out that though Nehru did not believe in any religion he did uphold humanism and wanted to root out poverty, ignorance, superstition, communal passions. All this meant that he stood for secularism and democracy. In an interesting exercise Sudhir Kumar "Secularising the literary space: Problems and possibilities", analyses the literary work of Muslim writers to understand the secular space in India. Justice Hosbet Suresh in Secularism Betrayed analyses the Supreme Court Judgment, popularly known as HIndutva Judgment and points out it shortcomings.

Rohini Hensman in her "Struggle Against Communalism: Defining a Positive Alternative" opines that "Creating a movement which puts forward a positive alternative to communalism also implies a critique of the sectionalism of most of the existing progressive movements, which oppose one form of oppression and authoritarianism but not others. Thus, the trade union movement is compromised by being seriously contaminated with communal elements, feminists have raised slogans amenable to a communal interpretation, and even Dalits have not proved immune to the false promises of Hindutva. On the other hand, anti-communal groups suffer from the same kind of narrowness, often indifferent to class, caste and gender oppression. The alternative is not that each individual has to participate in every struggle, but rather that all the diverse struggles should be linked together into a movement by shared principles and practical solidarity." Ram Puniyani in "Towards a Secular Society" analyses the politics of Sangh Parivar, the Hindutva politics and outlines the need to preserve secular democracy through the struggles for democratic rights. He articulates the need for a platform of social action for preserving the values of Indian Constitution.

V

The complex trajectory of the secularism in India has gone through ups and downs. While in nineteenth century the concept had to face major challenges from the declining sections of society in due course they organised themselves into communal organisations. These organisations were not part of freedom movement and constructed their nationalism based on societies of the past which was passed off as our glorious tradition. While the freedom and the later coming in of Indian Constitution rooted this concept firmly; its practice was mired by the landlord-clergy nexus which continued to dominate as the land reform measures were half hearted and ineffective.

These sections of society have been joined by other middle classes, small industrialists, rich peasants with urban ambitions and the rich professional amongst others. The emotive issue which these organisations project are a big obstacle to the implementation of secular values in a democracy which is mired by the gross social inequality. Today the challenges to these values have been strengthened by the global scenario where politics in the name of religion has come to the fore in a very prominent way. On one hand movements for caste and gender equality have become part of societal norms and on the other the social groups opposed to these movements have developed subtle language to oppose these changes and reassert the hierarchical values in the name of traditions.

The political forces are lined up on the opposite side of the battle lines and this is the major area of struggle in the contemporary times. Opposing secular values is done at low levels. More directly it is done by directly opposing the steps for security and equity of religious minorities. In a more subtle ways it stifles the process of equality of dalits and women. Scholars have been trying to grapple the issue and have been contributing to the understand the complexity of the phenomenon.

SECTION A
OVERVIEW

1

Indian Society and the Secular

—*Romila Thapar*

I would like to thank Mr Irfan Engineer for having done me the honour of inviting me to give the Asghar Ali Engineer Memorial lecture. I deem it a great privilege to have been asked, as it commemorates the work of a person deeply concerned with establishing a secular Indian society, and dedicating himself to the furtherance of this objective.

Let me say at the outset that secularism is not just a political slogan, although our political parties have attempted to reduce it to that. So, one party endorses it in theory but hesitates to apply it properly in practice, the other makes fun of it since its foundational ideology is anti-secular. Secularising a society is deeply tied to the question of the kind of society that we want. That is why perhaps it was widely discussed in the early years of independence, whereas now the attempt is not to give it attention, as it means seriously re-assessing the direction that we are currently giving to Indian society. There was even a tentative suggestion recently that it could be deleted from the Constitution, possibly motivated by the hope that the demand for its inclusion will be forgotten.

If, however, we want a secular society then that involves a change of mind-set, we would have to cease to think of ourselves as identified primarily by religion, caste, or language, and start thinking of ourselves primarily as equal citizens of one nation, both in theory and in practice. This involves mutual obligations between the state and the citizen applicable to all. The relationship of other identities such as religion, caste, language and region, will inevitably become secondary. These latter have to be adjusted so as to ensure that the rights of citizenship together with what they entail, remain primary. Eventually the state will not be expected to provide patronage to any religion or to support any religious organisation. This is a change that has barely begun and is already meeting with deliberate negations from some quarters.

In this lecture I would like to consider three aspects of what is involved in any discussion of Indian society and the secular. I would like initially to explain how I would define the secular, since I find that the generally accepted definition prevailing in India is inadequate and not everyone agrees on the definition. I shall then take up the question of how the social functioning of religions in India differed from the European experience and therefore in India religion has to be considered in association with caste and not in isolation from it. Finally, I shall say something on where the priorities lie for the process of secularising Indian society.

Definitions

I would like to begin by trying to explain what I mean by the terms secular, secularism, and secularising. Secular is that which relates to the world but is distinct from the religious. Secularism involves questioning the control that religious organisations have over social institutions. It does not deny the presence of religion in society but demarcates the social institutions over which religion can or cannot exercise control. This distinction is important. Secularising is the process by which society changes and recognises the distinction.

When the term was first used in 1851, 'secular' had only one basic meaning. It argued in support of the fact that laws relating to social ethics, values and morals; had been created by human society in order to ensure the well-being and harmonious functioning of the society. They were neither the creation of divine authority, nor did they require the sanction of divine authority. Religious authority may claim such a sanction but in effect the laws can exist without it. Authority lay in reasoning out what was best for society by those who constituted that society. Authority was exercised through laws. Social values therefore, frequently had their roots in reasoning and rational thinking. This was especially needed where the intention was and is to establish a moral code that required the agreement of the entire society and was not linked to any particular religion.

What this means is that the laws and social values that govern society should be observed as laws in themselves and not because they carry divine sanctions. They have their own authority distinct from religion or caste. Religion involving belief and faith in a deity and in an after-life, and such like, continued to exist. However, civil laws were promulgated and upheld by the secular authority. Secularism therefore is not a denial of religion but it is a curtailment of the control that religion has over social functioning, a control exercised through diverse religious organisations.

This theory had a variety of consequences. One was that it allowed people the freedom to think beyond what was told to them as being religiously correct. Again this did not mean throwing religion overboard, but disentangling the codes of social behaviour from religious control. This did not make people immoral as some had feared, since the threat of punishment for breaking laws was enforced, and punishment came immediately in this life. It was not postponed to the next life as in religious codes. So it made people think about the purpose of their laws and that is always useful. The observance of the law is strengthened when people understand why it exists.

Most people are socialised into religion from childhood and do not question it. It gradually becomes a psychological support and as such there is even less need to question the belief. Having to reason things out is never as easy as just accepting what one is told. It means that people have to learn to think independently. This can be facilitated if the kind of education they were given enabled them to reason out their decisions. The alternative was to make them dependent on an unknown supernatural power. The explanation of everything being part of divine plan and sanction was not always the answer to simple questions. Therefore, education involved searching for explanations other than those based on faith and belief, or possibly even honing these if there was evidence. But preferably social laws began to be drawn from enquiring into both the natural and human world in which we live. So the explanations for social laws became an essential part of education and of thinking about the implication of being secularised.

Religion had originated as a personal, emotional need. For many it remains so. This extended to explanations of how the universe functioned which was attributed to a supernatural power that was held in awe. Gradually however this personalised religion became a complex organised religion and took the form of institutions ambitious to control society and politics. With this change religion became powerful both as the focus of belief, and as an authority controlling social institutions through various religious organisations. In some places its power paralleled that of the governing authority – the state. It is this particular aspect of religion that the secular person wishes to see curtailed and kept separate from the functioning of the state. This makes it necessary to concede the presence of the secular in the constitution of a democracy. The distinction between religion and the religious control over social institutions is important because we often overlook it in saying that secularism denies religion altogether.

Secularism then takes on an additional meaning. The state having authority over the making and observing of laws by human agencies, should be distinct from religion since religion has its sanction from another source, namely faith and deity. The authority of each was clearly different. Let me repeat, that the secular is not a denial of religion. It is not the equivalent of atheism. Secularism does not mean expunging religion. But the control of religious organisations over social laws and institutions has to be limited.

Civil laws are the spine of a society. They should protect the rights to human life, and they should ensure that there is no discrimination that affects life and work. This is crucial to protecting the points of change in a human lifetime necessitating laws – birth, marriage or even its break-up, processes of education by which a child is socialised into society, occupation and employment, and inheritance particularly of what is thought of as property. These come under the jurisdiction of the civil law. To make this effective, such laws relating to the functioning of society and the social life of humans, have necessarily to provide the basic aspects of welfare in a modern state – the absolute minimum of which are: food and clean water, equal access to education and to healthcare for all members of society, and to employment. And this is to be irrespective of religion and caste. If civil laws are to be universal and uniform, as they would be in a secular society, then they must guarantee this. Discrimination on any count would be unacceptable.

So religious authority remains in a secular system but is restricted to governing religious belief and practice. It has been argued that there should be no rigid barrier between religion and the state, but that there can be a negotiated principled distance between them. This can allow for new alignments within the religion, or between the religions, or between religion and the state. The overall relationship would disallow the dominance of any one religion since each would have equal rights on the state and equal status before the law. Nevertheless, there would be a degree of stipulated separation in this arrangement, in as much as religious authority would no longer be controlling social laws.

This is not of course the same as what is sometimes described as the Indian definition of secularism, namely, the co-existence of all religions. Rulers in the past that supported this idea, such as the two who are always quoted – Ashoka and Akbar are spoken of as providing a kind of prelude to secularism. However, the mere co-existence of religions is insufficient as they can still be treated as unequal and some remain marginalised. When we speak of the religions of India today, we are seldom conscious of the religions of a quarter or more of the population who are at the lower edges of society. The acceptance of co-existence together with equal status before the law, can certainly be a first step. But we do have to ask how far it goes and what should be the next step.

This definition is incomplete since the question of the jurisdiction of religious authority over society, that is crucial, remains unanswered. The intention would in any case be not to put up barriers between state and religion. It would instead be to demarcate the activities that come under a civil jurisdiction and those that would continue to be controlled by the organisations representing religious authority. In a democratic system the equality would be essential, as essential as spelling out who controls which laws.

In contemporary India the co-existence of religions already exists but the secular is less evident and some might even say, virtually absent. Political and state patronage does not invariably distance itself from religious organisations. In fact, the two are sometimes closely tied.

Some oppose secularism by arguing that it is a western concept, not suited to India. Should the same be said about nationhood and democracy, both new to post-colonial India? And surely our internalising of the neo-liberal market economy is a far stronger imprint of the West. To support the secularising of society does not mean subordinating ourselves to a western or an alien concept, but rather trying to understand a process of change in our history after independence. Being a nation is a new experience of modern times, and is current now in virtually every part of the world. We have chosen democracy as the most feasible system despite its being a new experience, and a secular society is essential to democratic functioning.

Secularism is the necessary manifestation of a social change that comes with societies that begin to function with modern institutions that are the channels of new political, economic and social forms. It is a concept that accompanies modernisation. It assumes new directions in the functions of law and ethics and the relations between religion and the state. We should not look for it in its current form in our pre-modern history. But what we can search for and of which we have evidence was a long and evident tradition of questioning orthodoxies of various kinds, including religious orthodoxies in Indian religions. This began in the first millennium BC and continued unbroken to the present. A deeper study of these schools of thought would make reasoned thinking more familiar to us and would puncture the idea that Indians never questioned orthodoxy. When laws are recognised as made by human societies and not divinely dictated, then negotiating changes in these laws because of social change that has happened continuously in the past, also gets facilitated.

Colonial Readings of Indian Religions

Let me turn now to looking more closely at the specifically Indian aspect of the subject. I would like to comment on how I see the interaction of religions and society in the past, in order to compare it with how it is viewed in our times. Any deliberate social change with sizeable consequences becomes a little easier to handle if one can see the earlier historical forms of the society and its gradual mutation. The present after all emerges out of the past. My argument is that in the important area of the relationship between society and religion we have been nurtured on ideas about religion in India that were constructed by colonial thought on the subject. The colonial perception was in many ways a disjuncture in understanding how religion functioned in pre-modern Indian society. Yet, we have accepted it without adequate questioning. So a brief look at the past might be useful.

With reference to Europe, secularism is often described as the separation between Church and State. This is taken as a one-to-one relationship because generally the religion was a single monolithic religion – Christianity, either Catholic or Protestant. This was so strongly asserted that in past times before the rise of Protestantism, those that questioned Catholic belief and practice were heavily punished as heretics. Some were burnt at the stake, some had to recant and many faced the punitive actions required by the Inquisition. Although Protestantism later was perhaps more flexible the earlier experience was not forgotten. (Incidentally, this single monolithic religion facing the state, is now changing in many European countries with the coming of migrant communities bringing their own religions, and hence the frequent contestations over the secular in society).

This European perspective of religion being monolithic and identified with large pan-European communities, was what the colonisers brought to India, and was the perspective from which they viewed Indian religions. So their reading of Indian religion needs re-investigation. The colonial image of Indian society projected two monolithic religions, the Hindu and the Muslim, and the two religions defined the identity of two nations – the Hindu and the Muslim. They occupied the same territory. They were depicted as largely antagonistic to each other. It was maintained that because of their mutual hostility, a controlling authority from outside was required. This then became one of the justifications for colonial rule. As many historians have pointed out, this image was also imprinted on the history of India, especially on the medieval period, thus, reinforcing the distancing between the two religions and also in their ideologies. A shared history was not conceded in this approach to the past.

The concept of majority and minority communities identified by religion further consolidated the idea of religion being monolithic. In addition it fuelled the politics of religious identities. Claims of the majority community were juxtaposed with the aspirations of the minority communities. Social and political claims and demands were projected as religious. Such an understanding of society obstructs the functioning of democracy. Permanent majority and minority communities are contrary to the norms of democracy. The creation of caste and religion-based vote-banks in the electoral system, are not exactly conducive to democratic functioning. A majority that is viable as a democratically formed majority, requires the larger number of people to come together, in support of a particular issue, and irrespective of their other affiliations. The constituents of a democratic majority therefore change with each issue, and there is no permanent majority community with a specifically defined membership.

Anti-colonial nationalism tried to confront this image, since broad-based nationalism has to be inclusive and bring in a range of opinion and it draws on a shared history. The shared history is crucial. I would like to quote Eric Hobsbawm who wrote that history is to nationalisms what the poppy is to the opium addict. It is the source. It feeds, in this case, ideas of identity. Anti-colonial nationalism did not question the monolithic nature of religious communities. Instead it focused more on denying their antagonism, preferring to project just the co-existence of religious communities. This became central to its idea of secularism and has come to be called the Indian definition of secularism. But it did not succeed as we can see from the events of the present. One reason was that the colonial view of religion in India was (and it continues to be), also foundational to the ideologies of what are now referred to as religious nationalisms, those that went into the making of the communal landscape of India. A century or so ago the reference was to the Muslim League and the Hindu Mahasabha. These were perhaps fewer religious orthodoxies when compared to ideologies using religion for political mobilisation. Today religious nationalism includes a range of Hindu, Muslim, Sikh and other religious organisations, politically ambitious and anxious to continue their control over community laws to ensure a political constituency. History is not shared, it is divisive and it becomes the arena of battle.

We may well ask, was this actually the way in which religion functioned as part of Indian society from early times? Or have we not looked analytically at our past and that of the role of religion in our earlier social institutions. What forms did these organisations take, how did they exert authority, and why don't we examine which sections of society supported which kind of organisation?

I would like to argue that the historical picture of religions in India was complex and was not a simple binary. It seems to me that there were two sets of relationships that need to be examined.

One was the way in which religion and society interacted. Religious groups consisted of a range of sects rather than monolithic communities, and the social linkage was through caste. It was linked to forms such as *varna, jati, zat* and so on. This combination of sect and caste mediated in turn, the other relationship, that between the religious sect and the state. In this there was no Church to bring together the sects into a single entity. The state having to relate to individual sects gave the relationship a different flavour.

In the Indian scene the crucial relationship lay in the connection between multiple religious sects and many castes. The sect propagated belief, the caste often determined its social context. Status was measured through an inter-dependence of the two. Upper castes across religions, whether they observed caste restrictions strictly or not, tended to be more closely associated with the formal manifestations of the religions, generally text-based; whereas the lower castes that were much larger in number, tended to be more flexible in their religious identities. Caste determined the social code, maintained formally by those who claimed to be educated and knew the law. Few people knew the texts or the sources of the laws. For most people it was the hearsay of tradition, the lore maintained by the *jati,* and perhaps the experience of the daily routine. Codes after all are ultimately man made, however much they may be backed by claims to divine sanction as maintained by the voice of religion. The authority of caste and sect over the social code has to be replaced in our times by a civil law common and applicable to all. This will require looking afresh at civil law to ensure its secularity and its endorsement of social justice. Both are familiar as values but their application in social institutions is new.

Historical Perspectives of Religions in India

Many valuable and meticulous studies have been made of religious texts that have enhanced our understanding of these texts. However, less attention has been given to examining the institutions created by various religions, both to propagate their beliefs and as agencies of social control. Rather than focusing on monolithic, undifferentiated religious society in general, what may be more insightful would be if we study the link between caste and sect in order to comprehend the interface between religion and society in our past. The link between caste and sect had a flexibility or fluidity that monolithic religious communities lack. We could then ask whether rigidity lay less in religion and more in caste discrimination? In that case the colonial construction of religion in India that we have readily accepted, would have to be scrutinised afresh. Perhaps we need to look more carefully at how caste, or even elements of class, in past times and now, shaped and are shaping the relations between religion and society. Which groups in society support which politico-religious organisations and why?

In pre-Islamic times there are no references to any monolithic type of Hinduism. Interestingly what we today call religions are not mentioned as such, but what are mentioned are two broad categories of sects that propagated their distinctive ideas. These were the Brahmana and the Shramana. A basic differentiation was based on belief in or denial of, divinity; and theories about the after-life. Brahmana referred to Brahmanic beliefs and rituals. Shramana referred to the *shramanas* or Buddhist, Jaina and other monks of the heterodox orders, the *nastika* / non-believers, and their followers. These latter sects rejected the *Vedas,* divine sanctions and the concept of the soul, and were consequently associated with more rational explanations of the universe and human society. Within each of these two categories there was recognition of a range of distinct sects with varying beliefs.

This duality continues to be used with reference to what we call religion, over a period of 1500 years. The earliest mention is in the edicts of Ashoka (*bamhanam-samananam*). The later quotations from the account of the Greek visitor Megasthenes refer to his statement on the *Brachmanes* and *Sarmanes.* In the travel accounts of visits to India of the Chinese Buddhist monks in the latter part of the first millennium AD the distinction is present. It is also present in the book of Al-Biruni of the eleventh century AD, where the Shamaniyyas were said to cordially dislike the Brahmanas.

Kalhana's *Rajatarangini* of the twelfth century AD refers to earlier hostilities between Shaiva sects and some Buddhist monastic orders; and inscriptions from south India refer to violent disagreements between some Shaiva and Jaina sects. Interestingly they used the same abusive terms for each other. The grammarian Patanjali of the early centuries AD; refers to the two, adding that their relationship can be compared to that between the snake and the mongoose!

This underlines the fact that there were among the multiple sects some that adhered to the orthodoxy and others that were supporters of the heterodoxy. The advantage of sects over monolithic religions is that sects shade off from the very orthodox to those far less so. This allows the less orthodox to assimilate new beliefs and this is not treated as heresy. The heretics function in a stream of their own. This allows for the occasional, even if marginal overlaps at the edges of both categories. When confrontations became acute violence was resorted to.

A distinction ought to be made at this point between sect as used in the Christian sense and sect as used with reference to Indian religions. The words used more frequently in Sanskrit and in later Indian languages present a spectrum of meaning, suggesting that these were the more familiar concepts. Thus, *pashanda,* was originally neutral but gradually incorporated a sense of heresy and whereas opponents may use this term it was not used in self-definition. *Shakha,* suggests a branching off from a bigger organisation. But *patha, pantha, marga,* suggest followers along a path of thought and action that can be fairly freely formulated. *Sampradaya* is more often a doctrine transmitted through teaching. Sects therefore are not breakaways from monolithic religions. Their authority comes from independent founders, some being historical figures, they follow a distinctive organised form and much of their teaching is oral to begin with. Belonging to a sect is more frequently than not by individual choice. The larger body of people is often from the lower levels of society but this does not debar anyone from the upper castes.

A third category that is not listed as such in early texts was that of those that were discriminated against because of their low caste, or lack of it. They had their own belief system and forms of worship. The creation of a sect was open and led to a plurality that became characteristic of religion in India, irrespective of which religion. This constitutes an important aspect in understanding the relationship between religion and society. Such relationships differ from society to society. We cannot assume therefore that the role of religion that emerged for Europe can be applied automatically to India – a mistake made by colonial scholarship. This does not imply that the meaning of secularism can change, but that the manner in which it is introduced into a society may vary.

Whereas the history of Shramanism takes a more linear form with some segments branching off from existing segments, the history of Brahmanism is less linear and more complex. An early phase was Vedic Brahmanism focusing on the ritual of sacrifice, the *yajna*, invoking many deities and especially Indra and Agni, and performed by upper castes. These beliefs were questioned by a variety of heterodox sects pre-eminently the Buddhist and Jaina but including many others such as the Charvaka and Ajivika. This category came to be called Shramana. Incidentally the heterodox groups tended to provide generally rational explanations about the formation of social institutions and established a critical tradition of questioning orthodoxy, eventually establishing their own orthodoxies.

By the Christian era a more individualised belief system and ritual came into being with a focus on other deities – Shiva and Vishnu. Sects of worshippers came together differentiated by particular deities, as for example, the Vaishnava Bhagavatas and the Shaiva Pashupatas. From the seventh century onwards religious belief and worship was prevalent in the form of devotional sects, what we call the Bhakti sects. They arose at varying times in different parts of the sub-continent. The earliest recognisable as such were the Alvars and Nayyanars in the south. Subsequent to this were many in the north, with or without links to the southern tradition. Some among these reflect the striations of new religious ideas.

Both Brahmanism and Shramanism received hefty patronage and became wealthy, powerful, established religions. This gave them status and enabled them to control social laws.

Donations were made to individually named sects, rather than larger religious entities. This continued to be the norm even in later periods when references to monolithic religions begin to be mentioned.

Centres of the wealthy sects strengthened their identity when they also became the nucleus of education. This added to their authority and they could induct the elite and contribute towards elite culture. Frequently sects with large followings and authority began to function as castes in themselves, as for example, the Lingayat sect in Karnataka, and some would include the Varkaris of Maharashtra.

More loosely defined were the Kabirpantha, the Dadupantha and the Nathapantha in the north, among many others. Most kept their distance from the formal religions and only occasionally might draw from them. Some even opposed them, in part because the sect was the articulation of the lower castes with a smattering of upper castes that no longer conformed. Unlike the formal religions, some accepted the participation of the untouchables and most discarded caste segregation.

A few of these sects sought a connection between the dominant religions. A few others tried to revive earlier belief system but gave them a new form. Among these was the sect founded by Ramananda who resided in Varanasi in the mid-millennium. The Ramanandi sect revived the Vaishnava worship of Rama and re-introduced the conservative features of Bhakti in contra-distinction to the teaching of Kabir, Nanak and Dadu. In colonial records however, they tended to get assigned to one or the other of what were regarded as the two dominant religions.

There is a hesitation in recognising these sects as representing another way of articulating the connection between religion and society. Because of the multiplicity of sects it is sometimes difficult to demarcate clearly between them and what have been called the formal religions. The latter term refers more often to the religion as formulated by the upper castes or the dominant castes in a region.

Given this background I would like to differentiate between what I call formal religion and religion as practiced. Formal religion is heavily dependent on texts, on the correct performance of ritual as directed by priests and specialists, and on the organisations that emerge from these that become the centres of authority particularly in matters relating to the pattern of living. Religion as practiced, is observed by a far larger number of people. It refers less to texts and organisations of propagation and far more on oral traditions of teaching and worship.

In Indian social history the second form of religion has actually been more immanent than the first. The first was always prominent at the political level for obvious reasons of political identity and action, and status, as in court chronicles and more important inscriptions and religious texts. Modern writing on religion did not distinguish sufficiently between these forms of religion and the more popular ones. The former was therefore taken as representative of religion in general. Historians are now beginning to recognise the greater significance of the second form of religion for society at large.

Islam in India

With the arrival of Islam and more so the presence of the Sufis the exploration of religious ideas expanded as also the number of sects. There were more orthodoxies of various kinds but also more heterodoxies. The latter in some cases questioned the former or otherwise could hold out mixed belief and worship. This was rejected by the orthodox but was frequently popular with the larger number of ordinary people.

The new presence was indicated by the elaborate mosques and mausoleums built by royal patrons and the wealthy. The religious endowments became richer and richer as do all the endowments to well-patronised religions. As in the case of the Buddhist monasteries and the Hindu temples and *mathas*, these endowments tied to *khanqahs* and *madrassas*, also enabled their recipients to participate in the world of scholarship and in the world of politics. More detailed studies of new social institutions that came under the control of religious authority would be revealing.

As in earlier times the sect remained the popular religious identity among the majority of people. This becomes more evident if we look at two processes involving the coming of Islam – settlement and conversion. But before I do this let me comment on the single association that is frequently made on the coming of Islam to India, namely invasion.

At the popular level the arrival of Islam is projected largely in terms of invasion and conquest, mass enforced conversion, and the political events that followed. But even if we limit our sights to invasion, despite this being historically limited, there are aspects that we have to consider and which we willfully ignore. Invasion means traversing an area and negotiating with a variety of populations.

Invading armies from the North-West would have met large groups of people with varied patterns of living. There were many who were pastoralists, such as the Gujjars and Jats, some of whom were converted to Islam but a large number continued with their earlier religion. The reason for this needs investigation. Some of the pastoral Jats mutated into the peasantry of Sindh and Punjab and among them some groups converted and many did not. The same was the case with artisans in towns producing items for trade, where artisanal groups tended to convert in some trades, such as weaving and metal working, whereas the merchants involved in the commerce, remained as before. The continuity of caste names and ethnic identities common to more than one religion, as among the Jats, is a give-away of the process of conversion. The pattern is repeated in other parts of the country. Wherever there are common caste names among more than one religion, those castes that today are labelled as Hindu are usually in larger numbers. The picture that is presented of mass conversions in the wake of invading armies is an exaggeration often embroidered upon by eulogistic chroniclers of the rulers. Their figures cannot be taken at face-value and have to be seen in the context of other evidence. Armies do not convert and what is wanted at the point of the sword is not a convert but wealth.

There were other avenues of social mixing that presented different, more innovative social and religious forms that were often more long-lasting and built upon the values that people cherished. These were more easily found in the settlements of traders, migrants, Sufis and such like.

Mohammad bin Qasim conquered Sindh in the eighth century AD. There is a diversity of texts that speak of these times from different perspectives. The *Chachnama* comments on how the area is to be governed. Among its suggestions is that existing practices should not be heavily disturbed, and as it turned out, whether deliberately or accidentally, they were changed to some extent but were not over-turned in Sindh. The presence of pre-Islamic religions continued.

Another associated text is the *Devalasmriti* that shows a concern about problems of conversion and reconversion. It does not appear to be deeply concerned about the situation but does prescribe rituals for reconversion. What is significant is that these are referred to as *shuddhi* / purification, and the ritual itself is symbolic of a new birth out of being buried in dirt. *Shuddhi* would suggest an emphasis on caste purification for which the term was used, interestingly even in the nineteenth century by social reform organisations. Women abducted by the *mlecchas* were also taken back into their original caste after the ritual of *shuddhi*. Was caste purification more problematic for a reconversion, than religious commitment, or was it subsumed in such belief?

Shuddhi was necessary we are told because the person converted had lived with the *mlecchas* and as a consequence, had fallen out of caste. *Mleccha* again was the term often used in preference to using 'Muslim', even at times for rulers that were otherwise being eulogized. Its connotation was that of a social rather than a strictly religious identity.

But the new feature that reflects actual social and religious change was different from these two. It is reflected in other texts and in inscriptions from western India. This was the emergence of new sects from out of an amalgam of existing sects of various kinds with the belief system of those that settled among them generally connected with maritime trade and occupations. Inter-marriage together with the continuity of some rituals and beliefs often linked to local custom brought about new sects. The Bohras evolved from a mix of indigenous and imported belief systems, not surprising among traders, and inter-marriage with local communities. Some Bohras traced their origin to Shi'ah sects but there was a controversy as to whether they could claim to be Muslims as they also used Hindu rituals. Subsequently there were the Khojas emerging in a similar way in Gujarat and western India and also retaining some local belief and rituals. These diversions raise interesting questions.

What was historically significant during these centuries from the eighth to the thirteenth, and later in some cases, was the settlements of Arab traders and the occasional Persian, all down the west coast of India from Sindh to Kerala. Some Arabs entered the service of the Rashtrakuta kings of the Deccan. The senior officers among them exercised their right to give grants of land, and did so, to *brahmanas* and temples, as had been the prevailing custom. This is recorded in inscriptions from this period.

These Arabs inter-married locally and new communities evolved with a new take on existing religions. In traditional Indian style these became new sects. The Bohras and Khojas have a long history in western India. The Navayats further south in the Kanara region had links to Jaina trading communities and made a point of observing the caste rules of commensality. The Mapillas were important in Kerala and appropriated matrilineal forms and customary law of their caste equivalents. No two among the new sects were identical. Gujarati Bohras had little to do with Malayali Mapillas. Many such sects mushroomed elsewhere where belief, ritual and customary law adopted by settlers did not hesitate to draw from existing practice, especially in relation to civil law. But these have not been sufficiently studied as part of social and religious history, because we tend to look at religion only as monolithic forms. There is little reference to who formed the religious communities.

This pattern continued into later centuries at the level of the wider society. This was despite the emergence of other patterns that arose from political power and administration. Such dichotomies run through history and only their constituents change. The newly emerging teachers of various persuasions attracted support and followers. Until recently these remained the essentials of how a major part of Indians experienced religion, irrespective of having to declare their conformity to formal religions in colonial times. This was prior to the ingress of Hindutva and deliberate Islamisation that have considerably hardened the boundaries, and even at times altered practices. Many people today who identify themselves with a monolithic religion, when pressed further will mention their close if not closer, affiliation to a sect or the holy man or woman whom they revere, and who can be of any persuasion. This link is often more pertinent to the lives they actually live. It provides the emotional and psychological strength that is sought from religion. And interestingly, the sects they identify with are generally those that were established within the last thousand years.

The History of India in the Last Thousand Years

In the history of India, the history of approximately the last thousand years, referred to as the medieval period, has had a raw deal from religious extremists and politicians in being described as the age when "we were slaves". The implication of the statement is that it refers to a uniform tyranny of Islamic rule over a suppressed Hindu population. Viewed historically however, the scene differs at many levels. The inter-action between what we today call Hinduism and Islam, had its moments of confrontation and conflict in the face-offs between competing politics manifested in various ways. This was to be expected initially with the change in existing political authorities at the upper levels of society, and more so where it was accompanied by the introduction at these levels of a new language, religion and culture. Such disruption was by no means new to the Indian political scene, familiar with conflicts between sects of Brahmanas and Shramanas, nor was it uniform throughout the sub-continent. There was substantial variance with regard to where and why it happened and which groups were involved.

What these variations were and what caused them are matters we ignore in our sweeping generalisations about Hindus and Muslims in history. Nor was the experience of the coming in of settlers altogether unfamiliar, given that traders and migrants from West Asia and Central Asia had been known earlier in the borderlands and in the coastal areas. The unsettled period in the early second millennium gradually settled into more stable patterns.

Some of the earlier confrontations between groups continued and new ones were added to these. None of this is unexpected in any period of history. But what we often forget when we rush to say that it was a time when "we were slaves" and that the nastiness and oppression was unmitigated, is that it was also a time when striking creativity enriched facets of Indian culture, a creativity that we have made our own and internalised and that we actually respect, often without recognising its origins. It took two forms.

One was what has been often discussed by historians and has been labelled as the 'composite culture'. This was largely the mutual borrowing between what we today call Hindu and Muslim religious sects and various facets of cultural expression. It is displayed in an infinite number of ways through language, cultural idioms, customary law and forms of worship. It tends to be more conspicuous among the upper castes, but was probably more quietly internalised by the others. If one insists on the religious binary then where does one place the poetry of Sayyad Mohammad Jayasi's *Padmavat* or the *dohas* of the devotee of Krishna, Sayyad Ibrahim Ras Khan, both widely popular at various levels. The *gurus* and the *pirs* were such a striking feature of the landscape, were often intermeshed and worshipped by large numbers of common people, that one can't help but speak of a different religious tradition as the *guru-pir* tradition.

In some cases these extensions and exploration of ideas stemmed from contributions by diverse thinkers, writing in Sanskrit, Persian and the regional languages. Brahmana scholars writing in Sanskrit had close scholarly relations with the Mughals. Literary compendia were composed such as the *Kavindra-chandrodaya* during the reign of Shah Jahan, to which seventy such scholars contributed. This would not have been unusual given that the emperor is said to have had a voluminous library of works in Sanskrit in addition to his collection of other books. We should perhaps learn to appreciate the cultural achievements of some of those who were our rulers.

There were excursions into investigating theories in mathematics and astronomy going from Ujjain to Baghdad and beyond, with Indian scholars at the cutting edge of knowledge. In another area of interest classical Hindustani and Carnatic music was patronised by the courts of Maharajas and Mughals or in the homes of the wealthy. Many lyrics were dedicated to the praise of deities and were sung with fervor by musicians such as Tansen.

The other form that was equally significant was the virtual renaissance that took place in knowledge systems and cultural forms that reached back into the past and re-invigorated it into new forms. Let me give you a few examples of what happened in the tradition that is supposed to have been so oppressed that it almost vanished in the last one thousand years. Let's look briefly at the intellectual liveliness of the time with writing and thinking in Sanskrit and Persian, and in the regional languages, a liveliness that matched that of earlier times, although in different genres and forms of expression. It gave shape in various ways to much, although not all, that we now identify as Hindu in the landscape of our times.

Leaving aside for the moment the interaction of Hindu and Muslim cultures and religions, even the activities within the one tradition that is supposed to have been oppressed, is most impressive. Throughout the second millennium AD, from Kashmir to Kerala and in between, there were scholarly Sanskrit commentaries being composed on Brahmanical religious texts from the *Vedas* onwards. Obviously such scholarship was not without patronage. The exegesis on these texts illustrates the high level of scholarship being widely practiced and exchanged in many centres of that time. Sayana's explanation of the *Rig Veda* is a fascinating glimpse into the mind of a learned scholar of the fourteenth century with its mix of reality and fantasy. Kulluka's extensive commentary on the Manu *Dharmashastra* includes reactions to social changes involving caste and sect hierarchies. Many aspects are discussed at length, including for instance, an assessment of the status of temple priests. This was a new category of brahmanas since temples began to be built and manned by priests after the period when Manu wrote his *Dharmashastra*. The debate on the control and inheritance of land as substantial property and other forms of wealth, led to differences of opinion as in the Mitakshara and Dayabhaga schools of legal opinion. Clearly there were Hindus with substantial holdings of land for whom the laws of inheritance had to be formulated. There were multiple commentaries, digests, discussions on legal texts.

Commentaries from varied perspectives were written on the *Ramayana* and the *Mahabharata,* as also on the classics of Sanskrit poetry and drama. Such commentaries have not only been influential but have also facilitated the work on the modern critical editions of these texts. At another level of interest compositions in regional languages, carried much of the thought and creativity of their own times as is evident in the many versions of the Rama story as in the *Ramacaritamanas,* and the *Kritibas.*

Prior philosophical theories are summarised and the discourses on new schools of philosophy are widely discussed among philosophers. The *Sarvadarshana-samgraha* of Madhavacharya written in the fourteenth century provides a summary of on-going debates. The opening chapter begins with a long resume of the Charvaka system of materialist philosophy, and the author says this cannot be eradicated since many people are sympathetic to it. This was also the time when there was a flurry of discussion and writing on Advaita Vedanta.

At the more popular levels there were even alternate histories, sung as legends by folk poets and bards, very different from the court chronicles. The compositions of the Bhakti teachers were recited and sung throughout the sub-continent and are foundational to what is described as Hinduism today. The *sant* tradition has been in many ways a major force in the formulation of what we recognise as Hinduism today at the level of belief and worship. This was the tradition that evolved in the historical momentum of the last thousand years. The *bhajans* of Mira and Surdas and of Tyagaraja, and the *bandishes* of the Dhrupad *ragas* were not the compositions of an enslaved people.

Caste and Conversion

An impression has been created that because the Hindus were enslaved, it was easy to put them through enforced conversion to Islam. But historical evidence supports neither of these propositions. Even when there was conversion from a Hindu sect to a Muslim one, we have to keep in mind that often sects and castes were entwined. The chronicles of the Sultans claim that huge numbers were forcibly converted or decimated. Some would certainly have been forcibly converted in order to make the claim and some done away with as is common to invading armies, but certainly not fifty thousand at a time, or anywhere near that number, as the Chronicles of some Sultans claim. We should ask further as to who exactly was converted, and what does conversion mean in a society where the idea is alien, since the Brahmanic and Shramanic sects did not convert.

Our understanding of conversion would be more to the point if we could focus on sect and caste where the evidence exists. Which existing caste or sect converted to which sect of Islam, and what were the social consequences of conversion. This may provide a better explanation than merely referring to Hindus becoming Muslims and not investigating further.

Most of the individual conversions, in small numbers were from those in the upper castes. Many retained their caste identity to claim status. Some local ruling families converted and some married into the new Muslim ruling families although not necessarily converting. Mughal royalty marrying into Rajput royal families and where the women were not required to convert to Islam, is an indicator of negotiations in a politically complex situation. Shah Jahan had the advantage of a Mughal-Rajput descent.

Conversion in larger numbers occurred when a *jati*/caste converted. This was more frequent among lower castes who had been promised a better status but which status seldom materialised. Changing the over-all status of castes would have meant a major social upheaval.

If the converted caste continued with its caste name and occupation as most did, conversion would have had limited social advantage. Status depended on occupations as before and the rank remained virtually the same in the hierarchy. The litmus test of observing caste lay in arranging marriage and from this it is clear that the rules of caste largely continued, reinforced by social sanction. This would explain the overlapping mixed identities among those not regarded as upper caste and as recorded in the earlier census and in some colonial ethnography.

Sociologists working on societies in India other than those listed as Hindu find that they too function with the system of castes. Even those religions that claimed to be egalitarian could not entirely eliminate caste distinctions and more so between the higher and lower. Rules of endogamy and commensality are observed widely. The presence of caste is particularly strong in discriminating against and segregating Dalits. The excluded Dalit is found in every religion under different names. The Dalit is present even among those religions that claim all men to be equal in the eyes of God. So in addition to those now called Dalits in the broadly Hindu communities, there are the *pasmandas* – the fallen, the oppressed, among Muslims; the *mazhabis* of the Sikhs; and the *churahs* among others. Even places of worship were segregated.

Religions in India, irrespective of whether they originated in India or came in from elsewhere at a later stage, functioned in conformity with caste society, although not always according to the *Dharmashastra* rules. Some sects deliberately opposed these but many tacitly accepted them. Discrimination against the lowest castes or those outside caste society such as those we call Dalits today, and the *adivasis,* is characteristic of the formal religions. Similarly the assumption that women are inferior to men, indicated by social inferiority, was a marked feature of these religions, as indeed it was of the socially higher levels of society in general, with a few exceptions. This was despite the fact that in some religions there was the worship of goddesses and mother figures. Such worship made no difference. The worship of the *kuladevi* existed together with the insistence on *sati* and *jauhar*. In a secular, democratic system, uniform civil laws should ensure gender justice in endorsing the equality of all.

If a range of sects rather than monolithic religions was characteristic of pre-Islamic India, this phenomenon appears to have continued with the larger majority of people even after the coming of Islam. Were the umbrella terms more frequently a convenience when speaking of the other, until they were redefined into the neat binary in colonial times? Some recent scholars have argued that there were perhaps attempts to give definitions to these umbrella terms in the late second millennium, by suggesting a self-perception where similar sects would see themselves as part of a larger unit. The argument hinges on how Hindu is defined in these times as compared to now. The flexibility in the use of the term then and its relative rigidity now, is evident. The initial geographical term 'Hindu,' referring to the people of al-Hind, gradually came to be used not for a specific religion but for all those that did not identify with Islam. Terms for specific religions remained vague. Eknath's delightful banter, *Hindu-Turk Samvad,* written in the late sixteenth century, should perhaps be read less as referring to Hindu-Muslim relations as we understand them today, and more as the general approach of people of that time living in the same place, with varying sectarian identities. What is striking is the little attention that is given to what we emphasise today, namely conquest and conversion.

But the creation of monolithic communities, crystalised in the labels Hindu and Muslim as the identity of these communities, would seem to be the contribution of colonial policy. Resistance in some cases is recognisable largely from the upper castes. For them a new religion could threaten a loss of patronage and power. But the majority either let existing beliefs and rituals continue or else negotiated the change through a number of new sects in the usual way.

The World of Today

We now recognise that our understanding of the historical interactions that took place in the past, do mould current thinking about our identities in the present, to a large extent. They therefore deserve more analytical and precise historical explorations. We should not allow them to be dismissed by political slogans of various kinds.

In this rather scattered attempt to look at some aspects of the past, I have tried to underline the plurality in the articulation of religion in India, often in the form of sects and their inter-face with caste. I am also suggesting that possibly the weakening of the one is likely to weaken the other. To eventually disengage religious institutions from controlling the functions of civil society could bring about a more equitable society. The process of secularising society will have to address both religion and caste and to that extent it requires a different kind of analysis from that of religions elsewhere. Now that we have internalised the colonial version of our religions and are experiencing its aftermath in the stridency of dominant religious organisations, we have also allowed some of these to become mechanisms for political mobilisation. Secularisation therefore will have to be thought through with considerable sensitivity and care. Although it cannot be a rapid change nevertheless, a serious beginning has to be made through establishing confidence all round. Violent attacks are never a solution.

A secular society and polity does not mean abandoning religion. It does mean that the religious identity of the Indian, whatever it may be, has to give way to the primary secular identity of an Indian citizen. And the state has to guarantee the rights that come with this identity. This demands that the state provides and protects human rights, a requirement that at the moment cannot be taken for granted. Such an identity while adhering to human rights and social justice, would also be governed by a secular code of laws, applicable to all.

A beginning could be made in two ways. It would be necessary to ensure that both education and the civil laws are secular. Secular education means the availability of all branches of knowledge to all without discrimination. The content would have to be information giving access to knowledge, and knowledge that has been up-dated; and at the same time it involves training young people to use and understand what is meant by critical inquiry. Given that we are a democracy perhaps we can jointly work out how best this could be done.

Our laws were drawn up in colonial times, although we have made some changes after independence. In a turn to the secular we shall have to comb through the existing laws to ensure that they conform to equal rights for all citizens with no exceptions. Resolving the differences between civil and religious laws of each religion will obviously have to be discussed in the light of their existing social codes, and with those currently controlling these codes. In this process, injustices and discrimination against the minorities and the under-privileged, whether because of religion, gender or caste, will need to be annulled. The continuation of special laws for particular communities, whether they be the laws made by *khap panchayats* or the triple *talaq*, would need to be reconsidered. Law does not remain law if it can be manipulated to allow of discrepancies. This is likely to be the most problematic in our turn towards secularising society. Isn't it time now for a conscious beginning?

The overwhelming projection of religiosity in the world that surrounds us, sometimes appears to be a surrogate for not coming to terms with real life problems; or perhaps it is due to our having become a competitive society with all its unexpected insecurities.

The ostentation of rituals is taken to excessive lengths largely as a display of wealth, a display that most people can ill-afford. For the truly religious the simplest of rituals suffice and sometimes even these are not necessary. Rituals ultimately are an appeal to a supernatural authority to endorse our welfare. Can we instead consider how we can make the reality of citizenship a guarantee of our social welfare, our well-being, our understanding of our world and our wish to bring quality into our lives? The secularising of society is not an over-night revolution. It is a historical process, and will need time, but hopefully it will be assisted by the recognition that the state and society need to function in a new way. Implicit in democracy is the upholding of the ethic of human interaction. The secularising of society is an advancing of that ethic.

2

Secularism in India: Past and Future

—*Asghar Ali Engineer*

Introduction

India became a secular democratic State in 1950 when its Constitution was promulgated on 26th January of that year. In a way, it was in fulfillment of the promise made by the Congress leaders during freedom struggle. On promulgation of the Constitution, all citizens of India irrespective of their caste, creed, colour and sex got equal rights and became equal before law. It was a great social revolution for the people of India; a caste ridden hierarchical society where large number of people was treated as untouchables.

India had met with a great tragedy at the time of its independence, as the country was divided into two nations: India and Pakistan. Muhammad Ali Jinnah believed that Hindus and Muslims were two nations who could not live together and his view eminently suited the interests of the British colonialists and India was divided. Right from the colonial days, due both to the machinations of the British colonialists as well as the interests of Hindu and Muslim elite, Hindu-Muslim conflicts came to the fore and communal problem became one of the main problems of modern India.

The problem indeed was not religious but political and a result of struggle for political power between the educated middle and upper classes of both the communities. Had it been a religious problem, the religious leaders would have led it. But the two-nation theory was propounded by Jinnah, a Barrister at Law, who was almost an irreligious person and was, more or less, unaware of the teachings of Islam. Profoundly religious scholars like Maulana Abul Kalam Azad and the organisation of Islamic theologians, the *Jami'at al-Ulama-i-Hind* vehemently opposed partition and supported composite nationalism on religious grounds.

Thus, in its pre-independence days, India was confronted with communal problem which was, among others, a major obstacle for securing freedom from the Colonial rule. The Indian National Congress, however, was committed to a secular democratic State despite the communal problem and redeemed its promise on 26th January 1950 by promulgating the Constitution. It indeed was a milestone for multi-religious India.

However, if promulgation of the Constitution was redemption of the promise, it was also the beginning of new problems. To resolve to make a country secular is one thing and to manage successfully a multi-religious, multi-cultural and multi-caste society is something else. Also, nation-building is a far more complex and challenging process than securing nationhood. It is easy to declare a country as a "nation" but the task of *making it a nation* is extremely challenging.

In the above context, the real test lies in implementing the provisions of the Constitution. Although the Constitution gives equal fundamental rights to all castes and creeds, the upper caste Hindus who controlled all key political and bureaucratic positions, finance and industries did not show their readiness to share all resources equitably with others.

Factors and Actors Affecting the Secularism

A democratic society has to be equitable, if not egalitarian, and just; distributing jobs and economic resources equitably. And for this, politics have to be value-based so as to enforce the provisions of the Constitution honestly and with a sense of integrity. But, it is sad that our politicians violate these values and principles with utter impunity. Immediately after independence most of us were proud of being Indians. Today Indian identity has vanished into thin air.

We are today less Indian and more Hindu, Muslim, Christian or Sikh at one level; Brahmin or Rajput or OBC or Dalit, at another level, and Maharashtrian or Kannadiga or Tamilian etc. on a third level. We fight for power on the basis of these parochial identities. We are proud of these parochial identities and our politicians too appeal for votes on the basis of these parochial identities.

Those who often parade their patriotism are most guilty in this respect by appealing to Hindu and caste identities within its fold. Today the Bharatiya Janata Party (BJP) relies on Hindu and other caste identities within its fold most unabashedly.

And these identities are emphasised for distribution of power and economic resources as well as government jobs. There is no wonder that in the process the minorities suffer and develop a strong sense of being discriminated against. The situation has come to such a pass that now even the judicial system, more at the lower levels than at higher levels, is tainted with these identities. Thus, in multi-religious and multi-cultural societies it is much more challenging to have a smooth nation building process.

The real purpose of adopting a secular democratic Constitution for India was to do justice to all sections of the society, without discrimination against anyone. The leaders of the freedom movement were inspired by these secular democratic values and had assured all sections of the society that their being in minority or majority will not make any difference and all citizens would be treated equally.

When the Indian National Congress came into existence in 1885, all sections of the Indian society viz., Hindus, Muslims, Christians, Sikhs and Parsis, supported it whole-heartedly. The slogan raised in the freedom movement was "*Hindu-Muslim-Sikh-Isai, hain sab bhai bhai*" i.e. people of all these religions are brothers and united in their struggle against foreign rule. It is not widely known that Muslim theologians too supported Indian National Congress enthusiastically.

Maulana Rashid Ahmed Gangohi urged Indian Muslims to join the Indian National Congress and fight against the British colonialists. The Ulema of Deoband School also published a book *Nusrat al-Ahrar* (For the Help of the Freedom Fighters) in which they collected more such Fatwas. Badruddin Tyebji, a retired Chief Justice of the Bombay High Court joined Indian National Congress along with three hundred Muslim delegates. Justice Tyebji also became the President of the Indian National Congress.

By electing Justice Tyebji, Pherozshah Mehta, a Parsi, and W.C. Bonnerji, a Bengali Christian, as Presidents of the Congress Party, it was made clear that the INC was a secular and not a Hindu party. Though Mahatma Gandhi used to describe himself as a

Sanatan Hindu (an orthodox Hindu) he was secular to the core and believed in extending equal respect for all religions. Incidentally, it should be noted that in the Indian context, secularism never meant being religious or anti-religious but treating all religions with equal respect.

In his speech at Oxford in the mid-fifties, Jawaharlal Nehru, the first Prime Minister of India, himself an agnostic, had defined Indian Secularism as State giving equal protection to all religions while keeping equal distance from all religions. Nehru had a strong conviction for secularism and never deviated from his commitment to secularism. He was also committed to protecting minorities and giving them just share in political power as well as in the economic resources. In fact, he was the spirit behind the secular character of the Indian Constitution.

The Congress had committed itself to secular democracy and fundamental rights for all its citizens in its Karachi session of 1931 and it tried to assure the minorities that they will not be discriminated against. While Jinnah was not convinced, the Ulema (theologians) accepted this assurance and fully cooperated with the Congress during the freedom movement. And the Ulema have stood by their commitment till today. They have been allies of secular democratic Congress party.

Nehru, as pointed out before, remained committed to secular values but was surrounded by those congressmen who hardly had secular convictions and were in the Congress party, not because of their secular democratic convictions but because the Party delivered. In fact, most of them entertained, if not overtly exhibited, communal attitudes. Thus, Nehru's dream found great obstacles. He knew much depended on the educational system if one were to cultivate modern secular and scientific values.

But, the education system in post-independence India never changed. The education system in India was devised by Macaulay to produce clerks rather than critical intellect or scientific temper of mind. The British, in its own interest, made the education system divisive in character so as to rule over India. Thus, in post-independence India there was a need for a thorough change in the education system. Dr. Zakir Hussain, who later became the President of India, had devised a basic education system in consultation with Mahatma Gandhi. But it also remained on paper and was never implemented seriously.

Nehru believed that communalism will die its own natural death when scientific and technological education is imparted and scientific temper is cultivated. But it was only a pipe dream of Nehru. The Congressmen surrounding him never wanted such a radical change in the education system. They were more interested in retaining status quo in education as it served their interests much better. They were not at all interested in social change and refused to attack the age-old customs and traditions, and even the caste hierarchy.

Though the government appointed the Kothari Commission in the mid-fifties to make recommendations for bringing in changes in the education system, and Professor Kothari made excellent suggestions, they were totally ignored. Thus, the scientific temper and critical mind could never be developed. Also, access to education itself was, and still is, quite limited. Even primary education has still not been made compulsory after 61 years of independence.

Primary education in municipal and government schools is far from satisfactory. As the quality of primary education in municipal and government schools being poor, the middle and upper classes never send their children to these schools and opt for private schools, which, of course, are beyond the reach of the poor. The concept of neighbourhood schools was never accepted by the elite ruling class. Thus, let alone scientific temper, the government and municipal schools perpetrated caste hierarchy, as the poor mostly belonged to lower castes and minorities. It is impossible in modern India to transcend these barriers.

Thus, while the education system by and large continues to impart traditional values and perpetrate communal divisions, in the BJP-ruled States, the syllabus of social sciences openly promotes hatred against minorities, especially Muslims and Christians. Worse are the schools run by the Rashtriya Swayamsevak Sangh. Their textbooks are full of hatred for Muslims and declare Islam and Christianity as "outside religions", not part of India. For them Indian religions are Hinduism, Buddhism, Jainism and Sikhism. Thus, Hindu children studying in these schools are made to feel that Muslims and Christians are outsiders.

One textbook prescribed for XII standard in the State of Rajasthan (ruled by BJP) even praises fascism and says it is more desirable for India as it enables one leader to take right decision at the right time. The RSS-run schools teach children that Islam spread in India by shedding rivers of blood and with Qur'an in one hand, and sword in the other. What kind of mindset will it create among young children? They simply grow up with hatred for minorities. There is no emphasis on value education at all. Without value education children will not acquire healthy mind and secular and democratic values.

Role of Media

If political campaigns are heavily loaded in favour of religious and caste biases, even the Media has been communalised. Even the mainstream media, both English and vernacular, is biased in favour of the majority community, though the English media is comparatively better and more subtle. But, the vernacular media (Hindi, Gujarati, Marathi etc.) is much more biased and at times openly partisan. The role of regional or vernacular media during communal riots is highly partisan and at times very crudely so.

A detailed study and careful analysis of the role of the vernacular press during the several major riots, right from the Jabalpur riots of 1961 to the Gujarat riots of 2002, reveals that the it has unabashedly been partisan. Unfortunately despite provision in the law against provocative writings and speeches, the Police just look the other way. The Gujarati newspapers openly provoked riots especially during 1969, 1985 and 2002 and no action followed.

The role of Marathi media during post-Babri demolition riots of 1992-93, especially of *Samna* which is the mouthpiece of Shiv Sena, was highly objectionable. Unfortunately most of the policemen read *Samna* every morning, apart from the other Marathi-speaking public, making them develop a jaundiced view of the minorities. The policemen were highly communalised during 1992-93 riots in Mumbai and other places.

However, the role of English newspapers especially that of *Times of India* was very laudable. The whole editorial team at that time was highly committed to secularism. But the problem is that the English-language papers are read by very few people, the educated elite, but those who indulge in riots and the constabulary who handle law and order situation, read only the vernacular papers. Same thing happened in Gujarat. The Gujarati language papers which are highly communalised are read by the constabulary and the general mass of the people, who imbibe raw prejudices and misinformation through these vernacular papers.

And now the electronic media has made things even worse. If newspapers are read by educated people only, the electronic media is accessible even to the illiterate. Electronic media, even if not communalised (though the vernacular channels very much are) thrives by sensationalising the news and telecasting it repeatedly on their channels round the clock. Thus, it becomes highly provocative. Also, on these channels the minorities are stereotyped, further confirming the prejudices acquired through other sources as well.

Role of Politics

The political campaigns play even a worse role in this respect. As pointed out before, all appeals for votes are made on the basis of caste and religion. There is hardly any exception to this. Caste-based parties like the Samajwadi Party (SP), the Bahujan Samaj Party (BSP) and the Rashtriya Janata Dal (RJD) though claim to be secular but reinforce caste prejudices all the time. They *appear* to be pro-minorities; their convictions are not based on secularism but on the arithmetic of votes (combining Yadav and Muslim votes etc.).

Then of course the BJP is a Hindu right-wing party and its whole politics depends on hate campaign against Muslims and Christians. It primarily targeted the Muslims throughout the eighties, and from the nineties onwards has added Christians too. Its political influence has grown on the basis of its communal agenda alone. Its mainspring of ideology is the RSS (Rashtriya Swayamsevak Sangh) which wants to establish *Hindu Rashtra* in India. The RSS was founded in 1925 in Nagpur (Maharashtra) by Dr Hedgewar to 'counter Muslim communalism.' Earlier it was mainly based in urban areas but has now penetrated each and every village throughout the country.

The role of RSS is quite sinister and has grown gradually to great proportions. If there is any force in India today which impedes the growth of secularism and secular values, it is the RSS. The BJP (earlier known as Jan Sangh) has also grown so much thanks to the efforts of RSS. It cannot take any decision without consulting the RSS, although the RSS claims itself to be a non-political, cultural organisation. However, now the BJP does not even try to hide the fact (which it did earlier) that its connection with the RSS is that of umbilical cord.

In early fifties the Jan Sangh hardly wielded any influence. In the first election in 1952 after promulgation of the Constitution, it got no more than 3.1 per cent votes and won just three seats in the Parliament. There were many reasons for this. It was a newly formed party (though the Hindu Mahasabha of pre-independence days was its predecessor) and the Congress had tremendous prestige among the people as it had mainly led the freedom struggle and successfully liberated India from the British Rule.

In the next elections (1957) it won 5.9 per cent votes i.e. nearly doubled its percentage but won only 4 seats. At the 1962 elections, it got 6.4 per cent votes but won 14 seats. In 1967, it got 9.4 per cent votes but won 35 seats. This was so because the Congress had started losing its popularity and appeal. Nehru was dead already and the Congress Party was now faction-ridden, famine conditions had seen a rise in prices and the opposition parties had formed alliances in States like Uttar Pradesh, which is part of what is known as the Hindi or cow-belt and where the Hindu right had great influence.

In 1971, Mrs Indira Gandhi had acquired great prestige as she succeeded in breaking up Pakistan and creating Bangladesh. She successfully trounced the opposition in the 1971 elections and the Jansangh could get only 7.4 per cent of the votes and win 22 seats in the Parliament. However, things changed again due to emergency clamped by Mrs Indira Gandhi which was highly unpopular and a new political formation i.e. Janata Party came into being under the leadership of Jai Prakash Narain, a socialist leader. The Jansangh merged with the Janata Party and took a pledge to follow 'Gandhian Socialism' and 'Secularism'.

This was a highly opportunistic step taken by Jansangh as it knew that it will be wiped out if it did not change its ideological stance. However, it was only a tactical move. It never renounced its communal ideology as it refused to severe its relation with the RSS, its ideological mainspring. In fact, the Janata Party Government fell mainly because it refused to severe its connection with the RSS. It is known as double membership controversy (membership of the RSS along with that of the Janata Party).

The Jan Sangh now took another birth under a new name, the Bharatiya Janata Party, and again repeated – for tactical purposes of course - its pledge to accept Gandhian socialism and secularism. But soon it discovered that by accepting this ideological stance it lost its very identity. It very badly lost in the 1984 elections, wining only two seats in the Lok Sabha.

Thus, while in the Janata Party it had won 80 seats in 1977 elections (but mainly due to alliances with other parties), it was reduced to a political non-entity at the 1984 elections winning only two seats. Thus, it went back to its communal politics with a vengeance to rediscover its original identity. The RSS, the ideological arm of the BJP, was happy at the return of BJP to the Hindutva ideology.

In its new form, the BJP pretended to accept 'secularism' and Atal Bihari Vajpayee, who had cultivated an image as a 'moderate,' was made the President of the Party. But after the political disaster of 1984, there was change of guard and L.K. Advani known for his aggressive communal stance, was made the President. Advani tried to revive its original ideology of communalism with a new strategy i.e. questioning the very concept of Congress secularism.

Firstly, Advani described the very concept of secularism as Western in origin (which is what the RSS had always had maintained) and secondly he called the Congress secularism as 'pseudo-secularism' based on 'appeasement' of minorities. He alleged that the Congress appeases Muslims for their votes and discriminates against Hindus. He came out with a strange theory that the Hindus have been 'besieged' in their own country due to the politics of appeasement pursued by the Congress.

This appealed to the Hindu middle classes, who had developed a sense of insecurity for a number of reasons (the Khalistan separatist movement in the Punjab and the ASSU movement in Assam, the latter based on opposition to infiltration of Bangladeshi Muslims in large numbers). Also, the Muslim leadership played very opportunistic role during the Shah Bano movement based on the Supreme Court judgment for maintenance after the *iddah* (three months after divorce) period.

The opposition to the Shah Bano judgment made Hindu middle classes quite apprehensive about Muslims rejecting a secular judgment based on secular laws of the country and that made the Hindu middle classes believe that Advani's theory of 'appeasement' of Muslims was true. The issue of reservation was also quite unpopular among the newly emerging professionals among the upper caste Hindus and the BJP shrewdly utilised this controversy also in its own way.

Though it could not oppose the reservation openly, the BJP supported the policy from behind the scenes. And when the Mandal Commission Report was implemented by V.P. Singh, the then Prime Minister whom the BJP was supporting, and all hell was let loose. The BJP was in a dilemma. If the Mandal Commission Report was not acceptable to the upper caste Hindus who constituted the main political base for the BJP, the Party could not also oppose Mandal Commission openly for fear of losing the OBC (Other Backward Castes) votes, which the BJP was trying to woo.

The BJP came out of this dilemma by raising the issue of *Ramajanmabhoomi* temple which was unleashed by the Rajiv Gandhi Government by opening the doors of Babri Masjid for worship of Ram Lalla and laying the foundation stone for *Ramajanmabhoomi Mandir*. Thus, it would be seen that the Congress party showed no less opportunism for the sake of votes by starting a controversy that had great communalising potential. It had done so to fight the Hindu wrath as the Rajiv Gandhi Government had upturned the Supreme Court judgment on the Shah Bano issue.

Thus, at this juncture both the Congress and the BJP were competing with each other in destroying the secular values of Indian politics. It was this competitive communalism of the two major parties that made last two decades of twentieth century most communal in post-independence India.

Right from 1980 to 1992-93 several major communal riots took place from Moradabad (1980) to Biharsharif (1981) to Baroda and Meerut (1982) Neili, Assam (1983) to Mumbai, Delhi (1984) to Ahmedabad (1985) to Meerut (1987) to Bhagalpur (1989) to Mumbai (1992-93). It will be seen that most of these riots took place in North India which has been the major theatre of communal politics, as this has been the centre of Hindu communalism as well as of Muslim communalism before independence. Also, the States of U.P. and Bihar together have the largest population of Muslims in India compared to the Southern and Western States.

Basically, Congress is not a communal organisation. Ideologically it is committed to secularism and secular values in politics and even today its commitment stands out compared to BJP which is a Hindu communal party. But in practice the Congress has not been able to redeem its image and also because it has to compete with the BJP for votes, its actions are often determined by consideration of Hindu votes. Unlike the BJP which is quite aggressive in its communal politics, Congress does not exhibit similar aggressiveness in its secular politics.

Gujarat is the best example of soft communalism of the Congress. BJP is quite strong in Gujarat and plays its Hindu card quite aggressively. While the BJP has eminently succeeded in selling its communalism to the Hindu middle class, the Congress has lost all its political courage to win this middle class to secular values. It either becomes neutral to BJP politics or simply accepts it with slight murmur.

Fortunately one factor goes against the BJP on the all-India level: that is India's bewildering diversity. Had India not been diverse to the extent that it is, the BJP would have come to power on its own. This needs some elaboration, being a most interesting phenomenon.

The BJP (formerly Jan Sangh) started with a very narrow political base. It got only 3.1 per cent votes as the Congress enjoyed great prestige and secondly the educated middle class comprised a very thin layer to begin with. However, it expanded slowly as the Hindu middle class expanded, and as competition for developmental resources increased between Hindu middle classes and the middle classes of other communities, particularly that of Muslims, and also the competition for political power. Similarly, struggle for resources and power also increased between the upper caste Hindus and the scheduled castes and OBCs. In fact, Hindu communalism reached its peak at the end of the eighties when the government announced reservations for OBCs. Thus, it shows that communalism is the result of competition for political and economic resources.

Now coming back to diversity, the caste diversity, especially in northern India, acts as a great deterrent to BJP's communalism. The increased political awareness among Dalits and the OBCs has effectively checkmated BJP both in Uttar Pradesh as well as in Bihar. During the Ramajanmabhoomi campaign, northern India, particularly UP, was the main epicentre of Hindu communalism. The BJP won State legislative elections during the height of Ramajanmabhoomi campaign.

But Dalit leaders like Kanshi Ram and Mayawati were working hard to bring political awareness among the Dalits with a strong message against upper caste domination. This effectively weaned away Dalits from both the Congress as well as the BJP. Consequently, the BSP, a Dalit party, became a force to be reckoned with. If the Congress had lost out to the BJP at the height of the Ramajanmabhoomi movement (also because Muslims were unhappy with the Congress for laying the foundation stone for Ramajanmabhoomi temple), now BJP began to lose to the BSP. The BSP and SP (the party of Yadavs and other OBCs) came together to defeat BJP in the post-Babri Masjid demolition phase. Thus, the BJP lost to Dalit and OBC parties in its own heartland owing to caste diversity in India. Both in UP and Bihar the BJP has been completely marginalised and caste-based parties have come to power.

BJP in Southern India

Apart from religious diversity, the Hindu religion itself, as pointed out earlier, is far from homogenised entity through the length and breadth of India. Hinduism is also as diverse as India. For this reason, the BJP is unable to record an equal growth pattern simultaneously in all parts of India, even among Hindus themselves. Thus, it has been finding it very difficult to find entry in the southern States and it is only recently that the Party succeeded to form a government in Karnataka, one of the four southern States.

In the southern States, the Dravidian castes are supreme, particularly in Tamil Nadu. No party can succeed without support of one or the other Dravidian parties. At times the two major Dravidian parties, (the *Dravida Munnetra Kazhagam* (DMK) and the *All India Anna Dravida Munnetra Kazhagam* (AIADMK) have also entered into alliance with the BJP but the BJP has not been able to win more than couple of seats. In Tamil Nadu, some backward castes like the Thevars, a community of landlords, has its sharp contradictions with the Dalits and so it is supporting the Sangh Parivar.

In Andhra Pradesh, apart from caste contradictions, linguistic factor plays an important role. The main contenders for power in the State are the Congress and the Telugu Desam Party (TDP) (the State language is Telugu). Though at one point the TDP allied itself with the BJP, the BJP could not make much headway in the State politically. Also, after the alliance with BJP, the TDP lost power in the 2004 elections, as the Muslims of the State were angry with TDP for its truck with the BJP at the Centre and voted against it.

The State of Kerala has remained beyond BJP's reach for different reasons, though caste also plays its own role. Kerala has large segments of Muslim and Christian population, to the extent of 20 per cent each, with Dalits forming about 20 per cent of the population. Also, the Communist parties, particularly the CPM (Communist Party-Marxist), are quite strong. The Communists and the Congress alternate in seizing power and forming a government in Thiruvananthapuram. Though the RSS is trying very hard to penetrate the State, the BJP is yet to secure a respectable presence in the State. In Karnataka too the BJP could succeed in forming a government to the division of secular votes between two secular parties, the Congress and the Janata Dal (Secular) and also thanks to the opportunist alliance of JD (Secular) with the BJP in the previous government.

Thus, it will be seen that the BJP manages to widen its political space due to the lust for power of some of the secular parties, which enter into alliance with it. But for such opportunistic alliances by secular parties with the BJP, the latter would not have been able to widen its political space to such an extent. BJP once used to shun secular parties to protect its ideological purity. But once it realised that it cannot come to power on its own, it entered into alliances with secular parties compromising its ideological purity for political gains. This also helped to strengthen its various front organisations like RSS, VHP and Bajrang Dal.

The BJP is thus facing a very complex situation in the country today. On one hand, it has been checkmated due to diversity of castes and religions, and, on the other hand, it is trying to expand its political space through these alliances. The main advantage of coming to power even through such alliances lies in expanding the RSS base, an organisation committed to establishing Hindu Rashtra and its anti-minorities stand. Also, because of coming to power, the BJP has been able to infiltrate more and more of RSS cadres in various government services like teachers, police and bureaucracy. These are very crucial services. Today there are much more RSS people in these services and the States in which the BJP is in power it permits government employees to attend RSS *shakhas* (branches where RSS carries out brainwashing).

Another advantage of entering into political alliances has been that the BJP's front organisations like the VHP and Bajrang Dal have become much stronger than they were before and they have been emboldened to take very aggressive public postures. They are the storm troopers of BJP. In all communal riots these organisations attack minorities. In Gujarat riots VHP and Bajrang Dal mainly attacked Muslims and recently in Orissa these organisations were mainly involved in attacking Christians.

Conclusion

It will thus be seen that secular India has been considerably weakened in recent years and communal forces have grown. Also, the police, judiciary and bureaucracy have become more and more communalised and this has considerably increased the woes of the minorities. Whenever any terrorist attacks take place, even innocent Muslims become suspect and all rules of the law book are thrown to the winds and indiscriminate arrests are made and the arrested persons are tortured to obtain "confessions". Often the judiciary denies bail despite the lack of objective evidence because, thanks to the Sangh Parivar propaganda that Muslims are terrorists. The judiciary, especially at lower levels, also often falls prey to such propaganda.

It is again the result of more and more communalisation that while SIMI (Students Islamic Movement of India), a militant organisation, has been banned, the VHP and Bajrang Dal equally militant Hindu organisations have not been banned despite the existence of abundant proof of their involvement in various terrorist and violent activities. Justice demands that these organisations also be banned like SIMI so that terrorism and violent attacks could be more easily controlled.

There is no doubt that today minorities like Muslims and Christians feel much more insecure than during the decades following independence. Nehru had hoped that with greater education in the country there will be more and more secularisation of society but unfortunately, just the opposite has happened. There is more and more communalisation instead. Thus, there are contradictory forces working in the political processes today. Increasing democratisation should have meant more secularisation but increased democratisation is resulting in increased communalisation. We have tried to explain this contradiction above.

The Future of Secularism

Does it mean that there is no scope and future for secularism in India? That there is no scope and future will not be a correct conclusion. There is definite hope for secular future. As pointed out above, political processes are extremely complex and finely balanced. There are different factors which determine democratic polity of the country. These factors are regional, linguistic, cultural, religious and caste-based. The impact of these factors together does not favour infinite growth of communalism in India. In other words, the possibilities of Hinduisation of India are remote. Certain institutions of Indian democracy like the Supreme Court of India have proved to be strong pillars for protecting democracy and democratic values, including secularism.

In one of the judgements on Fundamental Rights (Golaknath case 1967 and Keshvanand Bharti case of Kerala State vs. Supreme Court 1973) the Supreme Court had observed that even a new Constituent Assembly cannot change the basic structure of the Constitution (i.e. its secular and democratic values, fundamental rights etc.). This judgment is of great value and it is because of this judgment that the NDA (National Democratic Alliance) government led by the BJP could not change the basic structure of the Constitution. It was otherwise on the agenda of the RSS and BJP to change the basic structure of the Constitution.

In other words, secularism will continue to be the basic feature of Indian democracy and no government will be able to change it. It is real strength of Indian democracy. Also when the NDA Government appointed a commission headed by the retired Chief Justice of India, it met with strong protest and NDA government had to modify the terms of reference of the Commission.

Thus, we see that functioning of secular democracy in India for last 61 years has generated a strong base, which cannot be tampered with. All the marginalised section of the Indian society, Tribals, Dalits, and Minorities and also sections of the upper caste majority community will never allow Indian Secularism to be weakened, let alone being replaced by Hindu Rashtra. It is secularism which guarantees the protection and security of the weaker sections of the society.

Apart from these weaker sections of the Indian society, the peripheral ethnic minorities as in the North-East and those in the

South will never accept to be ruled by Hindu Rashtra. It is because of ethnic, religious and caste-based minorities that the BJP could never get majority even in its hey days. The maximum percentage of votes BJP got was in 1998 when it won 25.6 per cent votes. It was reduced to 22.2 in 2004. Thus, 75 per cent of people do not support any such radical change in the Constitution and opt for Secularism.

Even among those who vote for BJP, many vote for reasons other than the core ideology of Hinduism. They vote because of caste and other considerations and so it is also difficult to say whether all the 23 per cent voters support the ideology of establishing a Hindu Rashtra and oppose secularism. It is for this reason that the BJP also has to maintain publicly that it accepts secularism. The future of secularism in India is safe and sound.

In view of the fact that most of the key posts in the administration, teaching and law enforcement are held by upper caste Hindus, many of whom are under the influence of RSS ideology, the enforcement of secular values and secular spirit of the Constitution appears to be wanting. That should not make one feel that the future of secularism is despairing in any way.

3

Secularism: Concept and Indian Scenario

—*Ram Puniyani*

Introduction

The concept and practice of secularism has come under heavy criticism and attack during last two decades or so. With the coming up of communal politics all over the world and also in India, the movement which aims at Religion-based Nationalism has posed various question marks on the concept of secularism as a state policy and secularism as a cultural attitude. In India there are different question marks on the 'practice' of secularism by the ruling party in the earlier years of the republic, the Congress. The interest, understanding and the process of deliberating on this theme always goes up during the communal violence and has persisted on a very high pitch from 1992 Mumbai violence. The theme has been extensively dealt with by social scientists. "Predictably, there has been no dearth of scholarly interest in the subject in recent months. Such interest is welcome as it helps to achieve clarity on what Indian secularism entails, well before we confront the next crisis." (Venktesan, 2010)

Diverse Meanings

Various meanings have been attributed to this crucial concept. On one hand secularism has meant 'the iron wall between state and religion' and on the other 'equal respect for all religions'. Sometimes it has also been used as synonym to atheism, particularly in Western countries. "India is a country where religion is very central to the life of the people. India's age old philosophy as expounded in Hindu scriptures called Upanishads is Sarva Dharma Sambhav, which means equal respect for all religions. The reason behind this approach is the fact that India has never been a mono-religious country. Even before Aryan invasion India was not a mono-religious country." (Asghar Ali Engineer, 2008, p. 35).

Secularism relates to the relationship between individual and religion on one hand, and religion and state on the other. "Sacculum, the ordinary Latin word for century, or age, took on a special meaning as applied to profane time, the time for ordinary historical succession." (Charles Taylor, *Modes of Secularism. In Secularism and its Critics*, Edited by Rajeev Bhargava, OUP, Delhi 1998, p. 32). Donald Smith's "*India as a secular state*" published in 1963 laid the debate on the topic here in India. "Smith argues that secularism entails the mutual exclusion of the state and religion in order that they may separate effectively and equally in their respective domains. A strict separation of religion and state, he suggests would help achieve religious liberty and equal citizenship." (V. Venkatesan, *ibid*). This formulation of his has been very contentious in the debates all through. The central point of disagreements on these formulations has been many. In two of the recent contributions on the topic, Rajeev Bhargava, '*The Promise of India's Secular Democracy*' OUP, 2010 and Rononjay Sen's "*Articles of Faith: Religion, Secularism and the Indian Supreme Court*" OUP 2009, the topic has found in-depth treatment. These authors point out several peculiarities of Indian Secularism. These are diversity of religious communities and consequent conflict over values, emphasis on practice rather than belief, many oppressive religious practices sanctioned by religion, due to which state intervention in these matters becomes imperative. (Venkatesan, *ibid*)

Many a debates about secularism restrict themselves to state policies alone, while secularisation is a deeper process and secularism is a flagship of new social relations. "Most of the recent debates have argued by focusing on secularism as a state sponsored ideology, side-tracking completely its relevance as a major social phenomenon, emerging at a particular historical juncture, as an outcome of various cultural, political, religious and economic forces in Europe." (Mehta Uday, 1998, p. 22)

The Beginnings

Secularism is a social phenomenon which emerged parallel to the rise of industrial society. From seventeenth century discoveries of science were challenging deeply held beliefs and faiths, which were integral part of the broad canvas of religion. The application of these technologies and rise of industrial societies necessitated the change in social equilibrium, which was prevalent at that time. The earlier society where agriculture was the dominant production activity and 'feudal' mode of production was prevalent; the major sectors of society were tied to land as poor peasants. Demands of newly developing industries required the peasants to be freed from land. What tied them to land was feudal social structure and the concomitant to ideological constructs, which were again part of the religion in the broad sense of the term. This laid the foundation of vast socio-political changes, which began as 'bourgeois revolutions' in different European countries. The monarchs, Kings, stuck to the system of hierarchies "...whose values it symbolised and incorporated, and on whose support it largely depended. Absolute monarchy was however free to do whatever it liked, in practice it belonged to the world which the enlightenment had baptized as feodolite or feudalism." (Hobsbawm, 1992, p. 37). With changing system of production, "There was thus a latent, and would be soon overt, conflict between forces of old and new 'bourgeois' society, which could not be settled within the framework of existing political regimes..." (Hobsbawm, *ibid*)

The clergy (Church is the most organised form of the same but similar role is played by Brahmins, and Mullahs also) supplemented the feudal structure, 'kingdoms' and fulfilled the need to ensure firm implementation of the ideology, which supplemented the feudal production norms. This was the time when social life was totally revolving around the dictates of the clergy.

With onset of industrialisation process, the earlier ideological chains proved to be an obstacle to the emerging industrial society. It is in this realm that one has to understand the loosening hold of clergy and some religious traditions on the totality of social life. One has to understand the social norms developing around modern rationality, ideas from science i.e. the beginning of 'age of reason', in contrast to 'age of faith'. The farmer having its roots in science and technology and later in the *clergy's* interpretation of the word of God, clergy's imposition of ideologies in the name of religion, clergy's use of emotions of people for smoothening the exploitative social system of feudalism. Historically this process first occurred in clear form in West, where the above phenomenon manifested itself in the struggle between church and the state. "Until the renaissance period the state was subservient to the church. It was only after a long struggle that state could free itself from the papal authority...it was possible for the state to free itself from the domination of the church due to emergence of a bourgeois class in Europe. Bourgeois class felt stifled under the domination of church. It required free society for its expansion. (Engineer, 1998, p. 2)

Church stood for the declining social force of feudal lords, stood for age of faith, while the emerging nation state (vis-à-vis kingdom) stood for 'age of reason', for industrialisation process based on science and technology, concretising newer social relations (industrialists and the workers) in the process. This process which was called 'Enlightenment' and is a part of secularisation process began as radical rationalist critique of some facets of religion, especially those pertaining to the mediation between people and God by the clergy. This process assumed the undisguised role of displacing aspects of religion and faith (manufactured by clergy) to the private lives of people, freeing the social life from the constraints of orthodoxy and obscurantism towards the emerging realms of modernity.

Secularisation

Thus, secularism is a product of social movement of industrial bourgeoisie and landless peasants, manifested initially (in West) as Renaissance and Enlightenment, it being the expression of man's urge to live life of his own, independent of the domination by Church, which was prevalent feature of medieval society. "The term secularism started being used as an ideology. G.L. Holyoake used the term secularism to define an ideology, wherein social and industrial morality "hitherto determined by reference to the transcending principles of religion were now to be determined by reason, and firmly anchored to the good of man in this life (Quoted in Mehta, *ibid*, p. 25). Starting from this premise secularism assumed a socio-historical context in mid nineteenth century, shaped by circumstances and philosophy of the time. Secularism was based on the values, which recognised the contribution of science as a major source of knowledge and considered technological progress, social amelioration and human welfare as the goals of life. The goals of life shifted to this world (secular, profane) from the other world (sacred). With crumbling of dogmas and supernaturalism under the wheels of science and reason, the repository of dogmas, the clergy took a back seat and modern secular democratic states began to occupy the 'drivers' seats. Secular ethos is not concerned about the other world (leaving them as a merry hunting ground for the custodians of dogmas, the clergy). In a sense secularism is the policy of modern nation states it is philosophy of secularisation process. A process through which man becomes a free person from his earlier domination by the blind faiths imposed on the society by the clergy to ensure the smooth running of kingdoms, which require divine legitimacy, conferred on them by clergy, to continue their crass exploitation of the peasantry, which is the main source of their wealth. Secularisation introduces instrumental values, rational procedures and technological methods, which bring along urbanisation, pragmatism, profanity, pluralism and mutual respect. Secularisation process brings in the concept that all value systems are a product of historical circumstances, without any claims of finality. As a part of the package, science replaces supernatural explanation of things with those in terms of natural laws and an intellectual attitude in which reality is accounted from worldly mode of thinking.

Secularisation is a process, which relegates clergy to the background, while many other components of religion survive in modified form despite secularisation and do not contradict it. Secularisation process is the accompaniment of democratisation, throwing the clutches of feudalism. If one is to regard religion as morality, code of conduct to fellow human beings and ethical values, there is no contradiction between secularism and religion. "Secularisation introduces instrumental values, rational procedures and technological methods that encourage urbanisation, pragmatism, profanity, pluralism and mutual respect." (Puniyani, 2003, p.186) Rudolf Heredia points out that secularisation implies, "...the development of autonomous social institutions that need no longer fall under the sacred 'canopy' of religion for their legitimating...this comes from the process of rationalisation which is instrumentally concerned with end-means relationship, and values-committed to this worldly human liberation." (Heredia, 1995, p. 18)

As such the word secular has been derived from Latin Sacculum, meaning span of time or age and by implication present age or the world. Thus, the word secular stands for this world or concerned with the affairs of this world. As such its antonym is 'other worldly' and not religion or religious. In societies which have undergone secularisation, religion does survive and state does not oppose people's faith. It occupies a place in personal life and social life and makes its presence felt in the 'social space'.

Secularism- Western or Modern

Some political streams see secularism just as a Western phenomenon; Secularism is unsuited for Indian conditions as it is profoundly Christian and Western in character. '...the very notion of 'secularism' as it originated in the west has no relevance in our country.' (Golwalkar, 1966, 214)

To see secularism as a principle of Christian west is a very simplistic way of looking at social phenomenon. It is true that for a brief while church overpowered the state power and controlled it, kings of Europe were subordinate to it for some time and then they revolted against the authority of the church to set them free. Charles Taylor points out that "The secularism of today is built on original distinction, but of course it involves transformation in it. The original point of Western secularism was the wars of religion...The need was felt for a ground of coexistence for Christians of different confessional speculations." (Taylor p. 32) Taylor further argues that there is a connection between secularism and modern democratic polity, which shifts from the hierarchical mediated access societies to horizontal direct access society, i.e. individual relating to the system not merely as a member of particular community.

As pointed out above secularism is an outcome of secularisation process, which is a comprehensive term for the changes in social values with the advent of industrialisation and accompanying social relations, introduction of science, technology and rationalist thinking in society. Secularism in that sense is a marker of modernity, overcoming of feudal relationships and value system and thereby is a battle cry of newer social classes interested in overthrowing the feudal relationships and the accompanying baggage of constraining ideologies which find their vehicle in the religious clergy. It is the political expression of democratic values, Liberty, Equality and Fraternity. So secularism is a must for India. As it has entered the modern era with the introduction of industrialisation and accompanying rationalism the logical values are those of secularism. Those propagating the above myth are the sections of society who stand to loose in the liberal ethos which are an accompaniment of secularism, those are the social elements who hold to religious nationalism in contrast to modern, secular democratic nationalism. No country can be a stagnant pool and with dynamic changes in society in progressive direction secularism comes in as an outcome of struggle of rising industrialist, poor peasant, worker and women against the obscurantist, dogmatic values and the feudal social system and further provides the base for enhancement of struggles of exploited and subalterns.

Indian Context

The process of secularisation in India was a bit different from the European experience. It was mainly for two reasons; one, in India the clergy was not as well organised as in Europe. And two, India was a colony of British. "The Indian state did not have to struggle to free itself from the power of the church, but only to locate itself in relation to the citizens who belonged to different religious denominations." (Panikkar, 1995, p. 120) During freedom struggle itself secularism was emerging as the most dominant principle of the 'Nation in the making', India. The leaders of Indian National Congress, Gandhi, Maulana Abul Kalam Azad, Nehru and others were deeply committed to the ideal of secularism though its expression was very different in all of them. As a matter of fact "The word 'secular' in political sense was used after the formation of Indian National Congress in 1885...Sir Syed, the advocate of Modern education amongst Indian Muslims, remained aloof from Congress and dubbed it as 'Hindu Organisation. The Indian National Congress leaders were keen to enlist Muslim support and hence, tried to convince them that the INC is a secular organisation" (Engineer, 1995, p. 39). It is not to be denied that some of the Hindu Nationalists also joined Congress and some other leaders in Congress were having ideologies coloured by communalism of different hue, but it is undoubted that Congress did represent secular ideology to a large extent. The constituent assembly debates made it amply clear, and secular principles were enshrined in our constitution. The social dynamics was very complex.

The process of secularisation/industrialisation was going on at slow pace. At this stage, though constitution was secular, state apparatus: bureaucracy, judiciary, army and police, was infiltrated by Hindu communal elements, government of Congress though predominantly secular was having many leaders in important positions that were influenced by Hindu communal ideology.

Secularism in India

There are many differences in the Western/Christian social situation and the Indian situation. Hinduism is not like Christianity as far as the organisation of its clergy is concerned. Since it is a collation of multiple sects it has diverse nature of its priestly class. "While no two social phenomenons can be exact duplicates, one can say that the basic premise of the clergy's role remains the same, cutting across all religions. In the hands of clergy, politics and jurisprudence were considered branches of theology and were treated alike according to principles prevailing in the latter." (Puniyani, 2005, pp. 34-35) Despite that, Hindu clergy did play a parallel role to the clergy in other religions, i.e. giving moral legitimacy to the power and authority of the king, though it may not have directly interfered in the affairs of the state. Many a Gurus and Acharyas have been the guiding lights to the kings. They acquired an advisory political role to the royalty and exercised considerable influence in the court of kings. They accompanied them to the battlefield and blessed them and mediated for godly favours.

The main difference in India comes in the arena that the industrialisation process. In India, it began during the colonial period, initially under the patronage of colonial masters. In West, secularisation process accompanied the industrialisation process and the culmination of this was diminution in the authority of the priestly class. Since India was not free, the movement for secularisation was very slow. Also since the clergy was scattered, society was plural and the state was colonial, the secularisation process went on in opposition to the overall hold of religious ideology and the clergy.

Freedom Movement and Secular Values

The secularisation of society though slow, its political reflection in the freedom struggle and the National movement was dominantly secular, though communal (Muslim and Hindu) nationalisms also came up in the wake as a reaction to the growth of secular nationalism. Initially secularisation process got reflected in movements of Jotiba Phule, Ambedkar and Ramaswamy Naiker. Caste and gender are core areas of secularisation process. "...Secularisation of caste, has detached caste from ritual status hierarchy on one hand, and has imparted to it the character of power-group functioning within a competitive democratic politics on the other. Changes of caste may be observed along two dimensions of secularisation: de-ritualisation and politicisation. These changes have (a) pushed the caste out of the traditional stratificatory system; (b) linked it to new structure of representational power; and (c) made it possible, in their cumulative impact for individual members of a caste to claim and achieve new economic interest and a class-like identity." (Sheth, 2000, p. 242).

The same process is seen in the women's issue with the beginning of education process amongst women, initiated by Savitribai Phule assisted by Fatima Bi and picked by various women despite heavy odds. It was a very difficult battle. During freedom movement both national movement and social reform processes were attempting to address the place of women in modern India. Upper caste Western educated men raised the questions related to upper caste women, sati, kulin polygamy, widow remarriage in particular. "At times, reform was symbolic rather than real, attempted through appealing to the shastras rather than changing the social circumstances. At another times female education was seen as an important lever to effect the change...The period of nationalist movement is also significant on several counts. It is often pointed out that, in the years of Gandhi's leadership women participated spontaneously in political struggle" (Seemanthini, p. 266). This is where the efforts of Savitribai Phule come in as the major point of transition and also the mass movement contributing to the secularisation process vis-à-vis women.

Secular nationalism was finding expression in the politics of Gandhi and Nehru while Muslim communalism found expression in the politics of Muslim League and Hindu communalism was manifested in Hindu Mahasabha and RSS. Some of the Hindu nationalists were the part of Indian National Congress as well. The social base of Muslim Communal nationalism was Muslim Zamindars and moneylenders; similarly Hindu communal nationalism had its base mainly in upper castes, amongst Hindu Zamindar and moneylenders. K.N. Panikkar points out that "the basic objectives of the early nationalist leaders were to lay the foundations of secular and democratic national movement...and to develop and propagate anti-colonial nationalist ideology." (Panikkar, 1988, p. 79)

Secular nationalism was rooted amongst the nascent industrialists, newer professionals and, vast sections of peasantry and the low castes. It was the aspirations of these classes, which gave strength to freedom struggle and were translated in the foundation of Indian State and its constitution. Thus, secularism is a principle of Indian society and not an artificial graft. It is result of the struggles of the rising industrial class and the section of peasantry and the shudras. The process of secularisation was too slow and the process of transformation of caste and gender was hampered by social forces within the society itself. "The movement for secularisation of society had enemies within the society itself. The weak secularisation movement, represented by Indian National Congress...was voicing, projecting the socio-economic needs of the rising nascent industrialists, a section of professionals and modern businessmen who came up in the wake of newer business environment. The opposition to their social aspirations came from the entrenched powers assuming communal manifestations. The newer developments were breaking the back of established social hierarchy of landlords and priests...these sectors of society threw up political formations like Muslim League and Hindu Mahasabha." (Ram, 1998, p. 101)

Secularism is a marker of modernity, overcoming of feudal relationships and value system and thereby is a battle cry of newer social classes interested in overthrowing the feudal relationships and the accompanying baggage of constraining ideologies which find their vehicle in the religious clergy. In India, with dynamic changes in society in progressive direction, secularism comes in as an outcome of struggle of rising industrialist, poor peasant, worker and women against the obscurantist, dogmatic values and the feudal social system and further provides the base for enhancement of struggles of exploited and subalterns.

Secularism: Freedom Movement

India won freedom under the aegis of secular democratic movement led by Indian National Congress under the leadership of Mahatma Gandhi, Jawaharlal Nehru and Maulana Abul Kalam Azad. Secularism was the guiding principle of anti-colonial struggle and it thereby succeeded in mobilising vast sections of this plural society. It was recognised as an essential element of platform for multi-religious, multi-caste, poly-ethnic population of the subcontinent, as an instrument for unity of the people at large.

The different strata of society, which were the main bulwark of this movement, were modern, i.e. industrial bourgeoisie, urban proletariat, poor peasants, women, shudras and modern intelligentsia. This core was able to mobilise sections of other population. After Independence many a nationalists had communal tinge and they tried to project Muslims as foreigners, alienating a section of Muslims. Despite these irritants of the national movement, it overall remained a secular one. National movement remained, "...on the whole, basically secular in its approach and ideology. And young nationalist Muslims like M.A. Jinnah and Maulana Abul Kalam Azad had little difficulty in accepting it as such and joining it. The secularism became sturdier with leaders like Gandhi, C.R. Das, Motilal Nehru, Jawaharlal Nehru, Dr. M.A. Ansari, Subhash Chandra Bose, Sardar Patel and Rajendra Prasad." (Bipan Chandra, p. 410)

Constituent Assembly: Indian Constitution

Constituent Assembly was formed which framed the constitution, which was diverse in nature, and represented the aspirations of majority of population. The constitution thus framed after prolonged debates made different provisions, which formed the base of secular practice. "The Constitution declares India to be a sovereign, socialist and democratic republic. Even though the terms secular (and socialist) were added only by the 42nd Amendment in 1976, the spirit embodying the Constitution was secular. In 1973, the Supreme Court held the secular character of Constriction to be one of the basic features of Constitution. Further the Fundamental Rights include prohibition of discrimination on the grounds of religion and right to freedom of religion including freedom of conscience and freed profession, practice and propagation of religion, freedom to manage religious affairs...". (Chandra, 1999, p. 48) These secular provisions of Indian constitution are,

(i) State by itself shall not espouse or establish or practice any religion,

(ii) Public revenues will not be used to promote any religion,

(iii) The state shall have the power to regulate any economic, financial or other secular activity associated with religious practice (Article 25 (2) (9) of Constitution),

(iv) every individual person will have, an equal right to freedom of conscience and religion.

Indian State

Ours is a secular state which has no particular religion of its own and must observe neutrality and equality in respect of all religions prevalent in the country. The state cannot discriminate between one religion and the other, or between their respective followers — regardless of their numerical strength in the country. At the same time constitution guarantees to individual and groups/ sections of citizens the fundamental right to religious freedom in all its facets. Thus, secularism, equality of religions and neutrality of state to various religions within the constitutional limits are the basic features and part and parcel of unalterable basic structure of constitution of India.

Thus, though the constitution-makers had not used the word secularism in the explicit fashion, Indian constitution was standing on the firm foundations of secular principles. Indira Gandhi merely added a descriptive word for something, which was already ingrained in the constitution. The spokesmen of Hindu Right taking advantage of the fact that the word was added during the much-dreaded 'emergency' are trying to throw mud on the very concept of secularism, which is anathema to their political interests.

Thus, "ours is a secular state which has no particular religion of its own and must observe neutrality and equality in respect of all religions prevalent in the country. The state cannot discriminate between one religion and the other, or between their respective followers — regardless of their numerical strength in the country. At the same time constitution guarantees to individual and groups/ sections of citizens the fundamental right to religious freedom in all its facets. Thus, secularism, equality of religions and neutrality of state to various religions within the constitutional limits are the basic features and part and parcel of unalterable basic structure of constitution of India." (Mahmood, 1996,1) Jawaharlal Nehru explained it thus "What it means is that it is a state which honours all faiths equally and gives them equal opportunities; that as a state, it does not allow itself to be attached to one faith or religion, which then becomes the state religion...In a country like India, no real nationalism can be built up except on the basis of secularity...narrow religious nationalisms are a relic of the past age and no longer relevant today" (Nehru, 1961) As per Nehru "...(secularism) does not obviously mean a state where religion as such is discouraged. It means freedom of religion and conscience, including freedom of those who may have no religion. It means free play of all religions, subject only to their not interfering with each other or with basic conceptions of our state." (Nehru, Quoted in Chopra, 94, 26)

Communalism

This resulted in a social development, which was mixed; on one hand secularism thrived and on the other communalism. Communalism though remained dormant, was never dead. With social changes during late 70's and early 80's communalism got a strong boost and it started attacking secularism in a big way. Its expression surfaced first through the policies of Indira and Rajiv, but in due course the Ram Janm Bhumi was taken up by BJP and during the course of this secularism came under severe attack.

BJP rose rapidly around the issue of Ram Janm Bhumi and the concept of Religion based Nationalism; Hindu Rashtra came up challenging the secular democratic nationalism. The nature of debate around secularism started changing. It was well captured by Professor Upendra Baxi, "The events of eighties have engulfed all hegemonic apparatuses of state and society rendering 'secularism' into a problematic category. Political parties, parliament and judiciary have all been in major ways, exposed to legitimisation crisis symbolised by events, such as, Shah Bano, Roop Kawar and Ram Janmbhumi-Babri Masjid issues, which have generated, both a rich theoretical discourses...Indian state has emerged as an arena for the struggle to redefine "Secularism", struggle which puts to severe test, not just hegemonic apparatuses but also repressive apparatuses as well. The relatively new Hindu political formations –the VHP and Bajrang Dal have emerged as ideologues and pedagogues of 'new secularism', which by combating the political appeasement of the minorities, strive to enhance the identity of Hinduism and Hindus." (Baxi, 1998, 153).

During this campaign for temple at the site of mosque an attack on secular ethos, syncretic culture and composite nationalism was also launched. It is in this backdrop that one has to understand as to why for so many decades after the independence 'secularism' was never on the firing line, as to why only during last decade and a half secularism has come under cloud and the concept of Hindu Rashtra is being asserted aggressively.

Indian Political Scene

Congress began as a secular party with the inclusion of people of all religions, and their continued association with this party during freedom movement. At the same time many a communalists formed the part of its leadership, Lala Lajpat Rai, Madan Mohan Malaviya and Dr. Moonje. Even the founder of RSS, K.B. Hedgewar was associated with it till 1934. At medium and grass root level many a Hindu communalists in particular remained and are part of this party. It is this which made Nehru to warn that Congress should be cautious of those members who sound secular but are communal in the real sense. At the level of policies Congress took quite a principled secular path till the demise of Pundit Nehru, after which it was compromised regularly. The problem became apparent with Indira Gandhi's election speeches in, Rajiv Gandhi's 'when a big tree falls'; Shah Bano, shilaynyas, and Narasimha Raos' afternoon siesta when the Babri was being razed to the ground. Many a riots took place during this regime when the ruling government either acted as the silent witness or colluded with the rioters.

While evaluating this it has to be kept in mind that the riots take place due to three major factors, the instigator and conductor, which according the inquiry commissions, (Jagmohan Reddy, Justice Madon, Vithayathil, Shrikrishna and Venugopal) mostly has been some organisation which is a offshoot of RSS. Teesta Setalvad (Communalism Combat March, 1998) points out that most of the inquiry commission reports point out the role of RSS affiliate in initiating and conducting the violence. The second factor is those who are supposed to control it, the political leadership. In this case the Congress when in power has been weak and ineffectual at places and active colluding at other. Mostly it has been lacking the political will to control it effectively. The third force is the police and bureaucracy, which has been regularly communalised and has become a force providing the umbrella to the rioters or the active participant in the execution of the pogroms. Communalism is not the program of Congress, its basic programme remains Secularism, but its execution of those values has been lacking in will power.

Left and CPM, has come in this arena of discussion after Nandigram, when in order to execute the global economic agenda, they used their cadres to settle the point by 'paying its opponents back in the same coin.' Its programme remains essentially secular, while the proactive will to counter the communal issues is not visible at all, be it the plight of minorities or the worsening hate against minorities in the states ruled by the left parties. The communalism prevalent in the minds has not been tackled at all. One will tend to uphold the argument of Aijaz Ahmad (In The Eye of the Storm, The Left chooses, EPW, June 1, 1996, pp. 1329-43) that there is a core difference between the communalism of Congress and BJP. While Congress employs it pragmatically, BJP is programmatically communal, its agenda and goal are driven in that direction.

BJP is the political child of RSS, which has the agenda of Hindu nation. Irrespective of its temporary mask of Gandhian Socialism, it does lapse in to the 'Hate minorities' mind set at the drop of the hat. It has the patriarch RSS and associates; VHP, Bajrang Dal, Vanvasi Kalyan Ashram, etc, who have been communalising the mind set, which is the base of communal violence. This RSS combine has been actively initiating situations which bring in violence. It has led many a carnages and with the help of certain elements of Congress and the helpful state machinery, has been polarising the communities along religious lines. The scholars of communal violence have made the observation that in the aftermath of most of the communal violence RSS combine becomes stronger in the areas, where the violence has taken place. Communalism, in overt and covert language is its political vehicle towards the Hindu nation. Its communalism is programmatic.

In our semi-secularised society, where the values of liberty equality and fraternity are not fully rooted, where the transformation of the caste and gender equations are not fully achieved, one can classify the secular formations, individuals in to four broad categories on the scale of secularism. The first category exists as a rarefied group this category belongs to the party/individual who proactively strive to bring in caste and gender equality in a substantive way. Here land reforms are the key and the endeavour to bring in the unity between communities is the hall mark of this group. Some dalit formations, gender right groups, groups working for communal harmony fall here. A synthesis of values of Bhagat Singh, Gandhi and Ambedkar can best describe this group, which today is not in a very good state of its health.

The formations like Left are genuinely secular but they have ignored the proactive measures to pursue this. Congress is mired by too many power seekers to be able to stand firmly to oppose the communal elements and lands up being the accomplice, in part or in full, of the phenomenon. BJP is the aggressive, intimidating opponent of democracy and secularism, whatever its expression. Its biggest 'achievement' is that some of the political workers compare it with other electoral formations. That's the bankruptcy of our times and cleverness of this party. It is effectively using the electoral space to do away with democratic values in due course. It is the Indian face of fascism.

The anti-Sikh violence was a sort of single go phenomenon, which had more to do with the ethno-regional factors. The Nandigram carnage is more of economic massacre, while the BJP led pogroms are targeted at the minorities as minorities, to consolidate their political hegemony. To be sure none of the violence can be condoned. The subtleties of these differences point out that while we do not have the real good choice for electoral arena, we will have to keep putting the civic pressure for bringing in better and better political policies through the grass root campaigns. All the same to compare BJP with other electoral formations will be undermining the threat of the agenda of RSS, which seeks to abolish democratic space and build a society in the image of glorious Hindu past.

One can very well say, today in electoral arena we do not have a choice among good, better and the best. We are riddled with bad, worse, worst and BJP!

Conclusion: Challenges to Secularism

Today the scenario is very complex. The communal forces in the form of various organisations doing politics in the name of religion have become dominant. The threat of attack to secularism is not only from the communal political party but it is deeper. It operates through communalisation of social space, by spreading myths and stereotypes against minorities, and by practicing a divisive ideological propaganda and politics. It also operates through different cultural mechanisms, through attack on rational values and culture, through increase of blind religiosity. The section of media and the continuation of many textbooks based on communal historiography and sociology is also a big threat to secular values.

If we wish to strength the secular ethos, it has to be an all round effort, through all platforms of society with a multilayered approach. The issues which undermine the secular values, like Article 370, Uniform Civil Code, allegation of appeasement of minorities, all these need to be handled at humane level by putting across the honest attitude to all sections of society. It has to be firmly aligned with the values of freedom movement and the values of Indian constitution. The attacks on secular values are the determined attempts by section of society to do away with the rights of the weaker sections of society, dalits, women, workers and Adivasis. We have to ensure that their self assertions, their rights are preserved and strengthened. Secularism has a much broader meaning in the sense of overcoming sectarian faith-based impositions to ensure that all sections of society are able to have access to justice and equity. Anandhi S. points out that "...secularism is a part of the wider struggle against socio-political domination as well as struggle against class, caste, gender and ethnic oppressions. Pluralism, one of the basic elements in construction of secular identity, cannot remain a mere rhetoric, instead it has to be embodied in active political struggles so that transformation potential of identities as well as voices of oppressed will get fore grounded. Since the dominant groups tend to entrench their hegemony by inculcating an image of inferiority in the subjugated, the struggle for secular values must be a revision of these values." (Anandhi, 1995, 183)

So today while we try to understand the inter-community relations, the deeper issues related to secularisation i.e. land reforms, issues related to caste and gender transformation towards equality cannot by undermined.

References

Anandhi, S. Contending Identities, Indian Social Institute, Delhi, 1995, 183.

Ahmad, Aijaz, "In The Eye of the Storm, The Left chooses", Economic and Political Weekly, June 1, 1996, pp. 1329-43

Asghar Ali Engineer, Secularism in India: Theory and Practice, in Heredia and Mathais, Secularism and Secularisation, in Secularism and Liberation, ISI 1995, p. 39.

—, "Religion and Secularism", in State Secularism and Religion, Ajanta, 1998, Engineer and Mehta, p. 2.

—, "Secularism in India", in Communalism in India, Ed. Vatsala Shukla, Hope Gurgaon, 2008, p. 35.

Baxi, Upendra, "The Struggle for redefinition of secularism in India", Paper presented at Jaipur 1993, Quoted in Engineer and Mehta, State Secularism and Religion, Ajanta 1998, p. 153.

Chandra Bipan, India After Indpendence, Penguin, Delhi, 1999, p. 48.

Golwalkar, Madhav Sadashiv, Bunch of Thoughts, Jagran Prakashan, Bangalore, 1966, 214.

Rudolf C. Heredia, Secularism and Secularisation, in Secularism and Liberation, Ed Heredia and Mathais, ISI Delhi, 1995, p. 18.

E.J. Hobsbawm, The Age of Revolution 1789-188, Rupa, Calcutta, 1992, p. 37.

Mehta Uday, Secularism, Secularisation and modernity in Engineer and Mehta, p. 22.

Nehru, Jawaharlal, Quoted in V. D. Chopra, Religious Fundamentalism in Asia, Gyan, New Delhi, 1994, p. 26.

Panikkar, K. N., "Towards an Agenda for Secularism, In Tranceding Boundaries, Edi Raendra Sail and Aji Muricken, Vikas Adhyan Kendra, 1995, p. 120.

P.R. Ram, Hindutva Onslaught on Secularism in State Secularism and Religion, (Engineer and Mehta) Ajanta, Delhi, 1998, p. 101).

Panikkar, K.N., Foundation of Indian National Congress; The reality, in Bipan Chandra, India's Struggle for independence, Penguin, Delhi, 1988, p. 79.

Puniyani, Ram, Communal Politics, Sage, Delhi, 2003, p. 186.

Puniyani, Ram, Religion: Opium of the masses or..., in Puniyani, Religion Power and Violence, Sage, 2005, Delhi, pp. 34-35.

Setalvad, Teesta, "Who Casts the first Stone", Communalism Combat, March 1998.

Sheth, D.L. Caste and Secularisation Process in India, in Contemporary Transitions, Edi; Peter Ronaldo deSouza, Sage, Delhi, 2000, p. 242.

Seemanthini Neeranjana, On the Women's Movement in India, in Contemporary India, p. 266.

Venktesan, V, Frontline, Volume 27 - Issue 08: April 10-23, 2010.

Taylor, Charles, "Modes of Secularism". In Secularism and its Critics, Edited by Rajeev Bhargava, OUP, Delhi, 1998, p. 32.

Section - B

Concept and Genesis

4

Secularism, Secularisation and Modernity: A Sociological Perspective of the Western Model

—UDAY MEHTA

This article attempts to make somewhat elaborate appraisal of the Western model of secularism. We thought of undertaking this exercise for three important reasons, one, in recent debate on the "crisis of secularism" in this country, some of the critics, like Madan and Ashis Nandy base their critique, assuming that the West provides" a model of secularism" rooted in some identical socio-culture and religious processes even in leading European, paving way for distinct models of development.

Secondly, most of these critics in recent debate have urged by focusing on secularism as a state sponsored ideology, side-tracking completely its relevance as a major social phenomenon, emerging at a particular historical juncture, as an outcome of forces in Europe. Restricting the focus of the debate on secularism as a state ideology or using it as an instrument of rationality, or as a value-structure leading to perverse, irreligious and inhuman process of development, distorts our understanding of the implications of the secularisation as a social process with its distinct characteristics and mode of development in different nations of Europe.

Thirdly, the recent debate on secularism in this country also overlooks the dual role of religion in society right from its inception. In classical Marxist perspective also, distinction is usually made between religions on the one hand as a complex organisation owing its existence and influence to the state patronage and in turn, becoming instrumental in strengthening and consolidating the prevailing class and power structure, and on the other hand religion, as located in popular, religious and social movements of the oppressed strata of the society articulating their grievances and registering their protest against unjust, inhuman, exploitative practices of the dominant classes and striving to 'restore' just, egalitarian social order. Religion, as Marx and Engels noted, was probably the only effective and easily accessible institutional mechanism, that majority of oppressed masses could use in traditional societies for articulating their grievances. Even in modern societies, such movements of the continue to play revitalising role as reflected (those struggles inspired by the liberation theology) in Latin America and social and religious movements of the oppressed strata even in this country, right from the early period of Indian history. Numerous sects and cults right from the Mauryan and even earlier period, such as *Lokayat, Ajivikas,* Buddhist, *Nath* and *Siddha* cults, various Tantric sects, medieval Bhakti and Sufi movement culminating in religio-reform movement by Mahatma Phule and other social reformers in nineteenth century, articulated the aspirations of the oppressed strata in this country. Recent debate hardly recognises this dual role of religion in this as well as in Western world. As a matter of fact, Madan and others hardly even take note of such parallel trend in Indian religious traditions. Hence, this debate often becomes too abstract and academic for large sections of this country.

Finally, as stated earlier, we have done a little elaborate appraisal of Reformation, the French and Industrial Revolution, in spite of the fact that sufficient literature is available on these major historical phenomena nevertheless, our propose is reexamining the implication of these significant epoch making events, is to focus on different implications of these events for major European nations, like Germany, France and England and to indicate their relevance for the proper appraisal of the event debate on secularism, which has, by and large, overlooked their significance.

The study is broadly divided into five sections. The first section deals with the Protestant Reformation in Europe and specifically with the Reformation in Germany. We have done detailed appraisal of the Reformation in Germany, keeping in view the peculiar features of the Germans economy, its feudal structure and quality. Inspite of its backward economy and weak political structure, the Reformation made the first initial dent in Germany. Secondly, revolutionary, insurrectionary movement found the most powerful and militant expression in Germany, despite or because of its backward economy and weak polity. Marx and Engel appraisal of the German situation and peasant wars, even today, sound so refreshing and revealing. Engels particularly, has given considerable weightage to radical role of the religion, especially the early Christianity in inspiring revolutionary movement in Europe. As noted earlier, till the advent of the capitalism, religion probably provided the only effective and easily accessible mechanism to ventilate the aspirations, as well as the protest of the oppressed strata. Even after the advent of the capitalism, its significance as the "weapon of weak" should not minimised. Keeping this consideration in view, we have dealt with the Reformation in Germany more exhaustively.

Second section provides with appraisal of the Reformation in England and also deal with the impact of Industrial Revolution in UK.

Third section deals with the French Revolution and Reformation in France. We have gone into causes and consequences of the French Revolution and their impact on secularisation process, religious institutions and practices. This survey of the French Revolution, we thought, is relevant in the context of understanding distinct features of the secularisation process, secular state and religious institutions and practices in Europe.

The Fourth section focusses on the recent studies on popular religious revival movements in Europe and specifically in France. The emergence of new studies of religion in Europe in last over a decade has significantly altered our understanding of rise and decline in religious influence in the West, since the French and Industrial Revolution.

In this context particularly, recent studies on "feminisation of religion" in terms of changes in devotional practices in Catholic Europe especially in France, that led to increasing involvement of women in religious practices are quite revealing and these studies also bring out how religious institutions have become instrumental in empowerment of women and religion being used as an effective "weapon of weak" by women in large numbers in France during the nineteenth century.

The last section deals with the emergence of numerous radical, militant religious sects in England since the advent of the Industrial Revolution. It also deals with their decline and cooption with the established religious or social institutional structure over a period of time in UK.

Etymologically, the word secular originates from the Latin *seculum* which implied "great span of time" or the 'spirit of the age' subsequently, it acquired different meaning, that of belonging to 'This World'. Thus, two worlds are conceptualised i.e. the secular and the religious or the temporal and the spiritual. In the Christian discourse, the spiritual order is regarded as decisive in terms of ultimate truth. The term secularisation was the subsequent outcome. It was coined in 1648 after the Peace of Westphalla which originally referred to the transfer of ecclesiastical lands to civic control. By the nineteenth century, in the context of strong powerful hold of enlightenment values, G.L. Holyoake used the term secularism to define an ideology, where in social and industrial morality. "hitherto determined by reference to the good of man in this life.[1] Secularism was subsequently projected as a rationalist movement, agnostic or indifferent to religion.

Secularisation, as argued by Liana Gorgi, is a loaded concept, both theoretically and emotionally, and has been used in diverse ways and is rightly referred as a multidimensional concept.[2] Some critics as David Martin and others have also strongly disapproved of the projection of secularisation, as involving a more or less unified syndrome of characteristics, subject to an irreversible master – trend.[3]

It is true, that the secularisation process has not proceeded in a uniform, linear way in industrially advanced nations of Europe. The United States of America has altogether distinct religious traditions, because of its peculiar historical situation. At the same time, it would be too native to ignore the major focus of the socio-economic changes with Reformation, culminating in the French and the Industrial Revolutions. Although, historical context in terms of social structure, nature of polity, technological or industrial development and socio-cultural traditions were strikingly different in major countries of Europe such as France, England and Germany, one could notice the major contours of changes that took place in these nations, since Reformation. We shall briefly examine the peculiar historical context during medieval period in major European countries, such as, Germany, France and England in order to properly comprehend the nature of transformation that took place in these nations, since Reformation.

Section – 1

Reformation

Protestant Reformation, as widely acclaimed, was one of the most important movements which inaugurated what is called the 'modern West' just as the idea of popular participation in the government was established with the French Revolution and large-scale mechanical production with the Industrial Revolution. Individualism in the religious sphere similarly, began to assert itself from 1517, with Martin Luther's revolt[4] hence, the Reformation provides useful clue to understand the modern Wet. The Reformation had a remote, as well as a proximate social background. The remote background consisted of the general economic change affecting Europe, such as the Crusades, the Black Death, the new trade routes, the medieval frontiers and the internal contradictions of the feudal structure.[5]

Medieval period witnessed the consolidation of the nation-states in many parts of Europe, partly, at least, as a response to the growing economic demands of these regions. The emergent new political structure undermined the age-old relations between the church and the state. The new nations with despotic monarchs started challenging the overlordship of Rome. These changes were actually shaped by the peculiar political and economic conditions of each region. Thus, the kings of France could obtain the cooperation of all the three 'Estates' in their resistance against the Roman papacy. The kings of England, on the other hand, had several rounds of talks and had to negotiate with the Popes although some of them defied the Popes – others obtained the cooperation of the church to contain the barons, culminating in Henry VIII openly breaking with Rome. But Germany was politically and economically much weaker than either France or England and had to submit themselves to the Pope on several occasions. Typical was the case of Henry IV, who in 1077, had to wait three days in the winter with a rope around his neck as a penitent before he was admitted to the presence of the Pope in his Castle at Canossa. But this economic and political weakness of Germany itself, as argued out by Robert Varickayil, became the immediate prop for the success of the Reformation. In a nutshell, an excessive drain of money from an economically weak nation, prepared the necessary ground for a successful protest movement. This drain included the papal taxes, the veneration of relic and the sale of indulgences.[6]

Similarly, the feudal possessions of the church too differed from nation to nation. Thus, the Catholic Church owned a half of Germany, while only a fifth of France (estimated at value three quarters of the wealth of France) and only one-third of the Italian peninsula. Such possessions were still smaller in other nations though they included vast estates of immense wealth. Obviously, the ecclesiastical possessions as well as exactions were resented by every nation concerned, mainly because it strangulated the emerging merchant capitalism. The monarchs of these nations too, depended on the merchants. Hence, one could see that an attack on financial drainage became the rallying point of religious Reformation in feudal Europe. Further, the Reformation broke out in Germany because that region had suffered the worst form of papal exactions. This probably was also the main reason why Luther could initially succeed in Germany, whereas, his forerunners had limited impact in other countries.

The Lutheran revolt was actually preceded by a number of attempts at the purification of the church. The Catholic Church itself had made repeated attempts at Reformation from within. But the Popes, the College of Cardinals and the bureaucracy of the church could not agree upon a common formula, as the economic interests of each party or group could not coincide with the interests of other groups. Reformation with external pressure had thus become unavoidable. Reformation in a sense was actually the outcome of joint endeavours by kings, priests, intellectuals and mass of ordinary people.

Louis of Bavaria (1314 to 1347) was probably the first king to challenge the authority of the Church. He advocated, that marriage was a purely civil affair and granted divorce on his own authority. He patronised the first well known intellectual, William among the reformers who declared with the help of king, that the Pope had no infallibility as he claimed to have. Two more, Wycliff and Huss joined him. Wycliff (1370 - 1384) was a priest teaching theology at the University of Oxford. He taught, among other things, that there was no need for such intermediaries as the Pope and the bishop to stand between God and the faithful. Wycliff received protection from

John of Gaunt, the king of England. John was badly in need of money to defend his country against French man. Wycliff taking advantage of the situation, published a pamphlet advocating the retention of the Church dues and the severance of the English Church from Rome. Actually, Wycliff preached almost every precept Luther and Calvin stood for later. But as suggested, the social base in England was not ripe for a complete break with the Rome Church. A revolt of the lower classes demanded a strengthening of the *status quo* in England. The state, subsequently discouraged Wycliff from pursuing his radical teachings but he got protection from government, so as to die in peace.

Martin Luther in Germany

At this juncture, Martin Luther popularly known as the leader of the Reformation, appeared on the scene in Germany. One of the main reasons why Luther could succeed in Germany was a tremendous change in the socio-economic situation in Europe, which was favourable to new ideas by his time. Europe was no more a closed continent, which it was for centuries. The Europeans had already penetrated into African continent on the hand and crossed the Atlantic on the other. The sixteenth century, the century of Luther, witnessed the maturing of the mercantile capitalism. Nationalism too was stronger in the sixteenth century than earlier Portugal, Spain, France, the Netherlands, England and even Russia had gained a new awareness from the medieval lethargy. As Holborn notes, "Everywhere the secular authorities tried to counter the papal policy and they found support even among the devout."[7] Germany, of course, was far behind France and England in national solidarity. But even here, the princes had started establishing universities, a function that was strictly reserved for the Church till then.

A few distinct characteristics, marked Germany off her neighbours such as, France and England. Germany was declining because the continental economy, in terms of mining and commerce, was losing ground to the maritime economy, controlled by Spain, the Netherlands and others. Secondly, the Church was giving less concessions to Germany because she had a weaker central government compared to France or England. Thirdly, the weakness of the central government meant, that the local princes were more powerful. There was actually, no one Germany that was bargaining with the Pope, but a number of regions under various leaders.

When it came to Reformation too, it was side, than to convert the king or the whole of Germany.[8]

Printing Press – Far-reaching Impact

The theses of Luther were originally written in Latin, but were translated in Germany for circulation among the masses. Perhaps, for the first time, the press was used for propaganda. The power of the press was just emerging into the open. The presence of the press was one of marked differences between the world of Luther and that of earlier reformers. This became evident from the fact, that between 1457 and 1517 over 400 editions of the Bible were published. The opponents of Luther too had the same facility and they too printed and circulated their counter theses. Luthers theses appeared on 31st October 1517. Tetzds 106 counter theses appeared in December 1517. When the counter theses reached the university students, they were burned. Thus, what was intended as a modest debate, soon assumed a violent form.

Each offensive against Luther led to stronger reaction from him. Within a short time, he advocated the placement of an ecumenical council above the Pope and practically rejected the arbitrary mode of auction of religious relic by the Roman Church. Luther also focused on economic issues. Thus, in his very first thesis he declared, if the Pope knew the poverty of the German people, he would prefer St. Peter's in ashes so that it should be built out of the blood and hide of his sheep. To this, all Germans would agree.... Rome is the greatest thief and robber that has ever appeared on earth, or ever will. Poor Germans that we are... we were born to be masters, and we have been compelled to bow beneath the yoke of our tyrants. It is time that the glorious Teutonic people should cease to be the puppet of the Roman pontiff.[9] Thus, as observed by Robert, the Reformation from the beginning was a fight for political as well as economic freedom. Religion in this sense was only secondary. The exploitation was in the name of religion. Hence, the revolt too had to use the same mask.[10]

Engels on Medieval Church

Referring to the medieval religious conflicts, F. Engels also written:

Even the so-called religious wars of the sixteenth century involved primarily positive material class interests: These were class.

wars, too just as the later internal collisions in England and France were. Although the class struggles of that day were carried on under religious shibboleths, and though the interests, requirements, and demands of the various classes were concealed behind a religious screen, this changed nothing in the matter and is easily explained by the condition of the time.

Further, the middle ages had developed altogether from the raw. They wiped the old civilisation, the old philosophy, politics and jurisprudence off the state to begin anew in everything. The only thing they kept from the old shattered world was Christianity and a number of half-ruined towns, divested of all their civilisation. As a consequence just as in every primitive stage of development, the clergy had a monopoly on intellectual education, and education itself became essentially theological. In the hands of the clergy, politics and jurisprudence, much like all other sciences, remained mere branches of theology, and were treated according to the principles prevailing in the latter. Church dogmas were at the same time political axioms, and Bible quotations had the force of the law in any court. Even as special estate of jurists was taking shape, jurisprudence long remained under the tutelage of theology. And this supremacy of theology in entire realm of intellectual activity, was at the same time, an inevitable consequences of the place held by the Church, as the most general synthesis and sanction of the existing feudal denomination.[11] Under the circumstances, all the general attacks against the Church, and it is not surprising that all social, political and even revolutionary doctrines found manifestations mainly in theological heresies. Revolutionary opposition to feudalism lasted throughout the Middle Ages. It took the shape of mysticism, open heresy, or armed insurrection, all depending on conditions of the time. Sixteenth century reforms heavily leaned on mysticism. Munzer, who led peasant revolts against the feudal oppression, himself derived deep inspiration from it. The town heresy which was actually the official heresy of the Middle Ages was directed against the clergy whose wealth and political importance it affected. As bourgeoisie demanded, at a later stage, 'cheap governments', the medieval burghers mainly demanded 'cheap Church'. Reactionary in form, like any heresy that sees only degeneration in the further development of church and dogma, the burgher heresy demanded the revival of the simple, Christian Church constitution and abolition of monks, prelates, and the Roman court, in short, everything in the Church that was expensive.

The Plebian Heresy

The heresy that articulated the peasant and plebeian aspirations, and almost invariably accompanied an insurrection, was of a totally different nature. Though it shared all the demands of burgher heresy with regards to the clergy, the Papacy, and revival of the early Christian Church constitution, it also went much further. It demanded the restoration of early Christian equality among members of the community and the recognition of this equality as a prescript for the burgher world as well. From 'equality of the children of God' it inferred civil equality, and partly even equality of property. Equality of nobleman and peasant, of patrician, privileged burgher and plebian, abolition of the corvee, ground-rents, taxes, privileges and at least the most crying differences in property, these were the demands advanced with more or less determination, as natural implications of the early Christian doctrine.[12]

Engles classifies the various responses to the growing social and political crisis of the Middle Ages in terms of emergence of the three camps. The first of these, he calls the conservative Catholic camp that embraced all the elements interested in maintaining the existing conditions, i.e., the Imperial authorities the ecclesiastical and a section of the prelates and the city patricians. The second camp of burgher like-moderate Lutheran reforms, attracted all the propertied elements of the opposition, the bulk of the lesser nobility and even a portion of the lay princes who hoped to enrich themselves through confiscation of Church estates and wanted to seize the opportunity of gaining greater independence from the empire. Peasants and plebians who constituted the third radical camp were united in a revolutionary party whose demands were most clearly articulated by Munzer.[13]

Luther by translating the Bible in German had placed a powerful weapon into the hands of the plebian movement. Through the Bible, he showed the contrast between the feudalised Christianity of his time and the unassuming Christianity of the first century; and between the decaying feudal society and a picture of a society that hardly knew anything about the complex and artificial feudal hierarchy. The Peasants revolt during the medieval period were largely inspired by the aspirations drawn from such version of the old, the original spirit of Christianity. There were peasant revolts in France in the thirteenth century in England in the fourteenth century and in Bohemia in the fifteenth century. But none of these could succeed. The same fate awaited the revolt of the German peasants in the fifteenth century. By April 1525, no less than 800,000 peasants were under arms in Germany. They looked up to Luther for support. Luther, by this time, had become a symbol of the new social order. Luther initially supported the revolt and challenged the princes. But he soon realised that Germany was ready for such a radical change, not at least for another few hundred year. Princes and Knights joined hands together to defeat the peasants, rebellion. Luther quickly changed his stance and openly advocated crushing and killing of rebels and told and the princes that thereby they would please the God.

Revolutionary leadership to rising peasant rebellion was provide by Thomas Munzer who treated the Church dogmas and rites with the greatest contempt. He drew inspiration from medieval mystics and particularly the Chiliastic work of Joachim. Munzer's philosophical' theological doctrine attacked all the main points, not only of Catholicism, but of the Christianity generally. Under the cloak of Christian forms, he preached a kind of pan theism. He repudiated the Bible, both, as the only and the infallible revelation. The real and living revelations, he argued, was reason, a revelation which has always existed among all peoples at all times. To hold up the Bible against reason, he maintained, was to kill the spirit by the letter, for the Holy Spirit of which the Bible speaks is not something that exists outside, the Holy Spirit is our reason. Faith is nothing else but reason come to life in man, and pagans could therefore also have faith. Through this faith, through reason come to life, man became Godlike and blessed. Heaven is, therefore, not a thing of another world, and is to be sought in this life and it is the task of believers to establish this Heaven, The Kingdom of God, is here on earth. Just as there is no Heaven in the beyond, there is also no Hell and no domination. Similarly, there is no devil but men's evil lusts and greed. Christ was a man as we are, a prophet and a teacher, and His Eucharist is mere commemoration meal wherein bread and wine are consumed without any mystic garnishing. Munzer preached these doctrines mostly cloaked in the same Christian phraseology, under which the new philosophy had to hide for some time.

Munzer's political doctrine also followed his revolutionary religious conceptions very closely, and just as his theology overstepped the current conceptions of his age, so his political doctrine went far beyond the prevailing social and political conditions. Just as Munzer's religious philosophy approached atheism, so his political programme approached communism. This programming was much less a compilation of the demands of the plebians of his time and was more an anticipatory vision of the conditions for the emancipation of the proletarian elements that had just emerged among the plebians. This programme called for the immediate establishment of the Kingdom of God, of the prophesied millennium, by restoring the Church to its original condition by the Kingdom of God. Munzer understood a society in which there would be no class differences or private property and no state authority independent of or foreign to the members of society. It aimed at establishing a union to implement this programme, not only throughout Germany, but throughout Christendom. Princes and lords were to be invited to join, and if they refuse, the union was to take up arms and overthrow or kill them at the first opportunity.[14] Nevertheless, Munzer's Utopia could not have succeeded in his time, He lost the battle and the growing peasant revolt was crushed and about 30,000 peasants were murdered in cold blood.

This created a situation where the Reformation was left only with two options, either to carry the princes or perish. Luther openly preached that the subjects of the princes had no right to insurrection even if their lords were evil and unjust. In one word, the Bible and the rules of Christian morality were placed at the service of the temporal authority. Thus, the union between the Church and the empire was broken. The new Church decided to serve minor lords and local interest. International Church became national, an important step toward a bourgeois Church. It is not that Luther consciously visualised such outcome. He actually desired a better Church. But the unanticipated consequence of this wish was a territorial Church. Later, the nation became a union between the king, the parliament and the burgher. The Reformed Church as argued by Robert, was in the frontline to bless that union. Thus, Luther laid the foundation unknowingly for the triple alliance between religion, nation state and bourgeois.[15]

In Norway, it was the king who needed money badly, found easiest source through acquisition and sale of the Church property.

Hence, he imposed the Reformation on Norway and Iceland in 1537 and secularised the properties of the clergy.

The reform in Switzerland was welcomed by Zwingli, a military chaplain who came to power in 1529. He was against the Papal authority, image worship and the veneration of the saints and also mercenary work abroad.

Section-II

Protestant Reformation in England

The sixteenth century saw the integration of English towns into a single national unit. London was unique in terms of its economic and political importance and contributed as much to a parliamentary subsidy as all other towns put together. Moreover, in the sixteenth century, the 800 or so market towns in England and Wales came under the control of oligarchies of their richer burghers, as the latter grew in strength and ambition. They had emerged as a class by this time to rule in their own right, against the feudal ruling class.

The significant expansion of London, and its growing power as a unifying force was quite visible in the post-Reformation era. It furnished a market for food which could be supplied only by improved means of cultivation. This paved way for enclosure and the investment of capital in farming for the market, gradually over the whole kingdom. The standards and morality of the market-place were increasingly drawn from London. "Individualism", city doctrine soon became respectable, as London merchants brought more and more of the county into a single market.

Throughout the Middle Ages, as noted, there had been a tug-of-war over control of royal administration. Government was located in the King's households. As business became more complex, formal departments began to be differentiated.

The Church had been a source of power, patronage and wealth to rulers of major powers like France and Spain for a long period. These governments, which broke with Rome in the early sixteenth century were on the fringes of Catholic civilisation, secondary powers whose rulers had not been strong enough to effectively bargain with the papacy, like England, Sweden, Denmark, Switzerland and Scotland. Before the Reformation, English kings had to join hands with the Pope in order to control their bigger clergy who also were privileged land owners and franchise- holders.

Since Reformation, they were reduced to royal servants, and played a much less independent role in political life. In 1540, Henry VIII proclaimed himself King of Ireland, to do away with any consideration of Ireland as a papal patrimony. The King became, in theory, as well as in practice head of Church and state, leading to the concept of national sovereignty.

The Reformation thus nationalised the Church, and thereby prohibited any appeal outside England. It reduced the franchises and privileges of the Church. Post-Reformation bishops, were reduced to the status of royal civil servants. The Church could exercise coercive power since servants. The Church could exercise coercive power since Reformation only in alliance with and dependence on the Crown. Long run consequences, which followed from the break with Rome were momentous. Sir Lewis Namier went to extent of even suggesting that, 'Religion is sixteenth century word for nationalism.' The early Protestant reformers were staunch supporters of the English monarchy. This is evident from the statement of the Protestant martyr William Tyndale, that the King is, in this world, without law, and may at his lust do right and wrong, and shall give account, but to God only. As a matter of fact reformers preferred a tyrant to a weak king, as in contest against the Roman Pope authority, powerful monarch war far more useful than a timid emperor. But this situation created a deep dilemma in Protestant attitudes, which simultaneously sought to elevate both, the monarch and the conscience of the individual.

Printing press enabled the Protestantism to spread dissemination of vernacular translations of the Bible, some in pocket edition, made possible study of Scriptures to people at large. In the sixteenth century increase in middle class wealth was reflected in more domestic comforts and more privacy, the economic achievements made possible more widespread study and discussion of the Bible. As celibacy was not regarded as compulsory for intellectuals, and printing made books easily accessible to the middle class, the home could become a cultural and discussion centre. Closed parish churches and family worship were both characteristics of protestantism.

The Protestants stress on Bible-reading, vernacular preaching and congregational participation in worship encouraged higher educational standards, in clergy and laity alike. The whole trend of educational advance during the century before the Reformation had been towards a more secular, lay-controlled education in the vernacular. Gentlemen's sons, who previously had the exclusive privilege of learning in monasteries, now sat side by side with plebeians in village and grammar schools, and flocked in to the universities. However, over a period, the gentry managed to monopolise the better schools, Oxford and Cambridge Colleges, to the great detriment of the lower stratum in English society.

Protestant theology in all possible ways, appealed to the individualism of the middle class. The abolition of mediating saints and a mediating priesthood placed individual consciences face to face with God. It also popularised the idea of the individual spiritual balance sheet, the profit and loss book keeping of diaries. The assumption is that of an atomic society of individuals fighting for their own salvation and no longer a community working for their salvation. The phrase 'The individual' as suggested, in its modern sense emerges in the late sixteenth or early seventeenth centuries. This also gets reflected in the emphases on puritan and dramatists on the right to choose one's matrimonial partner, which proved so liberating for women, in more realistic portraiture and sculpture, resulting from post-Reformation secular patronage of the arts.

The Reformation stimulated not only individualism but also gave impetus to a scientific world view. Protestants had imbibed long standing lollard tradition of skepticism about the miracle of the mass. Tyndale denounced the Pope as a magician. There was a sharp decline in appeal for magical power of shrines and saints. But the attempt was made to transfer such power to monarchy. This also could not be sustained for a long period, with the advancement of industrial and scientific age. But as suggested, it finally disappeared only after the establishment of parliamentary sovereignty. Another byproduct of the Reformation was a hatred towards cruelty. The great puritan preacher William Perkins for instance, even condemned cock-fighting on humanitarian grounds. Nevertheless, in spite of this humanism, English law remained harsh and brutal, especially to the lower classes.[16]

SECTION – III

French Scenario

Development in France proceeded on a different line than England. Main reasons for this distinct pattern of the French development, was the sharp contrast in socio-economic conditions and the technological breakthrough in these two important nations of Europe, in medieval and post-medieval periods.

As aptly suggested by Hobsbawm, if the economy of the nineteenth-century world was formed mainly under the influence of the British Industrial Revolution, its politics and ideology were formed mainly by the French. French actually provided the vocabulary and the issues of liberal and radical – democratic politics for almost the entire world. France provided the codes of law, the model of scientific and technical organisation and the metric system of measurement.[17]

The French Revolution, although was not an isolated phenomenon, had far reaching consequences throughout Europe. The French Revolution was a major social revolution and was far more radical than any other comparable development in Europe. It is no accident that the American Revolutionaries, and the British 'jacobins' who migrated to France because of their political sympathies, found themselves moderates in France. For instance, Tom Paine, was an extremist in Britain and America, but in Paris he was among the most moderate of the Girondins. The American Revolution, compared to the French, remained a crucial event, but left a few major traces elsewhere. The French Revolution was a landmark for all countries. It aspired as far as social reformers like Raja Ram Mohan Roy in India, who insisted in 1830 on travelling in a French ship to demonstrate his enthusiasm for its principles of equality, liberty, fraternity and social justice. Throughout the eighteenth century 'France was the major economic rival to Britain; her colonial system was in certain respects far more dynamic than the British. Yet, France was not a power like Britain which was technically far more advanced and whose foreign policy was substantially determined by the interest of capitalist expansion. France in a sense, was the most powerful and in many ways was the most typical of the old aristocratic absolute monarchies of Europe. In other words, as suggested, the conflict between the official framework and the vested interests of the old regime and the rising social forces was more acute in France than elsewhere.[18]

The New Forces

The new forces were quite clear in terms of changes they desired, for example, Turgot, the physiocrat economist, advocated for an efficient exploitation of the land, for free enterprise and trade, for a standardised, efficient administration of a single homogeneous national territory, and the abolition of all restrictions and social inequalities which stood in the way of the development of national resources and rational, equitable administration and taxation. Yet, his attempt, not surprisingly, to apply such a programme as the first minister of Louis XVI in 1774-6 failed miserably. Reforms of this nature, Hobsbawm argues, in modest dose, were not incompatible with absolute monarchies. They were widely propagated during this period among the so called 'enlightened despotism.' Such reforms were inapplicable, and therefore restricted to mere theoretical formulation, as also they failed in the face of the resistance of the local aristocracies and other vested interest. In France they failed in the face of the resistance of the vested interests was more effective. But the results of this failure proved to be far more catastrophic for the monarchy; and the forces of bourgeois transformation were far too strong to relapse into inactivity.[19]

However, in order to understand, why the revolution broke out when it did, as the same author suggests, it is most useful to consider the so-called 'feudal reaction' which actually provided the spark to explode the power-barrei of France. The French nobility consisted of around 4,00,000 persons in a total population of twenty-three million in France. They enjoyed considerable privileges, including exemption from several taxes, (although clergy enjoyed still more concessions), and the right to receive feudal dues. But politically their situation was not so comfortable. Absolute monarchy, while entirely aristocratic and even feudal in its ethos, had deprived the nobles of political independence and responsibility and cut down their estates. Economically, the noble's worries were by no means negligible. Nobles, being fighters by birth and traditions, were even formally debarred from taking up trade or profession, hence depended exclusively on the income of their estates. This too was possible if they happened to belong to the favoured minority of court nobles or through wealthy marriage, or court pensions, and gifts. They found increasingly difficult to manage their rising expenses. Throughout the eighteenth century therefore, it is not surprising to find that in France as in many other countries, they encroached steadily upon the official posts, which the absolute monarchy had preferred to fill with technically competent and politically harmless middle class men. By the 1780's large chunk of the army commission assign} ents, all bishop posts and even the keystone of royal administration were captured by nobles. As a result the nobility not merely exasperated the feelings of the middle class by their successful competition for official posts, they also undermined the state itself by frequent attempts to take over provincial and central administration. Similarly, they did everything possible to extract maximum money by squeezing the peasantry. Hence, the nobility exasperated not only the middle class but also the peasantry.

The position of this vast strata, constituting nearly 80 per cent of the French population, was also far from satisfactory. They were, in general free and also often landowners. Noble estates covered only one-fifth of the land, clerical estates probably another six per cent, with some religional variations. In fact, great majority were landless or with insufficient holdings, and technically backward. Land hunger was getting intensified with rising population. Feudal dues, tithes and taxes took a large and rising proportion of the peasants income. Only the minority of peasants who had a constant surplus for sale benefited from the rising prices; the rest in one way or other suffered from them, especially in the times of bad harvest. The twenty years preceding the revolution, undoubtedly, the situation of the peasants grew worse for these reasons.

The financial troubles of the monarchy precipitated the matter to a head. The administrative and fiscal structure of the Empire was grossly absolute, and attempts to remedy it by the reforms did not succeed. France's involvement in the American War of Independence was economically a big setback. Victory over England was gained at the cost of financial bankruptcy, various attempts were made to tide over the financial crisis, but nothing short of a fundamental reform, which could mobilise the taxable capacity of the country that could cope with a situation in which expenditure outran revenue by at least 20 per cent. The government's crisis provided good opportunity to the aristocracy and the parliaments to exercise enough pressure on the monarchy. They refused to pay without extension of their privileges. The first breach in the front of absolutism was an attempt to call assembly of nobles in 1787 to consider government's demands. The second was the desperate decision to call the States General – the old feudal assembly that had become defunct since 1614. The revolution thus began, as Hobsbawm aptly suggests, as an aristocratic attempt to recapture the state. However, the aristocracy totally underestimated the strength of the 'Third Estate'- the entity that demanded to represent all who were neither nobles nor clergy, but in fact was dominated by the middle-class.[20]

The French Revolution, surprisingly, was not made or led by organised party or movement as we now understand these terms. Nevertheless, a basic consensus of general ideas among a fairly coherent section of people provided the revolutionary movement, an effective unity. This section consisted of the 'bourgeoisie' who articulated ideas of classical liberalism.

Bourgeois Declaration of 1789

The demands of the bourgeoisie of 1789 were specifically laid down in the famous Declaration of the Rights of Man and Citizens. This document proved to be a manifesto against the hierarchical society of nobles and privileged, but still it did not stand for democratic of egalitarian society. "Men are born live free and equal under the laws" stated its first article; but it also provided for the existence of social distinctions. Private property was accepted as a natural right, sacred, inalienable and inviolable. A constitutional monarchy based on a propertied oligarchy expressing itself through a representative assembly still appeared more congenial to most bourgeois of 1789, was not a democrat but a believer in constitutionalism, a secular state with civil liberties and guarantees for private enterprise, and stood for the government by tax-payers and property-owners.

However, formally such a regime was supposed to express not simply his class interests, but also the general will of 'the people; which was identified as the French nation'.

Since the peasants and toiling poor were illiterate, politically modest and the process of election indirect, around 610 men got elected to represent the Third Estate, most of whom were lawyers and about 100 were capitalists and businessmen. The middle class, although representing overwhelming mass of people, bad fought bitterly and effectively to win representation as large as that of combined strength of both nobility and allergy. The Third Estate succeeded, in spite of united resistance of the King and the privileged orders, as it represented not merely the views of an educated and militant minority, but far more powerful forces; the labouring poor of the cities and also the revolutionary peasantry. The later 1780s had been, for practically all branches of the French economy. A bad harvest in 1788-89 and very difficult winter made this crisis more acute. Bad harvest hurt the peasantry, as it meant that large produce. The majority of them, because of their small holding had to eat up their seed-corn, and buy food at exorbitant prices. It also hurt the urban poor, with bread prices shooting very high. The impoverishment of the countryside reduced the market for manufacturers and hence also produced an industrial depression. The country's poor, under the circumstances were desperate and took to riot and banditry. The urban poor were all the more restless as work ceased at the very moment when the cost of living soared. The outcome was an epidemic of peasant unrest, combined with provincial town risings that spread rapidly across vast stretches of the country. By July, 1789 the social structure of the French rural feudalism and the state machine of royal France was totally shattered. By the end of August 1789, the Revolution had also acquired its formal manifesto, the Declaration of the Rights of Man and Citizen. The King resisted with his usual stupidity, and sections of the middle class revolutionaries, frightened by the social implications of the mass upheaval, felt that the time for conservatism had come to an end.

"Sansculottes"

In short, the main contours of French and even all subsequent bourgeois revolutions had become now clearly visible. Time and again, one could see moderate middle class reformers mobilising the masses against die-hard resistance or counter-revolution, masses pushing beyond the moderates to their own social revolutions, and the moderates in turn splitting into a conservative camp. In most subsequent bourgeois revolutions the moderate liberals, as suggested, shifted to conservative camp, at a very early stage. In the nineteenth century we increasingly find, especially in Germany, that they become unwilling to begin revolution at all, for apprehension of its incalculable consequences and preferred to compromise with King and aristocracy. The peculiarity of the French Revolution is that one section of the liberal middle class called the Jacobins was prepared to remain revolutionary even beyond the brink of anti-bourgeois revolution: Since the French Revolution, the new Jacobins became a symbol for radical revolution everywhere. After 1794, it became clear to moderates that the Jacobin regime had driven the Revolution too far for bourgeois comfort and prospects.

Jocobins could afford radicalism also because, in their time no class existed that could provide a coherent social alternative. Such a class could arise only in the course of the Industrial Revolution with the emergence of the 'proletariat'. In the French Revolution the working class or to be more precise, toiling strata consisted only of the aggregate of hired, but mostly non-industrial wage – earners, which had not played an independent role. The only alternative to bourgeois radicalism where the "Sansculottes", a shapeless, mostly urban movement of the labouring poor, small craftsmen, shopkeepers, artisans, tiny entrepreneurs and such other categories. The "Sansculottes" were organised, especially in the 'sections' of Paris and the local political clubs, and provided the main striking force of the Revolution, the actual demonstrator, rioters, constructor of barricades. They also formulated a policy which reflected their contradictory ideals, combining respect for (small) private property, with hostility to the rich, government guaranteed work, wages and social security for the poor man, and extreme egalitarian and libertarian democracy. As Hobsbawm argues, the "sansculottes" in fact, were one branch of that universal an important political friend which sought to express the interest of great mass of 'little men' who existed between the poles of the 'bourgeois' and the 'proletarian', often nearer the latter than the former because they were, after all, mostly poor. One can observed such trend in the United States (as Jeffersonianism and Jacksonion democracy or populism) in Britain (as 'radicalism'), in Italy (as Mezzanines and Garibaldians). Mostly, it tended to settled down in post-revolutionary period, as a left wing of middle class liberalism.

Sansculottism could provide no real alternative in France. Its idea, a golden past of villagers and small craftsmen or a golden future of small farmers and artisans undisturbed by bankers and millionaires, was unrealisable. History moved ahead against them.

Between 1789 and 1791 the victorious moderate bourgeois, operating through the Constituent Assembly, introduced the gigantic rationalisation and reform in France. Most of the lasting institutional achievements of the Revolution date from this period, the metric system and the emancipation of the Jews, as well as its other striking international results. Economically, the perspectives of the Constituent Assembly were entirely liberal: for the peasantry, it adopted the policy of the enclosure of common lands and the promotion of rural entrepreneurs, for the working class, the banning of trade unions, for the small crafts, the abolition of guilds and corporations. It actually provided hardly any concrete measure, for the common people, except, from 1790, by means of the secularisation and sale of Church lands as also of those of the emigrant nobility, which had the triple advantage of weakening clericalism, strengthening the provincial and peasant entrepreneur, and giving sizeable section of peasants, a measurable return for their revolutionary activity.

The post-revolutionary generations witnessed attempts to create a bourgeois non-Christian morality that could be a substitute to that of the Christian. This could be seen in a Rousseauist cult of the Supreme being (Roberpierre for instance in 1794) and several such pseudo-religions constructed on rationalist non-Christian foundation, but still retaining the ritual apparatus as Comte's "Religion of Humanity."

Victory of Secular Forces

The bourgeois actually remained divided in its ideology between a minority of increasingly frank free-thinkers and a majority of the pious Protestant, Jewish and Catholic. As Hobsbawm argues, although in purely quantitative terms, religion remained immensely strong, and grew stronger, yet it was no longer dominant, had become recessive and has remained so to this day.[21] This was strikingly demonstrated by the decisive victory of secular over religious ideology. With the American and the French Revolution as suggested, major political and social transformations secularised. The issues of the Dutch and English Revolutions of the sixteenth and seventeenth centuries had been discussed and fought out still in the traditional language of Christianity, orthodox, schismatic or heretical. In the ideologies of the American and French. Revolutions, for the first time in European history, Christianity became irrelevant. The language, the symbolism, the costume of 1789 were purely non-Christian, if we leave aside, a few popular-archaic efforts to create cults of saints and martyrs, analogous to the old ones, out of dead Sansculotte heroes. This secularism, at the same time also demonstrated the remarkable political hegemony of the liberal middle class that imposed its particular ideological form on the much vaster social movement of the masses. Bourgeois dominance imbued the French Revolution with the agnostic or secular-moral ideology of the eighteenth century enlightenment. The French revolutionary idioms also in turn inspired all subsequent social revolutionary movements to imbibe secularist ethos in them. The same author further notes that with a few exceptions, among intellectuals like the Saint-Simonians and a few (Christian-Communist sectarians like the tailor Wrestling (1808-1871), the ideology of the new working class and socialist movements of the nineteenth century was secularist from the inception. The pre-dominant ideology of modern labour is based on eighteenth century rationalism.[22]

Secularisation and the Masses

It should be noted that this secularisation trend in the industrial working class was in sharp contrast to the masses who remained predominantly religious. This should not sound very surprising, because the natural revolutionary idiom of the masses brought up in a traditional Christian society is one of rebellion, as articulated through social heresy, millennialism and the like, as the Bible leaves enough room for such interpretations.

Nevertheless, as Hobsbawm writes, by modern standards the working classes and urban masses who grew up in the period of the Industrial Revolution, were no doubt rather strongly influenced by religion; by the standards of the first half of the nineteenth century there was no precedent for their remoteness from, ignorance of, and indifference to organised religion. The British religious census of 1851 clearly indicated this. However, one of the main reasons for this indifference was the utter failure of the traditional established churches to cope with agglomerations, the new industrial settlements and with new social classes like the proletariat, which were foreign to their routines and experience. By 1815, there were Church places available for only 34 per cent of the inhabitants of Sheffield, only 31.2 per cent of those in Liverpool and Manchester, and only 29 per cent in Birmingham. The problems of being a parish in an agricultural village could not really help much to cure souls in an industrial town or urban slum. The established churches hence, neglected these new communities and classes, thus leaving them particularly in Catholic and Lutheran countries almost entirely to the secular faith of the new labour movements. The Protestant sects were more successful, especially in countries like Britain, where such sectarianism was a well-established phenomenon. But they were more influential particularly, in traditional small town village communities, as among the farm labourers, miners and fisherman.

Among the industrial workers, the sect's influence was quite marginal. Hence, according to Hobsbawm and several other Marxist scholars, the general trend of the period from 1789 to 1848 was one of distinct secularisation. Science came increasingly in clash with the scriptures, as it ventured into evolutionary fields. Historical scholarship which applied to the Bible especially from the 1830s questioned the validity of the document as a single inspired text of the Lord. David Strauss's controversial life of Jesus (1835) eliminated the supernatural element from Jesus's biography. By 1841, as suggested, educated Europe was almost ripe for the shock of Charles Darwin. This trend was further reinforced by the direct official attack on the property and legal privileges of the established Churches and their clergy, coupled with the increasingly tendency for government or other secular agencies to take over functions like education and social welfare, hitherto left largely to organised religious institutions, especially in Roman Catholic countries. Between 1789 and 1848 monasteries from Naples to Nicaragua were dissolved and their property auctioned.[23]

Section IV

Recent Studies on Popular Religious Revival

The far reaching significance of the French Revolution in promoting the secularisation process in France and other countries of Europe has been sufficiently highlighted by various scholars. These studies knowingly or unknowingly convey impression that secularisation has proceeded as an irreversible process in France, England and other European nations. Although the decline of religion, in the sense that increasing reversal in the role and influence of the organised State in Church, clergy and monasteries was witnessed in most of the European countries and some of the vital functions were taken over by the secular agencies, interference of the organised State sponsored religious institutions were taken over by the secular agencies, interference of the organised State-sponsored religious institutions in private affair of individuals such as choice of a marriage partner, divorce and occupation was minimised. Citizen's rights of equality, liberty and social justice and the states obligation of maintaining and promoting them were incorporated in the constitution. Nevertheless, if one gathers the impression that this resulted in the perpetual decline of religious influence in general, over a period of time even in most advanced industrial nations it would be a misleading interpretation. As suggested by Caroline Ford, although the two centuries following the French Revolution have seen periods of great popular religious revival, the tale most often told by historians has been one of the ineluctable "secularisation of the European mind."[24] The emergence of new studies on religion in Europe in the past over a decade, have significantly altered our understanding of the rise and decline in religious influence in the West, since the French and the Industrial Revolution. These studies include, Thomas Ksciman's, "Miracles and Prophecies in Nineteenth-Century France", Edward Berenson's, "Popular Religion and Left Wing Politics in France, 1830-1852", Judith Devlin's "The Superstitous Mind", French Peasant and the Supernatural, Suzanne Desan's, "Reclaiming the Sacred:" Lay Religion" and Popular Politics in France. These studies highlight the persistence of popular religious enthusiasm, the relationship between popular religion and politics, and the larger, social and cultural meanings of spiritual belief.[25]

Gender as a Category of Historical Analysis

Recent literature on religion and popular culture in Modern Europe as suggested, has also shaped by development in the gender history and with a focus to make gender a genuine category of historical analysis. Natalie Zemon Davis's pioneering contribution on women in Reformation and Caroline Walker Bynum's remarkable appraisal of the religious significance of food among medieval women, serve as models for understanding modern European history. A historical survey of formal religious practices, autobiographies, and records of female associational organisation, sufficiently demonstrate that religion occupied a central place in the lives of European women. Cholvy and Hilaire's the first consists of two volumes which span from 1800 to 1930, which depart substantially from earlier Dansette's classic account, as their central focus is on the religion of the people, rather than that of political and religious elites. Cholvy and Hilaire's work focuses on the history of religious France from the perspective of both, Paris and the provinces and not restricting their account only in terms of the political conflicts between the Catholic Church and the French state. The regional perspective brings out the evidence of both persistence and disappearance of religious practices. But they do not provide any caused explanations for such phenomena. Ralph Gibson's Social

History of French Catholicism as suggested, bridges this gap by exploring the relationship between the old regime and nineteenth century religious beliefs and practices.[26] Similarly, Lannon provides a comprehensive history of Spanish Catholicism. One of the most significant insights these works provide is, as brought by Lannon's, that to be religious could and did mean quite different things according to place, local culture, education and class.[27] Caroline Ford adds one more, but very important dimension to this. According to her, religions also meant different things according to gender. All of them argue against reduction of cultural or religious beliefs to economic or social determinants. The nineteenth was punctuated by a series of religious revivals in France as well as by a process of rechristianisation among certain social classes, especially the bourgeois. All the four of them share in common, a view that there were sharp regional disparities. In France, statistics of religious practice do not show any immutable boundary between practicing and non-practicing France. The well known St. Malo/Geneva line that identified a literate, enlightened and industrial France in the north from an illiterate, rural, underdeveloped France to the south, did not create two geographically distinct areas in terms of religious behaviour. However, certain parts of the French west and the Central portions of the southwest have demonstrated their continued allegiance to the Catholic faith in the nineteenth and twentieth centuries.[28]

Religious Practices - Cultural and Political Clues

As socio-economic and educational status do not help in predicting religious behaviour, historians have begun to turn to cultural and political clues to resolve the riddles of religious practices. In some cases, it seems that the relationship between the clergy and the laity was of central importance in determining the strength of religious devotion. In others, the collective memory of a single historical event or series of events, such as the French Revolution in the Vendee and conflicts between Catholics and Protestants in the Rhone Valley in the sixteenth century, appear to have made religious affiliation a vital element in the identity of a community. In France, as well as in Spain the growing religious indifference of the working classes is attributed to the growth of anti-clericalism. But the intensity of anti-clericalism has to be seen in the context of the peculiar traditions, historical events and other allied factors in a given country or even a region. Lannon suggests that the intensity of Spanish anti-clericalism had a great deal to do with the formal relationship between the Catholic Church and the state, particularly the Franco's regime. In Spain, the Spanish Church as Lannon argues was intimately tied to the cultural identity of the nation throughout the supported one authoritarian regime after another during this period, and as it was intimately associated with the propertied classes, it bred an unparalleled resistance and contempt among the Left in all areas, except the Basque region. In France, in contrast, one of the legacies of the French Revolution and of twentieth century republicanism was that the Catholic Church failed to become a national Church and Catholicism never became a constituent element of French national identity. Besides this, the secularisation of educational and welfare institutions as well as the separation of Church and State in 1905 put the Church on the defensive during much of Third, Fourth and Fifth Republic.[29]

In Contrast to Cholvy, Hilaire and Gisbon, Ravitch's History of the French Catholic Church from Henry IV to the bicentennial of the Revolution, adopts a more holistic approach. According to Caroline Ford, Ravitch's theological view prevents him from seeing the more variegated, complicated, and ambiguous religious world that Cholvy, Hilaire and Gibson reveal. Ravitch holds that the Church's alleged support of ultra conservative positions, particularly fascism. His argument that the Catholic leadership embraced the Vichy regime and fascism appears to be of a doubtful proposition, in view of the fact, that the leadership of the first mass-based Christian Democratic Party in France, the Parti Democrate Populaire, emphatically rejected such a regime. The creation of populist religious and social organisations in the 1920s and 1950s that challenged the right wing Action Franchise, is conveniently overlooked by Ravitch. Ravitch also can't give any adequate explanation for the continued vitality of popular devotions as it does not fit into his linear view of the progressive alienation of more and more Catholics from the Catholic religion. He downplays the role of the people in shaping developments within the Church. The 'religion of the people' finds only a cursory reference and here also he equates 'popular religion' with "superstitions" which shuts out fascinating area of historical enquiry.[30]

Chovly, Hilaire, Lannon and Gibson on the basis of their study, argue, in contrast to that of Ravitch, for the healthy survival of the

Church. While it lost some adherents, it also won others. By exploring the complicated and changing relationship between clergy and laity and the persistence of religious belief, they suggest that the process of rechristianisation is as important a subject of historical study, as that of secularisation in the modern period. While the notion of dechristianisation has received a fair amount of attention, that of rechristianisation and the persistence of religious enthusiasm, whether within or outside an institutionalised Church, needs as Caroline suggests, further enquiry.[31]

Persistence of Supernatural Belief: Pilgrimage Shrines

The history of post-revolutionary Europe is rife with evidence, that points to the persistence of supernatural beliefs. It is not possible for us to examine numerous studies that vindicate such interferences. However, we shall refer to some major such findings that deserve serious consideration. Nolan and Nolan have provided historians with quite significant information about the evolution of the Christian pilgrimage, during a long historical span from 1099 to 1980. The active pilgrimage shrines in Europe were established, as they suggest, in five major periods, the Early Christian (to 1099), the High Medieval (1100-1399), Renaissance (1400-1529), Catholic Reformation (1530-1779), and Modern Periods (1780-1980). Although these divisions are somewhat arbitrary; but the authors have been able to assess changes in the pilgrimage phenomenon over many centuries. They have found, for instance, that some of the significant differences between modern visions and those of the pre-1780 period correlate with changes in patterns of age and gender among the visionaries. Only 22 per cent of the visionary experiences that resulted in the establishment of pilgrimage shrines in the past 200 years were those of men. Women and young children have become the principal visionaries of the modern period. Nolan and Nolan suggest that increasing creditability is given to female testimony and the 'feminisations' of the Roman Catholic Church in the modern period. But still, the larger meaning of such a change appears a mystery to them.[32]

According to Nolan and Nolan, the European pilgrimage has been predominantly Marian in orientation. Since the Renaissance, sixty-five per cent of all holy places are devoted the Virgin Mary, and the largest number of shrines are located in Italy, France and Spain, followed by West Germany, Austria and Portugal.

Saint shrines are more numerous in Ireland and in the Protestant regions of northern Europe.

Hilaire, Cholvy, and Gibson provide exhaustive accounts of the expansion, particularly during the 1830s; the cults of saints and the growing importance of the Virgin Mary as subject of veneration during the course of the nineteenth century. Festivals in honour of the Virgin Mary-Purification, Annunciation, Visitation, Assumption, and the Immaculate Conception, were celebrated with renewed enthusiasm. Confreries and congregations devoted to the Virgin Mary proliferated from the 1840s onward, and so also the celebration of the month of May as the *"mois de Marie"* since 1830. The Catholic publicist Louise Veuillot proclaimed that the epoch following the century of Mary.[33]

In a period during which the Catholic Church, as suggested, increasingly worried about empty benches, the clergy encouraged this popular Mariolatry. The nineteenth century, surprisingly, saw a growing trend on the part of the Church to institutionalise popular forms of piety might have been deemed, as argued by Caroline 'superstition' by a prerevolutionary clergy, but the nineteenth century Church chose in many cases to embrace, rather than suppress them for pastoral purposes. It is interesting to note that the clergy's task and the spread of new religious practices were helped, rather than hindered by economic modernisations and the Industrial Revolution. Lithography and the printing press considerably facilitated dissemination of the new devotional practices. The railway lines laid from the 1840s to the 1860s, helped an increasing number of pilgrims to reach remote shrines. Finally, the mass production of the idols allowed the humblest household to acquire images of the Virgin Mary.

Cholvy suggests that the exaltation of Mary was a part of larger cult of feminity that characterised the nineteenth century. According to Cholvy and Hilaire, the nineteenth century witnessed a 'Veritabel sacralisaton of women and this was reflected not only in Catholic devotions of the period, but also in the writings of Jules Michelet and in the followers of Saint-Simon and August Comte.[34] "One also notices the growing social role that women occupied in Churches through social work and particularly in education. They argue that despite the civil code, in spite of the relative degradation that the working class woman experienced, in spite of the growing number of 'kept women' among the bourgeoisie, it can be hardly refuted that the family acquired a growing importance, which got translated into the greater influence of the Atlantic have indicated the growing 'feminisaton of piety' throughout post-revolutionary Europe.[35] Ellen Badone for instance, claimed, that in contempory Brittany religion is perceived to be primarily women's responsibility.[36]

Feminisation of Religion

The 'feminisation of religion' has been defined in terms of changes in devotional practices in Catholic Europe. Two of the indications, most frequently cited by historians of Catholic Europe as evidence of this Phenomenon, are the unprecedented growth in the number of women entering religious orders and congregations and the marked dimorphism observable in statistics concerning formal religious practice. Women increasingly performed Catholic rites, more faithfully and regularly, than men during the nineteenth century. These facts have been distinctly documented by Yves-Marie Hilaire in his work *"Materiaux pour l'historie religieuse* and by Claude Langlois and Caitrona clear in their studies on female religious congregations in France and Ireland.[37]

Between the end of French Revolution and the early 1880s 200,000 women represented only one third of the members of the Church, as a whole on the eve of the French Revolution. By 1880, women constituted almost three-fifths of the personnel of the Church. Catholic Spain also shows similar patterns.[38]

In Odile Arnold's Le corps *et l'ame* her exploration of the cultural and social world of female religious communities in retreat in the nineteenth century brings out the profound impact of the contemplative orders on their roles, both as women and as women in the Church. In a broader sense, Arnold indicates how religion shaped the understanding of gender differences and thereby provided a broad framework of the cultural construction of gender identities.[39]

Arnold's book is based on a wide range of primary sources that include autobiographies, biographies, the rules and constitutions of orders, memories, courtesy books and educational manuals. It is supplemented by an appendix documenting innumerable rules concerning postures, gaze and gesture that were expected to be followed by the nun in their routine life. Nuns were cautioned, as in the flesh with the exception of their own hands. The refactory was regarded as a place of penitence. The rules and manuals meant for the nun were replete with references to mortification. But in course of time, the mortification began to be articulated less in terms of the body than in terms of spiritual obedience. As Arnold points out, "It is interesting to note that the asceticism in the control of gesture and emotion, which was in turn, an inherent part of the religious education of young girls, contrast sharply with the exuberant, expressive 'feminisation of religious devotion that the nineteenth century ostensibly inaugurated:" It is no wonder, under the circumstances, contrary to the view that the nun was often placed in a convent against her will one funds that the vocation was freely chosen by her, at times even against the will of parents and peers.[40]

This reference to Arnold's study on the convent and female religious piety, although exhaustive, provides useful insight in understanding the vital role played by women in moulding religious institutions in nineteenth century France.

Yvonne Turin in her study explores the subjective motivations of congregationists and the consequences of such a choice for women themselves. Using the private archives of two congregations, those of the Soeursdela Doctrine Chretienne de Nancy and of Saint, Joseph du Bon Pasteur de Clermond-Ferrand – she scrutinised the transformation and growth of both lay female associations and religious communities form the eighteenth to nineteenth centuries. She found that many of these associations, consisting of unmarried or widowed women, were in essence work cooperatives whose ostensible religious purpose ensured their social acceptance. She poses the question whether, the formation of these communities represent protective pacts for single women, or were they a means for women to assert their independence? They probably represented both. Many of these female alongside communities with more explicit religious purposes by providing educational and social services to the laity. Despite the crisis of the revolutionary decade, as suggested, which sent the clergy into hiding or to the guillotine, themselves under the "benevolent" eye of the Napoleonic regime.[41]

Religious life, as argued provided opportunities and avenues of social mobility, which were otherwise not available elsewhere. In a practical way, apart from spiritual considerations, they created networks of female sociability, and security, as well as professional opportunities in the domains of education and medicine unavailable elsewhere. As Olwen Hutton so effectively brings out, women's role in reconstructing the Church in France during the nineteenth century, can in part, be linked to what religion offered in spiritual and practical terms in the context of the post-revolutionary settlement, Revolutionary legislation since 1792, and thereafter, the Napoleonic Civil Code excluded women from the public world of politics and relegated them to narrowly circumscribed social and economic orders. Religion and the vacation it offered and provided French women a means of transcending those roles and the isolation that they created. Irrespective of the authoritarian and retrogressive role of the organised Church and the clergy, it is not difficult to argue, that for French women religion was also a "weapon of the weak".[42]

Turin's book subtitled 'Feminism in Religion' has come as a challenge to the view that the 'feminisation of religion' was a reflection first and foremost of clerical domination. Turin actually seeks to restore the human agency to the religious women and argues that religion or the religious vocation was a source of empowerment. This is illustrated in the vivid cameos of a number, like case of a sister Bonnard, who protested against the attempt to lower the numbers of the clerical staff and to reduce the remuneration of the nuns who staffed the hospital in 1832. Whereas Claude Langlois reffered to the congregation as a model that mobilised elite women in the Church. Turin argues, for an inverse process, it was a self-created elite of women, not necessarily drawn from the social elite of French society, who found in the Church a way of acting and taking hold of themselves. Entry into a religious congregation represented a kind of feminism *'avant la letter'*. However, it should be noted that Turin makes a distinction between the unself-conscious feminism of her womens religious organisations an da more strident' egoistical, contemporary Feminism.

Turin's work acquires distinct significance because it also challenges the rather questionable attempts to link women's religious proclivity to the biological differences between the sexes, which allegedly put them in closer proximity to birth and death. It is most certainly true that women have often assumed the role of bearers of tradition within the family and were the guarantors of family unity, but such extreme views that link gender difference to biology cannot explain; why female religiosity assumed the particular forms, and why it disappeared at certain other historical moments.

SECTION IV

Radical Sects in England

As in case of France, in England also the religion sponsored and patronised by the state and religious sects which masses imbibed or adopted were strikingly distinct. In England, for the last over 300 years, the attempt had been made, to bring the entire population, within on comprehensive religious political institution, the Anglican Church. The Act of Uniformity of 1662 made the terms 'citizen' and 'Anglican' synonymous. This actually was attempted when all religious bodies, Anglican included were in fact minorities within a predominantly non-Church English society. The largest single component in the religiously pluralistic society, as is the case with several other Western countries, is the unaffiliated, non-ecclestical majority.[43]

As against the fictional state of affairs legalised in the Act of Uniformity the real religious situation in the seventeenth and the first half of the eighteenth centuries was the fact that large numbers of the ordinary people adhered to an interconnected system of supernatural belief and practices which could be called popular paganism. The term paganism, as suggested, is widely appropriate for a situation in which at least 80 per cent of the population lived in the county side, and experienced the human sufferings of a rural, pre-industrial society.

Under the Act of Uniformity, it was illegal even in 1662 to be absent from Anglican worship. Non-attendance could entail the future of two-thirds of a man's estate. Those who could most likely suffer such loss of property were the Catholic landed gentry. These penalties, however, were not usually enforced after 1660. The main intention in imposing such penalties was to exclude non-Anglicans from positions of influence in the state. This was in order to neutralise what was felt to be the continuing political danger to the state, posed by the presence of Puritans and Papists and also to establish strong government with the aid of a politically reliable Church. Its significance has to be seen also in the context of the possibility of religious beliefs and organisations to be used to justify revolt. Penalties of non-conformist religious belief and affiliation were therefore proportionate to the political danger they represented. Thus, the idea was allowed to gain currency that in England, all those who are not actively non-conformist were *de jure* recognised as adherents of the Church of England irrespective of their fulfilling their ritual obligations.

The practical consequence of the Act of Uniformity had been to reinforce the division between Anglican and non-conformists. The hostile attitude of Puritans towards the Church of England during the restoration of the Monarchy in 1660, was a powerful factor for the Anglican hostility towards Puritans since 1660. Puritans subsequently emerged under the name of Protestant dissenters and came to form a subordinate element in the cultural life of England.[44]

Divisions among Non-conformists

Non-cognisance of religious pluralism under the Act of 1662, led to the polarisation of the distinctively ecclesiastic bodies between conformist and non-conformist. The non-conformist, was extended to all, whether they were Catholic, Jewish, Muslim, Hindu Pentecostal or any other. But non-conformists could broadly be divided into two main types; (1) Protestant dissenters and later, the secular dissenters; and (2) Catholics, Jews and various Asian minorities. The former type can be viewed as contra-cultures; whereas the second are basically sub-cultures. Between the two categories, there was hardly any affinity or cooperation, except that in certain respects the sub-cultures were at times beneficiaries of the achievement of the contra-cultures in resisting the monopoly claims of the Church of England.[45]

Since 1660, Anglicanism was identified as the upper-class religion, while Protestant non-conformists consisted largely of men and women 'who used to rather pride themselves on their independence'. They were largely found in town than in the countryside. Some were artisans, others were merchants. Their social solidarity was also essentially a response to their social solidarity was also essentially a response to the concerted attempts of the Anglican State Church to destroy them altogether. The culture that developed among them was appropriately described as a contra-culture. It emerged in contradistinction from and the hostility to the upper-class Anglican culture of the gentlemen of England and their faithful, rustic dependents. Barred from universities and schools, as T. Ling argues, Non-conformist organised their own academies, from which eventually came the ministers of the Non-conformist congregations, supported financially by the contributions of the local congregation. Such congregations were mostly concentrated in towns and cities, as it was easier to gather a number of members sufficiently large to support a minister economically. These two cultures developed and persisted, side by side, as 'church' and 'chapel', almost to the end of the Victorian period and also continued to correspond with divisions in party politics, socialethics, and economic roles.'[46]

The Catholic non-conformists also were subject to civil discrimination, till the enactment of the 'Catholic Emancipation Act' in 1829. Nevertheless, the social position of the Catholics who were largely landowners, gave them some immunity from the contempt which the Anglican upper classes showered on Protestant dissenters. But still they remained politically suspect and religiously obnoxious to majority of the Anglicans. The Catholic community, often an extension of the aristocratic or land owning Catholic families, supported the priest and provided the chapel for the celebration of Catholic sacraments. Rather than developing as a contra-culture, as Travor Ling suggests, Catholicism contributed within the English environment until the early nineteenth century as a distinct sub-culture.

The English Revolution of the seventeenth century as noted earlier, dissolved the monasteries and deprived them most of their land which was almost one-fifth of the English land, crown and Church land. This land went directly to member of the gentry, merchants and wealthy. They used the money thus earned from the acquisition of landed property to finance a commercial policy that won the shipping trade of the Europe from the Dutch, and removed several restrictions on trade and industry. It actually gave the English bourgeoisie a tremendous head start over the bourgeoisie of the other European countries. Like the French Revolution, as argued by Paul N. Siegal, it gained a good deal of its impetus from the pressure of the plebian masses. This pressure exerted through numerous sects estimated to be around 29 in London and as many as 199 in England. This estimate may not be entirely reliable. But it shows the extent of influence exercised by numerous religious sects, radical in nature and quite popular among the masses.

Calvinism had proclaimed that wordly success was a sign of membership in the elect arbitrarily chosen by God. The sects denied that the poor were damned, and asserted that salvation came through an intense religious experience, which was more likely to come to those not corrupted by wealth. Calvinism had substituted the authority of the Bible for the authority of the Catholic Church enabling the educated to monopolise religion. The sects argued that it was not through burning the midnight oil that one can attain a knowledge of divinity, but through the innerlight, the spiritual spark that could be the possession of every human being.

Although the sects spoke in terms of mystical revelations of god, they sought to reform the educational system, to make learning accessible to all and there is discernible in some of their writing the beginning of scientific materialism. For the Digger leader Winstanley the "inner light" came to be pretty close to the light of reason through which man could perceive the workings of nature. Similarly, Richard Overton's pamphlet 'Man's Morality' affirmed that man is a compound wholly mortal contrary to the common distinction of soul and body and that of heaven and hell which are a mere fiction'. Thus, while using theological phraseology, they remained committed basically to materialist interpretation in philosophy. In this sense, both Winstanley and Overton were like the sixteenth century German Anabaptist Munzer.[47]

Contemporary works dealing with seventeenth and eighteenth centuries sects with faith in the "Inner faith' have shown "the barbarous outrages committed by the sectarians" by preaching that 'god hath now opened their eyes and discovered unto them their Christian liberty; and therefore it is now fit that the nobility and gentry should serve their servants or at least work for their own maintenance. The reversal of the roles of the servants being served, reminds one of Jesus's words about the first becoming last and the last becoming first at the millennium, which was confidently expected by the various sect. "I tell you, Jesus Christ is the head Leveller." The idea of bringing the mighty down from articulated in a frequently used phrase of the 'the world turned upside down'. Today, we have, as suggested by Siegal, the word 'revolution'.[48]

The radical sects of the seventeenth century, whose members overwhelmingly came from the poorer artisans, journey men and apprentices, disintegrated with the advance of capitalism or were absorbed by the Quakers. The Quakers whose name projected their trembling with excitement during their religious meetings, and their name was a term of opprobrium labelled on them by their opponents, originated in the seventeenth century with the other radical sects.

They refused to take their hats off before a leader. George Fox, a Quaker who was a cobbler, the son of a weaver and who became the richest man of the kingdom, warned the rich in the vein of the prophets of the Old Testament and Jesus that misery would come upon them. Fox later took to non-violence as it happened to the German Anabaptists, after the failure of their uprising.[49]

With the Restoration, Fox concluded that the kingdom of God was not of the world. The Quakers gave up the expectations of their early million and their early enthusiasts who had appeared in public in the nude to demonstrate their adherence to the plain truth became responsible. Quakerism later became the religion of those artisans and petty tradesmen who, under the conditions of expanding capitalism became well to do businessmen. Quakers acquired fame for their sobriety, industry, orderliness, and (in the tradition of their earlier civil disobedience) their dislike for legal proceedings. Quakerism, basically remained a religion of the middle class. Those Quaker families who became well-to-do usually gave up their religion in the course of time.[50]

Methodism

The Quakers set the pattern for the Methodists of the eighteenth century. Methodism focused on man's corruption, but advocated that by relying on divine power one can change one's nature. It found its original support among artisans and a portion of the new industrial working class. The aristocratic and commercial oligarchy showed contempt towards them because of the mass hysteria that prevailed at its revival meetings and also due to the social composition of its membership. Their doctrines, said the Duchess of Buckingham, is most repulsive. It is monstrous to be told that you have a heart as sinful as the common wretches that crawl the earth. However, quite a few of the capitalists realised the advantage that could accrue to them, through Methodist virtues. The Industrial Revolution by destroying rural domestic industry and along with it the lingering patriarchal relationship, had congregated large masses of dispossessed peasants and artisans in the cities. Like the Black Muslims of a later time who took lumpen proletarians and instilled them with self respect, ridding them of their dependence on drugs, the Methodists liberated their converts, often disoriented by their new lives in the cities, from their addiction to drink, turning them into dependable workers. In the Methodist preaching-houses, as observed by a contemporary, the worker finds stimulus ..... not less powerful than what he formerly sought at the alehouse but, that has no morning headache. Methodist conducted their lives by rule and method and worked zealously with a sober exaltation, unmarred by hangeovers.[51]

This naturally was to the liking of employers, who often recruited Methodists to impose the rule and method of the factory on their workers. However, many Methodists, despite the Toryism of its founder John Wesley, on account of its earlier mass base among the workers were influenced by the eighteenth century radicalism and agitated for greater democracy within their movement. In the next century, Engels referring to the Salvation Army, which was founded by the Methodist preacher William Booth, precisely because Methodism had no hold on unskilled workers or on the lumpen proletariat.

"The English bourgeois.. accepted the dangerous aid of the Salvation Army, which... appeals to the poor as the elect..... and thus fosters an element of early Christian class antagonism, which one day, may become troublesome to the well-to-do people who now find the ready money.[52]

The authoritarian structures of the Methodists as well as the Salvation Army, facilitated the suppression of the protest movement they led against the rich. The Methodists lost their militancy, just as the Salvation Army lost its earlier radicalism and was reduced to a charitable organisation for tax deductable donations. As was true of Quakerism, Methodism also became the religion of the middle class.

Wesley's teachings stressed the gain of all one can, and the saving of all one can, 'but likewise give all one can, so that one will grow in grace. But as the Methodist grew in wealth they conveniently forgot about the principle of giving back to the community, everything beyond one's necessities. The richest Methodists came to dominate chapels. The habits of austerity and frugality were a good deal lost. Methodism, like Quakerism, also became respectable.

The religious situation in England, particularly in terms of affiliation to the various ecclesiastical bodies, Anglican and non-Anglican had significantly changed by the middle of the nineteenth century. The major transformation that occurred was the large extent of secularisation of the working people. Briefly, what had happened was the erosion of popular paganism under the gradually growing influence of scientific ideas and, more particularly, technological invention, the mechanisation of workshops, and the increase in the number of industrial towns and cities. Magical and astrological beliefs and practices certainly did not disappear completely, but many aspects of their appeal lost ground as it became possible for human misfortune to be alleviated in other than magical ways. The spread of secularism along with the growth of Methodism, affected the relative strength of the religious establishment, vis-à-vis the total population.

The growth of secularism among the large majority of the working class, since the period of Industrial Revolution had also the marks of a contra-culture, as it was also based on rejection of Anglican conformity.

The extent of erosion of Anglicanism could be seen in the facts provided by the Census of 1851, which shocked the Anglican hierarchy. In 1840, it had been estimated that the percentage of non-Church goers among the urban working class differed from place to place, ranging between 75 and 90 per cent. In 1821, the total number of seats in Anglican churches in Sheffield was around 4000, of which hardly 300 were rent free, that is available for the working class.[53]

It would be pertinent to note that although in the major centres of urban industrial society and culture, non-Anglicans are minorities within a pre-dominantly secularised majority. Secularised majority here is defined in terms of those who are virtually without any religious affiliations. Hence, in modern England, as T. Ling argues, Anglicanism is the 'major' religious community, only in the sense, that it possesses major power, especially political and social. This inheritance of political power has been carefully guarded and, when it was possible to do so, has been used in order to check any growth in the rights or status of other bodies. As late as 1847, for instance, a parliamentary Bill for the removal of civil and religious disabilities affecting Jewish citizens met with strong opposition from the Anglican lobby. It was opposed in the House of Lords on the grounds that its affect would be to 'de-christianise the legislature and imperil the country's religion' and was rejected by 163 votes to 125.[54]

It has been argued that the Church of England has now declined in power, as it no longer in a position to affect the rights of or the freedom of the other religious minorities in this country. Although in terms of number of worshippers it has lost the advantage which once earlier it might have had over other religious bodies, however, socially, it is still a formidable force. Its dominance in industrial society of modern England is explained in terms of other factors, such as one, the monopolist claim which was implied in the Act of Uniformity and the continuance of this claim by the Church of England during the succeeding centuries, and the fact that the Church is established by law. The Anglican clergy are also more numerous than other clergy. This along with the special position of bishops in political life, gives them a major religious body in this country is made by commentators, who themselves come predominantly from the middle class, and in whose milieu it still retains 'major' status. Such commentators are usually representatives of an influential professional class whose adherence to Anglicanism is more of a cultural and social kind, and which does not necessarily imply the Church attendance. So far as the national life as a whole is concerned, the predominant element is what may be called secular. But as the same author argues, a better word would be 'profane' in its original sense of 'outside' the temple' or not belonging to a sacred community. That seems to be the most common characteristic of this now a predominant class- the 'unchurched'. This does not imply that they have no interest in religion. Young people in this 'unchurched' class will often be found to be those who have consciously rejected some conventional, institutional form of religion, but who have a strong interest in religious issues and in finding a satisfactory religious view of life. Not a few are attracted by an Eastern religion, usually in its more mystical forms as Yoga, Zen, Sufism and such other religious traditions. For every one of the fairly small number of English members of local Buddhist and some other Asian faith, there are many more who have taken a serious interest in the ideas, and the way of life represented by these non-Western faiths. The contribution which such religious concerns make to the emerging 'alternate culture'— what Ling calls, contra-culture among young people, deserve serious consideration.[55]

Our perusal of secularism and secularisation and religion in three important nations viz., Germany, France and England, reveals that these processes have not proceeded in uniform, identical ways in any of these nations. Reformations also assumed different directions depending on the peculiar socio-economic and historical context in which they operated in these countries. Besides, that the response of different social strata such as nobility, monarchy, various plebian groups, peasantry, artisans and others also have strikingly differed in these nations. There could be no comparison for instance, with the militant, heroic peasant struggles led by Munzer with similar movements in England or France. The radical programme of social transformation unleased by the French Revolution, has no parallel either in England or Germany.

Similarly, decline of religion, either before or since the Reformation, has not been an irreversible process. One also finds that with the decline of the feudal Church, monasteries, and state patronised religious structures, parallel emergence of religious movements in the form of rise of numerous radical sects as in the case of England, feminisation of religion as in the case of France, and radical, heroic prolonged peasant war under the religious guise in Germany. Similarly, the connotations of the term, secular, is also not identical. Certainly, it does not imply non-religious or anti-religious phenomenon, unless by religion, reference is restricted to the state sponsored, established monolithic religious institutional structures, such as the Catholic Church and monastery in medieval period and the State Church and religious institutions, even in post-Reformation period.

Our perusal also indicates that during the Reformation, post-Reformation and even modern periods, with the decline of the state sponsored religious structures and the spread of the secularisation process in civil society, culminating in secular polity, vast bulk of oppressed and weaker strata in Western society, inclusive of women, have found it convenient and legitimate to articulate their aspirations, as well as to register their protest against social and economic exploitation and to gain social and economic exploitation and to gain social recognition and approval through varied religious and social movements. In this respect even in India one finds, right from the Vedic and the post-Vedic periods and even after the advent of the British rule, significant sections of oppressed strata registering their dissent, or protest and also thereby creating alternate forms of devotion, either by giving fresh interpretation to dominant religious traditions or by paving the way for alternate, more democratic, egalitarian religious traditions through their social and religious movements.

Our appraisal here is restricted only to three selected nations in Europe and that too it is confined to the far reaching impact of the French and Industrial Revolutions on religious and social institutions. We plan to examine the modern scenario in Europe, peculiar features of the secular state and secularisation process and the rise of new religious movements, especially in United States of America and elsewhere, as the time and space would not permit us to do the same in this appraisal.

References

1. Holyoake, G.L: Reproduced from Achin Vanaik Religion, Secularisational Manuscript. p. 1.
2. Gorgi, Liana:Religious Investment in a secularised society: article in British Journal of Sociology 43(4) Dec.1992.
3. David Martin : The Religious and the Secular London, Routledge and Kegan Paul, 1969, p.1614.
4. Varickayil, Robert : Social Origins of Protestant Reformation, p. 15 Article in Social Scientist June-1980.
5. *Ibid.*, pp. 15-16.
6. *Ibid.*, p. 18.
7. *Ibid.*, pp. 18-19.
8. *Ibid.*, p. 20.
9. *Ibid.*, pp. 20-21.
10. Engels, F. The Peasant War in Germany p. 87 from Marx Engels on Religion, Progress Publishers.
11. *Ibid.*, pp. 88-89.
12. *Ibid.*, p. 86.
13. *Ibid.*, pp. 88-89.
14. V. Robert, pp. 23-24.
15. Hill, Christopher: Reformation to Industrial Revolution Vol. II pp. 26-43 – Chap. 1 National Unification. Penguin Books, 1969.
16. Hobsbawm, E.J: The French Revolution, pp. 73-74 From his book. The Age of Revolution: 1784 -1848 Rupa and Co. Calcutta, 1992.
17. *Ibid.*, pp. 74-76.
18. *Ibid.*, pp. 77-78.
19. *Ibid.*, pp. 78-79.
20. *Ibid.*, pp. 83-85.
21. *Ibid.*, pp. 269-270.
22. *Ibid.*, pp. 271-272.
23. Owen, Chadwidkk: The Secularisation of the European Mind Cambridge, 1975.

24. Ford Caroline : Reference from her article Religion and Popular Culture in Modern Europe, Published in Journal of Modern History Vol. 65, March 1993.
25. Natalie Zemon Davis, Society and Culture in Early Modern France (Standford Calif. 1975).

    Carolin Walder Bynum Holy Feast and Holy Fast: The Religious significance of food to Medieval Women (Berkeley and Los Angeles, 1987). Recent significant works that focus on the religious dimension of women's lives since 1800 include Bonnie Smith, Ladies of the Leisure Class: The Bourgeoises of Northern France (Princeton, N.J. 1981) and Barbara Taylor- Eve and the New Jerusalem: Socialism and Feminism in the Nineteenth Century (New York, 1983) Gerad Cholvy Religion at Societe au XIX siècle? Lediocese d'Arras de-1840-1914 (Lille, 1977)- Adrien Dansehe's. Historic Religiouse dela France Contemporaine (Paris: 1918.51) Ralph Gibson: Part of new series on Christianity and Society in the Modern World, edited by Hugh Mcleod and Bob Scribner.
26. Ford, p. 136.
27. Ford, Caroline, p. 157.
28. Ford, p. 156.
29. Ford, C: p. 161.
30. *Ibid.*, p. 38.
31. Ford, C: p. 164.
32. Quoted in R. Gibson. Social History of French Catholicism, p. 255.
33. Cholvy and Hilaire eds 1:177.
34. Jane Rendell: The Origins of Modern Feminism: Women in Britain, Im 20 France and the United States, 1780-1860 (London, 1985), pp. 73-107; Olwen Hutton, "The Reconstruction of the Church, 1796-1801, in Beyond the Terror; Essays in French Regional History, 1794- 1815, ed Gwynne Lewis and Colin Lucas (Cambridge, 1983), pp. 21-52; and family fortunes; Men and Women of the English Middle Class (Chicago, 1987). Im 5.
35. Ford, C: p. 168.
36. Ford, C: p. 170.
37. Arnold, p. 15.
38. Ford, C: p. 171.
39. Ford, C: p. 172.
40. Ford, C: p. 173.
41. Ling, Trevor, Karl Marx and Religion. The Macmillan Press Ltd, London, 1980. p. 34.
42. *Ibid.*, p. 36.
43. *Ibid.*, p. 38.
44. *Ibid.*, p. 38.
45. Siegel, Paul. N. The Meek and the Militantzed Books. USA 1986, p. 94.

46. *Ibid.*, p. 94.
47. *Ibid.*, p. 95.
48. *Ibid.*, p. 98.
49. *Ibid.*, p. 96.
50. *Ibid.*, p. 96.
51. Ling, T, pp. 40-41.
52. *Ibid.*, p. 44.
53. *Ibid.*, pp. 43-44.
54. Karl Marx & Religion: Macmillan Press Lonon.
55. *Ibid.*

5

Secularism and Secularisation Nation Building in a Multi-religious Society

—Rudolf C. Heredia

Secularism has been very much associated with nation building in our post-colonial world. Little wonder then that as the process of national development has failed to meet the rising expectation of our people, secularism too has been mired in controversy. The validity of this concept for our society is being questioned and its practical usefulness, challenged both by the conservative right and the counter-culture radicals as well. And yet, if the burning issues of religious and ethnic conflict are to be addressed in any depth then an analysis of the secularism and its role in our society cannot be bypassed.

Indeed "the understanding of the phenomenon of secularism (or of the process of secularisation) has emerged as a major intellectual challenge before the new Asian nations. These nations as late-comers to the modernisation process can benefit not only from their own historical experiences regarding the factors - promoting or retarding - secularism. They can also benefit from the experience of the western countries and avoid many of the conflicts and tensions, pitfalls and predicaments, distortions and deformations, associated with the pursuit of the secular ideal."[1]

Secularism was once accepted in this country by a broad social consensus, that even the trauma of the partition seemed to strengthen rather than weaken, and it has been written into the basic structure of our Constitution. Yet the state and society in India since then have become increasingly and violently communal, with communal politics being projected onto the national scene and even threatening to rewrite our Constitution. However, abandoning our Constitutional secularism, is, a cure guaranteed to accentuate the disease. Rather what we need is a renewed commitment based on a rethinking and a revaluation of the concept and its relevance for us today. In other words, we need to critically contextualise our understanding of Secularism within the "Conflict of Contrasting Worldviews" that reflect the reality of "Indian Society in Transition".[2]

For whether it be "the ideal of liberalisation" or "the ideology of Hindutva" or "the rising subaltern voice"[3] — implicit in all these three prevalent worldviews today is an understanding of the secular and its relationship to economic development, to religious culture, to democratic equality. Clearly, we are in a crisis that cuts much deeper than some of the responses being addressed to it, secular and anti-secular. Hence our approach here is to treat secularism not just as a *sine qua non* for tolerance in a multi-cultural society but also as a project for liberation in a religiously oppressive one. For although secularism may be foreign in its origins, as an ideology, it is not alien in the aspiration it inspires among our people.

Moreover, in a complex differentiated society, there is very likely to be more than one set of ultimate ideals, religious or otherwise. When these conflict with each other "humanity has either got caught in an escalating spiral of ultimate ideals need to be limited". This realisation "is neither purely Christian nor peculiarly western. It grows wherever there is a persistent clash of ultimate ideals perceived to be incompatible."[4] In short, a certain minimal pluralism must be politically guaranteed. When this happens with regard to religious worldviews, then we speak of secularism — in this case political secularism.

Secularism as it arose in the Christian West was very much a power struggle between church and state, a struggle over the two swords of temporal and spiritual authority, both claimed by the Roman Pope and the Holy Roman Emperor. But with the dividing of Christendom and the fracturing of the Catholic faith into numerous schisms and heresies, the problem of freedom of conscience in a multi-religious society began to take centre-stage, especially among the Reformed Churches, where the state was unable to impose a single official faith on its multiplicity of warring churches. In all this confusions, the 'age of faith' yielded to the 'age of reason', the Enlightenment began a radical rationalist critique of religion with the undisguised goal of displacing all religion from public life and all faith from private life as well, and replacing both with a new secular consensus as the basis of the national community.

The understanding of secularism in a pluri-religious, multi-cultural society, like India, will certainly be different from that in the West, a difference not just in degree but in kind. However, to deny any relevance for our society of the realities of change that the concept attempts to capture, would be to fall into a kind of cultural solipsism of 'East is East' and 'West is West...',[5] that is hardly tenable in an interdependent world. What is required is a critical and fine-tuned analysis of the sweeping changes in our society in the context of the social processes that may not be exclusive or unique to it alone. For the relationship of religion to society is a problematic one in any differentiated society; though the concrete context may indeed make for more specific and significant differences.

Secularism and Secularisation

A good place to begin to unravel the complexity of the controversy over the 'Secular' and its role in our society and polity would be a clarification of terms. This will atleast help to locate the differences even if it is not possible to reconcile or integrate them into a more incisive understanding.

We would then at the outset distinguish 'secularisation' as a social process and 'secularism' as a socio-political ideal or ideology. Most of the controversy centres around the latter but it can hardly be grasped apart from the former. For the while, secularism is a value-loaded concept, its values derive from and must be contextualised in our understanding of the underlying social process we call secularisation. For viable ideals and ideologies must be grounded in the social context from which they derive and which in turn they affect. In actuality, secularism can become a reality in our social institutions only in so far as these are affected by secularisation. For

> *"the truism that there can be no secularism without a process of secularisation is now wisely (and perhaps 'limply') accepted, but the challenge of actualising it through concrete social, political, economic, and educational measures is an enormous task."*[6]

In this perspective then secularism is a Western concept to the extent that secularisation is a process that is located in western society. But then so is modernisation and modernism. Yet this does not make these irrelevant or alien to our present society, especially in the light of the pervasive global changes affecting all national societies today. Rather, what is needed is a creative and constructive contextualisation in our own contemporary situation. We can indeed find homologues' to these Western concepts and processes in our own context. And a comparative perspective can make our analysis much more incisive.

> *"Secularism in India (as, in fact, in Europe) is an intrinsic part of the process of giving shape to a modern identity for the people of a multi-language and multi-ethnic society, the necessity for which is being continuously generated by processes of industrialisation and urbanisation."*[7]

Here we make a modest attempt to theorise the process in the wider context of social change and development, as these have been associated with building modern nations.[8]

To begin then with secularisation — in the West this was hailed as "the liberation of modern man from religious tutelage" by some, while others bewail it "as de - Christianisation, paganisation and the like..."[9] But historically, the process of secularisation for the social scientists is intimately linked with the rise of modernity in the West and some would consider it as "perhaps the most significant development of the last several hundred years.[10] It was the apparent decline in traditional church-oriented religion in recent times that seemed to heighten the process of secularisation and bring it to its present culmination. Yet it is a process whose roots can be traced to the very founding of the major religions and in fact it stands in an ambiguous and dialectical relation to the very phenomena it supposedly undermines.

Originally 'secularisation' refered to the confiscation of Church property or the exclaustration of religious persons. However,

> *"secularisation is now understood as the process whereby various elements of human life (such as opinion, customs, social forms and even things and persons) or the whole of human life cease to be determined by religion."*[11]

This definition by a theologian is essentially similar to the ones prevalent among sociologists. Thus, Berger writes: "by secularisation we mean the process by which sections of society and culture are removed from the domination of religious institutions and symbols."[12]

Historically, this process has engendered conflict in three areas of controversy: faith and knowledge, church and state, this world and the other world as the goal of life. Obviously these need not represent mutually exclusive dichotomies. But rather areas of tension, even conflict. Correspondingly, we have the secularisation of science, politics and economics, However, these definitions of secularisation are essentially negative in that they define the concept in terms of the decline of religious hegemony, of social institutions coming out from under *The Sacred Canopy*[13] of legitimation which religion, once provided for them.

But with the widespread religious revivalism today, from aggressive fundamentalism to popular religiosity, from ecstatic spiritualists to committed liberationists, 'the decline' or the 'demise' of institutional religion is a far more complex and contested issue than was once thought. One is forced to the conclusion that "it is obvious no simple unilinear and one dimension 'theory of secularisation' in modern society can be maintained".[14]

For to maintain a theory of secularisation conceived as an inevitable and irreversible process away from 'religion' would require a clear statement of the criteria of secularity and a careful discussion of the historical trends in relation to each criterion. Attempts like this have produced such varied results that secularisation is as many sided as the sources that produce it; as multi-dimensional as the criteria that define it.[15]

The difficulty in defining the concept and the resulting confusion have led some sociologists to abandon the term 'secularisation' as a useful conceptualisation of socially relevant process. Thus, Younger would rather speak of 'religious change' than of secularisation.[16] And Martian argues emphatically that "secularisation should be erased from the sociological dictionary"[17] But such drastic solutions are not correspondingly helpful. It does seem that a good deal of the confusion comes not only from the complexity of the phenomena under discussion but also from a lack of a broader theoretical perspective even when ideological preoccupations are set aside.

In tracing the spirit of capitalism "to the Protestants Ethic"[18] establishes an affinity between modernity and secularisation. Both these are understood in the context of the most fundamental generalisation that emerges from Weber's work and his concept of the process of rationalisation[19] which includes both instrumental and value rationality *zwerckrationalitat and wertrationalitat* respectively.[20]

Following Weber, Berger isolates the 'process of rationalisation' as the "decisive variable for secularisation", in the Weberian perspective we can take a more decisive step: secularisation is the rationalisation of religion: it is concomitant with the rationalisation process that affects other social phenomena and is intimately bound up in a reciprocal causal relation with them. It is this process of rationalisation that results in the social differentiation and institutional specialisation that eventually makes possible the autonomy of social institutions apart from the 'sacred canopy' that religion once provided.

In this perspective, then, the limits to secularisation are the very ones inherent in the process of rationalisation itself. For the non-rational is not a residual category but an essential component of social action. Further being aware of the intrinsic antinomy between formal and substantive rationality, Weber is pessimistic about bureaucratic routinisation finally leading to the 'iron cage'. It is from the continued emergence of charisma. Which is not irrational but essentially non-rational or rather transnational, that he expects renewal and redemption. In this Weber anticipates much of the post-modernist, anti-rationalist criticism.

In a functionalist perspective like that of Dhurkheim, however, secularisation would imply the functional substitution of religion by some other symbolic reality capable of creating the moral consensus, the collective consciousness, the social society. This could be done by a "civil religion"[21] or an "ideology."[22] Obviously, there will be limitation to how functional such substitutes can be, especially if one considers religion to be a universal functional prerequisite, as some do.[23] Indeed in so far as these secular substitutes do perform the function of religion, they in fact become "sacralised"! Certainly this has happened with political ideologies and national symbols and rites. This brings us back to a de-secularisation or a re-sacralisation!

By Marxist understanding, secularisation is but the overcoming of religious alienation and as such it need have no limits to its rationalising potential. It is

> "a *many — sided (at both the material and the ideological levels) process involving the progressive decline of religious influence in the economic, political and the social life of human beings, and even over their private habits and motivations.*"[24]

Moreover, since religion is itself alienating it should have no substitutes to proxy for it. Hence, secularisation must mean the abolition of religion. However, Marx did not anticipate the resilience of religion and its capacity for revival, not just survival. For in the final analysis, Marxist rationality has been overly sanguine about dialectic materialism which now seems to be historically off course!

However, in our understanding secularisation is not premised on a Nietzschean 'death of God' or a Feuerbachean 'demise of religion'. Rather it implies the development of autonomous social institutions that need no longer fall under the 'sacred canopy' of religion for their legitimation. This comes not principally from tradition, or merely from power, but from a process of rationalisation which is instrumentally concerned with end-means relationships, and value-committed to this worldly human liberation. It is this process that must effectively ground our secular ideals and ideologies.

Not all rationalisation is liberating just as not all modernisation is egalitarian. For instrumental rationality by itself is not necessarily oriented to liberating values or goals. Thus, *laissez-faire* liberal capitalism rationalises the economy towards greater productivity, but it was hardly liberating for the 'proletariat'. So, too was caste a rationalisation of social interaction in terms of a hierarchy that was inhumanly oppressive of those at the bottom of the social pyramid. But here we are concerned with a value-premised understanding of secularism as a project for liberation for all, not just a class a caste or any single ethnic group. And such a project certainly need not be confined to the West.

Similarly not all religious, traditions are liberating. Indeed,

> *"It is possible to distinguish sharply between the religiosity of the propertied and oppressor classes on the one hand; and the religiosity of the petty propertied/propertyless and oppressed masses on the other. While the religiosity of the former type is truly 'the opium of the people',*

the religiosity of the latter is what Marx called 'the expression of real distress and 'the protest against real distress'; the sigh of the oppressed creature, the heart of a heartless world, just as it is the spirit of a spiritless situation. Religious symbolism of the latter type has a vastly energising and radicalising role for the people: it enables them to break away from false consciousness being imposed by the religiosity of the first type. This represents a stage in the qualitative transformation of mass consciousness; a break from their reconciliation to the status of object of historical forces and a movement towards becoming the 'subject' of historical processes.[25]

Religious traditions cannot but reflect the contradictions of its own society, and like "all cultural traditions are themselves ambivalent and contradictory."[26] Thus, while on the one hand, religious fundamentalism and conservatism have oppressed and contained the masses, on the other, liberation theology has inspired radical and even revolutionary responses among the people. Hence even for the critical left.

"the identification of secularism with rationalism and progress and of religion with unreason, social conservatism and political reaction is now undergoing a major revision and reformulation."[27]

Secular Ideologies

In India, the characterisation of traditional society as religious and of modern society as secular is as widespread as it is simplistic. The tradition-modernity and religious-secular dichotomies on which this seems to be based, amounts to superficial stereotyping, not useful ideal-typing. It would be "crude and mechanical" to label and categorise all such pre-modern thoughts patterns and trends, which do not convey the message of secularism."[28] Historically, the Indian situation is far more complex.

Thus, one can argue that the Upanishads were a secularisation of Vedic Religion and that Jainnism and Buddhism were Kshatriya attempts that successfully for a time, secularised/rationalised Brahmanic Hinduism with a non-theistic way of life. The Bhakti movement beginning in the Tamil south and spreading north "expressed the popular *aspirations for equality, the popular agony against oppression and exploitation"*.[29] The Sufi tradition is also very close to such expression and aspirations, and some would treat "Sufi-Bhakti poetry as 'the fixed deposits on which we can rely on in times of crisis.'[30]

More recently, diverse liberation theologies have begun to articulate the liberative, this worldly dimensions of our religious traditions. Here Asghar Ali Engineer for Islam, Swami Agnivesh for Hinduism and George Soares-Prabhu for Christianity deserve special mention. Indeed

> *"Asian civilisations existed, thrived and also survived the passage of time for thousands of years through inner creative tensions expressed in a series of intellectual movements and upheavals. These humanistic and life affirming stirring contributed towards moulding a secular outlook and consciousness in its formative period. They fertilised the cultural soil for the germination and growth of the modern concept of secularism."*[31]

However, the breakthrough to modernity happens only under the colonial impetus, and the Nationalist Freedom Movement, which makes a conscious and determined attempt to construct a modern India, as the *terminus ad quern* of a planned development process. Secularism as an ideal and an ideology was an integral part of this agenda. In fact, it is the failure of this developmental process and the consequent fragmentation of our society that has/polarised it into communal groups and fractured the consensus which has so far contained our differences, affirmed our communalities and inspired us to struggle for a sovereign, democratic, socialist and secular nation.

However, while political institution may be legally constituted, it requires the appropriate social conditions to survive. And it is here that Indian secularism has leaned too heavily on a Nehruvian rationalism, and remained an imposition from the outside even though it claimed constitutional legitimation for itself. It was not based on a consensus that

> *"emerged out of a creative dialogue between different communities. It was sui genesis. This archimedean existence gave secularism procedural priority but in doing so it gave it no abiding substantive authority."*[32]

A reactivation of this lost national consensus cannot be done in abstraction from the social processes in which it must be grounded. It cannot be imposed as part of a dominant hegemony, as liberal middle-class rationalists are wont to urge, if it is to be liberating for the religiously oppressed masses. A dichotomy between the "secular-minded elite and religiously oriented masses" cannot found a project for liberation — such secularism would be alien and oppressive as some anti-secularist have incisively demonstrated.

The rationalist secularism of Nehru is particularly vulnerable to this critique, as also to the Hindu backlash of the 'positive secularists', who denigrate this as 'pseudo secularist'. Indeed.

> *"the dharma-nirapekshata or indifference to religion, which is how secularism is generally translated though rarely used in everyday discourse...is completely at odds with the more accepted Indian' response to the term."*[33]

It was hardly ever likely to have sustained much mass support.

Gandhi rejected this elite-mass dichotomy. He "alone understood the meaning of religiosity of the masses as an attachment to the moral order, to moral economy, moral society and moral polity."[34] In other words, of dharma over adharma, The "old religious symbolism harnessed to a new secular purpose had an electrifying effect in releasing mass energy and removing fear and generating fearlessness."[35] In Gandhi's Swaraj through Ahimsa and Satyagraha, there was no separation of religion and politics. Rather he attempted to make religion more tolerant and politics more moral.

However, Gandhi's reformist Hinduism has its own inherent limitations. Particularly on the issue of the caste. Here his attempt to establish a basic social equality within the Varnasharma-Dharma was doomed to be rejected by the more radical and militant movements on the right and on the left. More recently his rediscovery by counter-cultural groups has called off a critical rethinking, not just an undiscerning repetition of his reformist programme. For we believe that there is still is a radical relevance to his message today for our destructive and violent age.

Gandhian secularism of Sarva-Dharma-Samabhav, equality to all religions and the essential tolerance and the openness it implies is much closer to the reality of the deep and multifaceted religiosity of our people. It is also more in tune with our Constitutional protection to the rights of religious minorities which has been reaffirmed in 83 judgments interpreting and applying legal principles to concrete cases.

Other Secularism

Nehruvian Dharma-Nirapekshata and Gandhian Sarvadharma-Samabhava represent the two most significant models of secular ideologies that were subsumed into the national consensus. Where "they are frequently mistaken for or conflated with each other."[36]

There were others too, like Tagore with his deep humanism, and Lohia with his committed socialism, that by and large supported rather than undermined this consensus. Eventually, the various tensions and contradictions between these diverse secularism were also fused or rather confused.

Yet today both Nehruvian and Gandhian versions are being dismissed by some as "pseudo-secularism" in favour of its very antithesis, i.e. "positive-secularism" of justice to all, 'discrimination against none'. — which is being urged in the guise of 'cultural nationalism'. This identifies India as Hindu, because this is the majority community, and so Hinduism must mean nationalism and vice versa! This would of course sacralise the state into a theocracy. But Hinduism is a very broad civilisational concept, whereas Hindutva is a narrow communal ideology. Indeed, there is till today only one "Hindu State" and that is outside the boundaries of the Indian Union, namely Nepal!

The majority versus the minorities conflict which this sets up is already tearing apart the fragile fabric of our society, perhaps beyond repair if this is not remedied soon. But for the majority community too, the "cultural nationalism," of Hindutva, implies a social homogenisation that can only lead to the hegemony of the dominant groups, of upper castes and classes in our society. Indeed, elites have only too easily been able to manipulate ethnic identities, from within the group and from without, to serve their own vested interests.[37]

Thus, to the extent that religion in this country has in the past been dominated by such elites, "positive secularism' is not really in discontinuity with this older tradition, and represents more a fundamentalist revival than a liberating secularism. Thus, Hindutva is a "cultural narcissism" that has nothing in common with the "critical/dialogical Hinduism" Gandhi symbolised.[38]

Certainly the dominance-subservience relationship this perpetuates, are in continuity with, and represents a consolidation of the inegalitarian development which has precipitated our crisis in the first place. For the national homogenisation it imposes is a remedy that can only deepen this crisis even farther and set us down the slippery slope to an authoritarian and fascist state.

However, when a state actively and aggressively promotes secularism, this easily becomes one more ideology imposed from above. Thus, for the anti-secularists, "the ideologies of secularism development and nationalism" begin to act "as faiths among other faiths", from which the modern state provides no protection.[39] These faiths may be different in content from the communalists and their 'cultural nationalism', but they are similar in the attempt to absorb diverse and marginal groups and people into homogeneous national society. Historically, rationalist secularism in the West has been at times, not just intolerant of religions, but actively anti-religious, and the stigma still sticks.

Certainly in the West, secularism has been used in the role of a nationalist ideology to motivate citizens towards building a modern state. This of course is a use of state power that the anti-secularist would consider to be an abuse and we are cautioned against it. Obviously "there can be no secularism in India today without a critique of the state."[40] For a state sponsored secularism cannot be a liberating secularism, if it frees people from a religious domination to bring them under apolitical or any other one.

However, in negating any liberating potential to secularism some anti-secularists seem to have exceeded themselves even to the point of denying any validity to the underlying process of secularisation as well. Their post-modernist opposition to development and nationalism at items seems to be exaggerated and uncritical. Of course, we need to evolve alternative models of development and ideologies of state power, just as we need to critically rethink our secular ideology. But to reject these outright easily adds up to romanticising traditional religious institutions and legitimating, albeit unintentionally (perhaps), much of their oppression. Some anti-secularists in "rubbishing secularism" seem insensitive to the "victims of patriarchy and religon", and to be seeking "merely for secure niches in cognitive markets."[41] At times they seem downright obscurantist, as when they make a distortion of religious tolerance that included a convoluted defense of practice like sati, from the believers' world view, if you please!

The lunatic fringe of anti-secularism may often express itself in religious fundamentalism and obscurantism which may well prove to be their own worst enemy. But the more sophisticated and subtle versions are finely tuned and do merit an appropriate response. Thus, for T N Madan, "the crisis of Indian secularism lies first in the failure of political leaders and intellectuals to distinguish between the two kinds of identity and the relevant context without opposing them,"[42] i.e. inborn religious identities and the civic/political ones. The state then becomes the "integrator"-of "rival group interest and parochial identities", not the "mediator" between them.[43]

This obviously refers to a nationalist secular identity imposed from above, which as we have seen may have an opposite content, but a similar function to the "cultural nationalism" of the Hindutva-wadis. In addressing the task, Nehruvian nationalism, sets itself, of "creating a secular state in a religious society." Madan feels that what

> *"deserves top priority today is to determine how human rights can be assured to one and all without sacrificing cultural pluralism, and how groups defined in terms of inborn identities may be replaced in the political arena by political majorities and minorities that exchange place though peaceful democratic means."*[44]

But such a liberal-democratic ideal seems like a fool's utopia in the rough-and-tumble of Indian Politics. Ashish Nandy's opposition to rationalist modernist secularism comes from a similar perspective with the same apprehensions. But going further, he identifies a Western meaning of secularism which "chalks out an area in public life where religion is not admitted."[45] "In contrast, the non-western meaning of secularism revolves around equal respect for all religions".[46] Nand's anti-secularist manifesto is really in opposition to the "import from nineteenth century Europe", which he regards as.

> *"definitionally ethnophobic and ethnocidal, unless of course cultures and those living by cultures are willing to show total subservience to the modern nation-state and become ornaments or adjuncts to modern living."*[47]

Such a state in treating religion as an ideology of mutually exclusive identities promotes a backlash of insecurity that eventually precipitates communal and ethnic violence. For Nandy, then, cultural nationalism and nationalist secularism are similar pathologies of civil society.

His response is to recover traditional religious tolerance, from the "hegemonic language of secularism."[48] For him,

> *"instead of trying to build religious tolerance on the good faith or conscience of small group of de-ethnicized, middle-class politicians, bureaucrats and intellectuals, a far more serious venture would be to*

explore the philosophy, the symbolism, and the theology of tolerance in the various faiths of the citizens and hope that the state systems in South Asia may learn something about religious tolerance from everyday Hinduism, Islam, Buddhism, and/or Sikhism, rather than wish that ordinary Hindus, Muslims, Buddhists and Sikhs will learn tolerance from the various fashionable secular theories of state craft."[49]

Nandy's preferred model is Emperor Ashoka who "based his tolerance on Buddhism not on secularism."[50] But Ashoka's Buddhism did have state patronage, albeit an enlightened one and Buddhism is a very 'rational' and not dogmatic as far as religions go. In putting his faith in "religion as a way of life", Nandy has chosen well against "religion as ideology." But one cannot help feeling that he is being too uncritical and over-romantic about popular religiosity.

For while it is true "that popular religion, being syncretic in nature, should be distinguished from communal ideology."[51] Yet it is not always or everywhere being or tolerant. It has its own demons that need; to be exorcised. In rejecting rationalist nationalism, Nandy has failed to appreciate the liberating potential of secularism and seems to throw out the baby-water. For our people need an "emancipation of the mind" no less than they do an "economic and political emancipation."[52]

Now if our Constitutional secularism is given a Nehruvian interpretation, it is difficult to see how the anti-secularists can be accommodated. However, a Gandhian understanding would allow its positive contribution to stand. However, to our mind. Hindutva's positive secularism' would require a rewriting of our basic constitutional framework.

For secularism in our Constitution though not adequately defined, minimally at least, has meant a guarantee of equal treatment to all religious communities by the state. Those who want to homogenise our society with a 'cultural nationalism' will inevitably be at odds with such a secularism. But our secular state is also committed to the reform of religious communities in view of establishing the fundamental rights of its members. Those who see their religious traditions endangered by such interventions of the state will surely be opposed to it.

In giving weightage to minority rights and the needs of socially and economically backward groups, the Constitution was recognising "the principle of equality between groups qua groups."[53]

This was an acknowledgement of collective rights with special consideration for the more vulnerable sections of our society. Certainly these cannot be absolutised, for their purpose was to expand citizen participation in national life not to allow an isolationist separatism, or divisive groupism. For the Constitutional protection to the minorities and weaker sections in our society cannot be used to vitiate the rights of other citizens, as guaranteed by this very constitution.

There is, indeed, the real possibility that "a cultural right be used to perpetuate thoroughly illiberal practices within the groups."[54] For the "right to culture" for a group can only be validly claimed in a "culture of right"[55] – such a culture does not accept "an ideology of enforced homogenisation nor seek violent methods of resolving conflicts of interest."[56] For collective groups rights cannot be allowed to violate fundamental individual ones or vitiate the legitimate interests of other groups or the national community of groups. This is the point at which state intervention would be constitutionally justified. In other words, in affirming national identity and universal rights of citizens in our society, at the level of *gesellschaft,* we must at the same time protect the ethnic identity of the socio-cultural groups and in particular their members in their communities, at the level of *gemeinschaft.*[57]

Apparently then that "the cultural and historical realities of the Indian situation call for a different relationship between state and civil society."[58] And this is what our Constitution has done:

> *"To sum up, the idea of secularism as expressed in our Constitution and as articulated over the years through the political process was embedded in the concepts of equality and democracy rather than in the Western concept of secularism which denies religion any space in the public sphere. This secularism, admittedly, was a peculiar Indian invention. But it was one necessitated by the historical conditions of Indian society in which a modern democratic state was being introduced by our national leadership and our Constitution-makers at the time of Independence."*[59]

Peoples' Movement

An adequate response to our social crisis cannot come merely from the elites on top impinging on the masses below. It is more likely to be precipitated from below by the motivation and mobilisation of our people to reach out to the elites on top. So too the communalisation of our society must be opposed not just by the dominant classes and castes over society, but by releasing the secular potential embedded in people's movements that struggle to empower and liberate our oppressed masses. Here we mention a few.

Mahatma Jotirao Phule (1872-1890) founded the Satyashodhak Samaj in Maharashtra, with its alliance of middle and low castes. shudra and ati-shudra — and stood the Aryan theory of race on its head. He used popular peasant myths and symbols from nineteenth century theism to contest the *prevailing brahmanic* religious hegemony.[60] This "gained widespread following throughout India in the 1920s, where it was used especially by untouchable groups throughout India as an assertion of equality and a rejection of a Hindu identity."[61]

In Tamil Nadu, Periyar E V Ramaswamy Naicker began the Self Respect Movement (1926) which he developed into the Dravida Kazhagam (1944) that "centred around the struggle for democratisation and secularisation of the hitherto inarticulate levels of Tamil society."[62] Periyar not only denounced Brahmanism, he explicitly proclaimed atheism. Unfortunately though, much of the liberating secular potential of this movement has today been stymied if not actually reversed as it has undergone several transformations—the Dravida Munetra Kazhagam (DMK, 1949) and the All India Anna DMK (AIADMK, 1977)."[63]

Babasaheb Ambedkar (1891-1956) attempted to organise a broad-based caste-class from dalits and non-brahmins but did not quite succeed. His Republican Party remained a Dalit organisation. His rejection of Hinduism, however, was total and he led a mass conversion to Buddhism, to which he "gave a secular-social liberation theology interpretation."[64] There were other attempts at redressing oppressive religious structures, like Ram Manohar Lohia, in the 1950s "trying to contrast the 'Vasistha' with the 'Vishvamitra' (liberal versus the conservative) traditions in Hinduism."[65]

J P Narayan's "Total Revolution" in Bihar in the 1970s gave a significant turn to the Sarvodaya movement and precipitated a student revolution for a socialist democracy with a strong secular component.[66]

In Maharashtra, the Shiv Sena has not completely succeeded in appropriating the popular Shivaji Maharaj. Phule and Ambedkar are still heroes, and

> *"it, is interesting that the new social movements' including the Dalit, women's, peasant and ecological movements which have been particularly strong in Maharashtra have consistently had an anti-Hindu cultural thrust."*[67]

Thus, the Shetkari Sanghatna has taken the mythical peasant king Bali Raja, not Ram Raja as its central symbol. Moreover, through the country there are numerous "secular seekers (of whom many artists, writers, and thinkers could be included)" whose secularism is not driven "by the imperative of any ideology,"[68] but for whom

> *"secularism is, first and foremost, an act of living. Its interventions need not be mediated through institutional one. They can be made at very human levels almost anywhere on the street. In animated discussions and 'addas' in the classroom, by responding to a film or play, in contesting communalism slurs in jokes and small talk."*[69]

This, indeed, makes for "the cultural preparation for the political ideology of secularism."[70]

It is not our contention here, that all these peoples' movements add up to a secular revolution. But they certainly are more than mere signs of hope in the midst of anti-secular and revivalist religious forces. What it does mean is that there are numerous centres of resistance to a hegemonic brahmanical Hinduism that is posing a real threat to our secular aspiration. And further that

> *"the ideology of militant Hinduism is on the rise only in the sense that it is becoming more aggressive not that it has become more predominant in our society."*[71]

This is crucially important for the future of secularism in our country, given the crucial predominance of the majority community here.

What we have here, then, are the indigenous strands of various liberative movements that can be woven into a strong support for a secularism that must be realistically grounded in, and be able to critically orient the secularisation process already at work in our society. For a multi-religious society there is an obvious "limitation to any secular intervention that fails to take into consideration other faiths."[72] But this will demand more than "a gingerly mix of political secularism and non-secular communities ."[73] As some like T N Madan seem to urge.[74]

What we need is a more enriching "pluralist version of ethical secularism which is both secular and communitarian."[75] In other words, we must have more than state neutrality vis-à-vis religious communities operating within an orderly framework.

Such tolerance is but the minimum for a multi-religious society if the groups in it are to live together and survive. But beyond this we must strive for an affirmation of the more universal liberative human values without negating the particular community identities – and vice versa. For the basis of participation in society as *geselleschaft* must be in terms of human universals, while the sense of belonging to a community as *gemeinschaft* must be in terms of group particulars.[76]

Conclusion: Commitment to Liberation

This is a project for liberation to which we must now commit ourselves. For in the final analysis, secularism in our country must mean more than mere religious tolerance. It must "be inscribed in other, more positive agendas, transcending the innate condescensions of tolerance through new modes of respecting and living with difference."[77] It must mean more than the commitment to religious reform and the end of all oppressive beliefs and practices that violate human rights. It must also mean a commitment to build this world, as a habitat for all humans without prejudices to caste, or creed. Indeed this is a project for liberation that is validated by the human, whose autonomy and value is affirmed.

Such a this-worldly commitment "need not be hostile to ultimate ideals."[78] It need not amount to a rationalist negation of religious faith, nor need it be bound to an exclusivism in favour of a particular community or nation-state. Rather it must be a secularism which must be grounded in the processes of secularisation as these obtain in our society now, as well as facilitate and foster this very process further. But like all social change, secularisation is ambiguous, and without a commitment to human liberation. It could become an anomic process with an alienating ideology, and eventually provoke an explosive religious backlash. Already our skewed modernisation has lead to an inegalitarian development and an uncritical consumerism, that has reinforced old hierarchies and mobilised caste loyalties. The communal crisis engulfing us today is but a reflection of the religious and group tension. Due to our failed development that has "prevented the consolidation of a secular society in India"[79] and precipitated the mobilisation of "disaffected groups by appeals to their religious identity."[80]

The insecurity consequent on such unresolved tensions does drive people to seek reassuring sense of belonging in a group. For "it seems a social identity can support a crumbling self the way a scaffolding can support a crumbling building."[81] Such "ethnic groups are not only a shelter for those mourning lost attachments but also vehicles for redressing narcissistic injuries for righting what are perceived as contemporary or historical wrongs,"[82] In other words, an alienation society only precipitates anomic communities. For in a complex "Division of Labour in Society", when 'organic solidarity' is compromised or destroyed, then 'mechanical solidarity' in its constituting groups is also undermined and negated.[83]

No wonder these find a sense of efficiency in violence against accessible scapegoats. This is regrettably regressive and not to be confused with a people's movement struggling for justice and liberation from their oppressors. Secularism is but one aspect of this struggle, specifically with regard to religious freedom and tolerance, with regard to conscience and faith.

In sum, we are identifying secularisation as a specific process of social change with regard to the relationship of religion and society of religious to other social institutions. The inherent ambiguities of such change can lead to a social insecurity, that can precipitate a backlash of religious fundamentalism and intolerance under various disguises. But it also has a liberating potential where the change is oriented by an ideology committed to freedom and tolerance. This ideology is what we identify as 'secularism'.

In the concrete context of the religiosity of India, such an ideology must not, indeed it cannot be a negation of religious faith. Rather what it demands is an affirmation of religious freedom against religious oppression, of religious tolerance against religious chauvinism. What this calls for is an open-ended but value-committed dialogue between believers of various faiths and followers of different traditions in an "heretical response" to our present challenges,[84] or in other words, in a search for collective alternatives to modernity and secularisation.

Neither the positive secularism of the Hindu right, nor the Nehruvian version of the liberal left, nor the anti-secularism of the anti-modernist are able to provide an adequate basis for such a guess in the changing socio-religious situation of our times. Rather this must be founded on our Constitutional guarantees as contained in its basic framework. It must also be grounded in the realities of social change and come to them with the contradictions of the developmental path we have espoused. Here we have, indeed, much to re-learn from a critical reappraisal of Gandhi.

References

1. PC Joshi, "Secularism and the Religiosity of the Oppressed: Some Reflections". *Man and Development*. Vol. 9, No. 4. Dec. 1987, p. 201.
2. Avijit Pathak, "Indian Society in Transition: Conflict of contrasting Worldviews", *Mainstream*, Vol. 32, No. 28, May 1994, p. 13.
3. *Ibid.*
4. Rajiv Bharagava, "Giving Secularism its Due", *Economic and Political Weekly*, Vol. 29, No. 28, 9 Jul. 1994, p. 1787.
5. *Ibid.*
6. Rustom Bharucha, "In the name of the Secular: Cultural Interactions and interventions", *Economic and Political Weekly*, Vol. 29, Nos. 45 and 48 5-2. Nov. 1994.
7. Nasir Tyabji, *Economic and Political Weekly*, Vol. 29, No. 28, 9 Jul 1994, p. 1298.
8. Cf. Rudolf C Heredia, "Religion and Modernisation in India, *Indica*, Vol. 18, No. 1, Mar. 1981, 26-50.
9. Peter Berger, *The Social Reality of Religion*, Faber and Faber, London, 1969, p. 106.
10. Thomas O'Dea, *The Sociology of Religion*, Prentice-Hall, Englewood Cliffs, New Jersey, 1966, p. 17.
11. Albert Keller "Secularisation", Sacramentum Mundi, Herder and Herder, New York, 1970, p. 64.
12. Berger, op. cit. 107.
13. Peter Berger, *The Sacred Canopy: Elements of a Sociological Theory of Religion*, Anchor Books, New York, 1969.
14. Thomas Luckmann, *Invisible Religion: The Problem of Religion in Modern Society*, Macmillan, New York, 1967, p. 35.
15. Bernard Meland, *The Secularisation of Culture*, Oxford University, Press, New York, 1966, p. 33.
16. Milton Younger, *Sociology Looks at Religion*, Macmilan, London, 1963, p. 67.

17. David Martin, *The Religious and the secular,* Penguin, London, 1969, p. 22.
18. Max Weber, *The Protestant Ethic and the Spirit of Capitalism,* Unwin University Books, London, 1930.
19. Talcott Parsons, *The Structure of Social Actin,* Macgraw-Hill, New York 1937, p. 752.
20. Ref. AM Henderson and Talcott Persons trans and Talcott Parson, ed., From Max Weber: *The Theory of Social and Economic Organisation,* Free Press, Glencoe, III, 1947, 112-123.
21. Robert Bellah, Beyond Belief, *Essays on Religion in a Past-traditional World,* Harper and Row, New York, 1970, 168-189.
22. Clifford Geertz, *The Interpretation of Culture,* Free Press, Glecoe, III, 1973, 193-233.
23. Talcott Parsons and Edward A. Shils, *Towards a General Theory of Social Action,* Harvard University Press, Cambridge, May, 1951.
24. PC Joshi, op. cit. p. 219, emphasis in text.
25. Albert Keller "Secularisation", Sacramentum Mundi, Herder and Herder, New York, 1970, p. 64.
26. Gail Omvedt, *Economic and Political Weekly,* Vol. 25, No. 14, 7 Apr. 1990, p. 725.
27. PC Joshi, op. cit., p. 209.
28. Joshi, op.cit. p. 202.
29. Omvedt, op. cit., p. 726.
30. Bharucha op. cit., p. 2930.
31. Joshi, op. cit., pp. 202-203.
32. Akeel Bilgrami, "Two concepts of Secularism: Reason, Modernity and Archimedean Ideal", *Economic and Political Weekly,* Vol. 29, No. 28, 9 July 1994, p. 1254.
33. Bharucha, op. cit., p. 2925.
34. Joshi, op. cit., p. 226.
35. *Ibid.*
36. Bharucha, op. cit., p. 2925.
37. Cf. Paul Brass Ethnicity and Nationalism Sage. Pub., N. Delhi, 1991, p. 15 and Rudolf C Heredia. *Tribal identity and minority Status: The Kathakari Nomads in Transition,* Concept Pub., N. Delhi, 1994, p. 15.
38. Pathak, op. cit, p. 15.
39. Ashish Nandy, "The Politics of Secularism and the Recovery of Religious Tolerance", in Veena Das, editor, *Mirrors of Violence: Communities, Riots and Survivors in South Asia.* Oxford University Press, Delhi, 1992, p. 80.
40. Bharucha, op. cit., p. 2928.
41. Upendra Baxi, "The Struggle for the Redefinition of Secularism in India: Some Preliminary Reflections". *Social Action,* Vol. 44. No. 1, Jan-March 1994, pp. 28-29.

42. T N Madan, "Will of the majority: Threatened identities and Secularism." *Times of India*, Bombay 23 Nov. 1993, p. 10.
43. *Ibid.*
44. *Ibid.*
45. Nandy, op. cit., p. 74.
46. *Ibid.*
47. *Ibid.*
48 *Ibid.*, p. 69.
49 *Ibid.*, p. 86.
50. *Ibid.*, p. 85.
51. Veena Das, op. cit., "Introduction Communities, Riots, Survivors. The South Asian Experience", p. 4.
52. Joshi, op. cit., p. 204.
53. D. L. Sheth, "On Communalism- The Communal Virus and the Problem of Reservations" *Lokayan Bulletin*, Vol. 4, No. l, 1987, p. 8.
54. Partha Chatterjee, "Secularism and Tolerance", *Economic and Political Weekly*, Vol. 29, No. 28, p. 1774, 9 July 1994, 1768-77.
55. Rajee Bhargave, "The Right to Culture", in K.N. Panikar, ed. *Communalism in India: History, Politics and Culture*, Manohar, N. Delhi, 1991, 165-172.
56 *Ibid.*, p. 171.
57. Ferdinand Tonnies, *Community and Society*, trans, and ed., Charles Loomis, Michigan State University Press, East Lansing, 1957.
58. Chatterjee, op. cit., p. 1773.
59. Sheth, op. cit., p. 8.
60. cf. Rosalind O'ttanla, *Caste, Conflict and Ideology*, Cambridge, University press, Cambridge, 1985.
61. Omvedt, op. cit., p. 727.
62. Anandhi, S, "Collective identity and Secularism,". "Discourse on the Dravidian Movement in Tamilnadu," *Social Action*, Vol. 44, No. 1, p. 59.
63. Cf *ibid.*, 54-68.
64. Omvedt, op. cit., p. 727.
65. *Ibid.*, p. 728.
66. Sebasti L. Raj. *Total Revolution: The Final Phase of the Political Philosophy of Jayprakash Narayon's*, Satya Nilayam pub. 1986.
67. Omvedt, op. cit., p. 729.
68. Bharucha, op. cit., p. 2926.
69. *Ibid*, op. cit., p. 2933.
70. *Ibid*, op. cit., p. 2932.
71. Omvedt, op. cit., p. 729.
72. Bharucha, op. cit., p. 2927.
73. Bharagava, op. cit., p. 1790.

74. Cf. Madan, op. cit.
75. *Ibid.*
76. Rudolf C Heredia, "Transition and Transformation: The Opposition between Industrial and Pre-industrial Types of Society in the Writings of Karl Marx, Ferdinand Tonnies, Emile Durkheim and Max Weber," *Sociological Bulletin*, Vol. 25, No. 1,1986, 29-43.
77. Bharucha, op. cit., p. 2926.
78. Bhargava "Giving Secularism its Due" op. cit., p. 1787.
79. Tyabji, op. cit., p. 1801.
80. *Ibid.*
81. Ernest Worf, *Treating the Self,* Guilfold Press, New York, 1988, p. 47.
82. Sudhir Kakar, "Reflections on Religions Group Identity". *Seminar* No. 402, Feb. 1993, p. 52.
83. Emile Durkheim, *The Division of Labour in Society,* trans., George Simpson, Macmillan, New York, 1933.
84. Peter L Berger, *The Heretical Response: Contemporary Possibilities of Religious Affirmation,* Doubleday, New York.

6

On the Roots of Secularism

—*Andreas D'souza*

Secularism as understood in the West is an ideology which consists of the conscious rejection of all forms of the supernatural and the sacred, as well as the promotion of non-religious or anti-religious principles as the basis for personal morality and social organisation. Secularism has contributed to the secularisation of our society, which in turn has contributed to the formation of a valueless society, encouraging the growth of various reactionary movements, including what many people presently call "fundamentalism". The term "secularisation" was first used in 1648 to describe the transfer of territories previously held under ecclesiastical control to the dominion of lay political authorities. However, the distinction between things religious and things "worldly" - the separation of the supernatural and sacred from the mundane or profane - began long before.

To understand secularism we must begin with the European Renaissance, for it is here that we find this ideology gradually unfolding itself in philosophical and religious writings. Starting in the fourteenth century, European thinkers began to be diverted from their concern with "the other world" to this world for, in the words of Theodore, Greene, "it began to be borne in upon the minds of men, so long darkened, that this world itself and its affairs are worthy of attention of the best men and that man himself is worthy of study."[1] This was a revolution: the authority of intellectual and religious tradition was being challenged by a positive and determined assertion of the freedom of the individual- freedom in social, political, intellectual and religious affairs. This spirit of freedom was founded on a new and extravagant belief in the power of "autonomous" reason and a strong conviction in the essential goodness and infinite perfectibility of human nature. The existing world was the best possible of all possible worlds and human reason was capable of finding ways to purify the human nature of evil influences. Faith in the old presuppositions soon gave way to a spirit of criticism based solely on logical and rational demonstration. Concepts and ideas which were surrounded by an air of mystery. including the indefinable and incalculable depths of life, were immediately suspect.

One of the key factors in this remarkable change was the Christian encounter with Hellenistic thought. During the Middle Ages, the Church predominantly followed Augustine and a theology based contemplation and illumination. According to this theology, the human intellect had the innate God-given power to receive illumination. However, with the infusion of Greek thought through the translation of Arabic works into Latin, a new and decidedly rational Christian theology emerged. Not only had the focus shifted from the next life to this, from the state of the human soul to man's essential humanity, the commentaries and incisive interpretations of Muslim philosophers like Ibn Sina and Ibn Rushd re-introduced Western Christian thinkers to the purest ideas of Aristotelian thought. The response was electric; Christian writers like Guillaume d'Auvergue, Alexander of Hal Albertus Magnus, St. Thomas, St. Bonaventure and Duns Scotus vigorously refuted Ibn Rushd's contention that Aristotle's philosophy conflicted with certain revealed truths such as the created nature the universe and the immortality of the soul. They went on to harmonize Greek philosophy with Christian revelation, giving rise a theology in which philosophy became the handmaid of theology, (philosphia ancilla theologiae). Thus, St. Thomas used Aristotelian reasoning quite extensive to prove the existence of God, and attempted to harmonize faith with reason, adopting Aristotelian categories express Christian doctrines. He rejected the primacy of illumination of the mind by the intellect,[2] but safe-guarded the authority of the scripture by considering all knowledge as having its source in the senses.

Almost unwittingly the rationalism of St. Thomas, which reached its golden age into the thirteenth century, also ushered in the radical secularisation of knowledge.[3] Men like William of Ockam, Rocelin of Compiegne and Peter Abelard resisted the arguments of the rationalists and taught that in human discourse the only universals are names (nomina), nouns or words, not things, common natures or ideas. The "Nominalists" held that universals existed only in the mind and not in things outside the mind - even fundamentally and potentially; an argument which led to the negation of the real in philosophy and theology.

Along with the conflict between Scholasticism and Nominalism, and the religious quarrels between the Roman Catholic Church and the forces supporting the Reformation came the post-medieval rise of modem science. New discoveries in biology, physics, astronomy and geology cast doubt on Biblical stories of creation, divine providence and the existence of God, and brought a deepening sense of uncertainty and chaos. Sixteenth century Western thinkers began to question the authenticity of scriptures and the authority of the Church. God's existence, God's relationship with the created world, supernatural forms of divine revelation, the immortality of the soul, heaven and hell - all that could not be observed or proved rationally was doubted, questioned and ultimately rejected as untenable. Since the metaphysical, supernatural order could not be proved through the scientific method, it was better to ignore it, or reinterpret it in terms of nature and physics, a trend that pervades modern society even today.

In the post-Renaissance period, the translation of Greek thought continued to offer fertile ground for philosophical and religious debate. The academic skepticism of Arcesilas (c.315-241 B.C) and Carneades (213-129 B.C) reached Western readers through Cicero's De Academia and De natura deorum, popularizing the idea that rational knowledge is impossible, and the one cannot distinguish truth from falsehood since there is no standard measure. This idea was further developed through the works of Sextus Empiricus (Outlines of Pyrrhonism and Against the Dogmatists) who introduced the thought of Pyrrho of Elis (360-275 B.C.; later given a theoretical form by Aenesidemus, 100-40 B.C.) Pyrrho held that no judgments were possible about scientific, mathematical, metaphysical, theological and ethical questions. This was comfort indeed for those seeking a defence of religion. As Erasmus held in his attack against Luther, we cannot know anything about free will nor can we pass judgment about theological issues; we accept instead the doctrines of the church as they are presented. This line of thought was pursued by others like Michael de Montaigne (1533-1592) who in his attacks on the science and theology of the time, argued that since our attempts to know the world end up in contradictions, we must accept on faith whatever knowledge God has given us.

The intellectual climate of seventeenth century Europe was tumultuous. Skepticism was having a field-day, and had sown doubt on the authority and source of philosophical, scientific and religious knowledge. The strongest attempts to challenge the influence of the skeptics in the field of epistemology came from men who upheld the primacy of human reason: Rene Descartes (1596-1650), Benedict Spinoza (1632-1677) and Gottfried Leibniz (1646-1716) being the most well-known. In Collins' words, these rationalist thinkers "agreed that the soundness of human reason can be fully vindicated against the skeptical attacks and that the scientific method can be accommodated within a philosophy where this vindicated reason is given the primacy in settling issues". Thus, they adopted a functional attitude to defend the possibility of human certitude and build a rational explanation of the real.[4]

It was Rene Descartes who, through his famous catch phrase "Cogito, ergo sum" ("I think, therefore I am")[5] laid the foundations for the new rational philosophy. This seemingly simple phrase revolutionised modern philosophy. By saying "I think, therefore lam," Descartes made the thinking self, with its experience and consciousness of thinking, the foundation of all epistemology and ontology. It was rational self which was source of certitude for, "if my very existence is dependent upon or proven by my thinking, then thinking is basic to everything that relates to me".[6] In other words, Descartes attributed the beginning of the process of knowledge to consciousness and assigned to reason the office of judging the truthfulness of this knowledge. People are thus thinking animals in quest of wisdom. Peace and happiness is a secondary goal, and is obtained when wisdom is acquired. Though Descartes himself was not an atheist, peoples' system of philosophy which he spawned banished God-consciousness from our thinking.

Benedict Spinoza, a Dutch Jewish scholar, continued on the lead given by Descartes, and worked out a rigorous, deductive naturalism on a pantheistic basis. In other words, he identified God with Nature and maintained that God is the substantial essence of all things in Nature. He proceeded to construct a scientifically- or demonstratively-based philosophy capable of assuring human happiness and ethical perfection.

With God as the unique substance entering into the instrinic constitution of all things, it was impossible to gain a true knowledge of them without conceiving them through God and in God. Expressed more positively, it now became possible to gain a unified knowledge of nature in its essential connections and thus insure the moral perfection of man, which consists precisely in this synoptic knowledge and union with God as the totality of nature.[7]

Spinoza declared that in the order of truth, reason alone is competent; revelation is concerned only with obedience and piety. He taught that "the task of theology must consist of defining dogmas of faith only in so far as they may be necessary for obedience... leaving reason to determine precisely how their truth is to be understood"[8]. For him, there was no place for supernatural revelation, and scriptures were certainly not sources of speculative truth. Spinoza also maintained that revelation does not add anything new to what human reason can already know; all it does is to assure the common person that blessedness can be achieved by simple obedience without philosophical study[9].

In his development of a philosophical explanation of the real, Gottfried Leibniz focussed on the primacy of essence, understood not as something static and abstract but as something dynamic and concrete. He saw essence as the same as substance; that is, the active centre of all operations and relations. Essence is the real basis which pre-contains all events, qualities and actions that will happen to the thing throughout its earthly existence. To know a thing we must know the reason for its being, i.e. its essential structure and relations. To know the reason of a given aspect of a thing we must know its connection with its essential nature or substance. The presumption, then, is that the intelligibility of a thing depends on our mind's ability to grasp the truth through analysis of its essential concepts and principles; also the conviction that if we know the real essence of a thing, we know its dynamic consequences.

It was in England that the rationalist spirit of Descartes, Spinoza and Leibniz was first consistently worked out in the religious realm. Already in 1624, Lord Herbert of Cherbury, known as the "father of Deism," took upon himself the task of finding an infallible criterion by which truth can be separated from error. Impelled not only by the prevailing Skepticism of the period but also by the ever-growing awareness of Eastern religions and the emergence of Christian polemical responses, Herbert tried to establish for truth certain unshakable foundations supported by universal consent. By adopting the method of his time, that is, by submitting every problem to the scrutiny of "Reason", "Nature" or "Truths of first inscription," he arrived at the principle of certainty in "natural instinct" and the "common notions" of mankind: "Thus universal consent will be the sovereign test of truth, and there is nothing of so great importance as to seek out these common notions, and to put them each in their place as indubitable truths"[10]. How does one arrive at this universal consent?

Now we derive this universal consent not only from laws, religion, philosophies, and written remains of all kinds of authors, but we claim further that there are certain faculties innate in us by means of which these truths are vouched for (conformees)...God has given these common notions in all times and in all places and to all men, as the means of his universal divine providence[11].

According to Herbert, there are two ways of discovering these common notions. One is to turn to true religion through a comparative method: "Religion is a common notion, for there has never been a century nor any nation without religion. We must, therefore, see what universal consent has brought to light in religion, and compare all that we find on this subject, so as to receive as common notions all the things which are recognisably present and constant in the true religion." But the best method to discover the fundamental religious notions common to mankind and indispensably necessary is "to retire into yourself and enter into your own faculties: you will find there God, and the other universal and eternal truths." After a comparative study of religions and searching his own heart, Herbert arrived at five fundamental religious principles which he claimed God had imprinted in us from the very beginning: the recognition of a sovereign Author of all things, and the resulting compunction to honour him, lead holy lives, repent of our crimes, and expect reward or punishment after death.

To truly understand secularism and the current religious and political situation in the world, we need to come to grips with the contributions of later apologists like Matthew Tindal (Christianity as Old as Creation or the Gospel, A Republication of the Religions of Nature), John Tillotson (1630-1694), Francis Bacon (1561-1626) and Locke (1632-1704), who accepted the distinction between natural and revealed religion and held that the former was the basis for the latter. Thus, they envisioned revelation to be nothing but the republication of truths of natural religion, and argued that reason was itself capable of discovering certain fundamental truths to which other "extra" Knowledge could be divinely disclosed, (donum super additum). We would also do well to fill in certain gaps in this historical summary; most notably the contribution of Immanuel Kant and the age of the Enlightenment, and modern philosophers like Hegel, Pascal and many others. These thinkers as well as those mentioned above nurtured the sprouting seeds of modern-day secularism. Today we are reaping the harvest.

References

1. Immanuel Kant, Religion Within the Limits of Reason Alone, trans. Theodore M. Greene and Hoyt H. Hudson (New York: Harper and Row, 1960), p. ix.
2. See Sayyid Husain Nasr, op.cit., p. 37.
3. *Ibid.*, p. 2.
4. Collins, get details from previous notes, p. 56.
5. Though this idea was conceived in 1619, it was first published in 1637 in his celebrated work Discourse de la Methode (Discourse on the Method).
6. See Richard H. Akeroyd, Reason and Revelation: from Paul to Pascal, (Gerogia: Mercer University Press, 1991), p. 54.
7. Collins, op.cit. p. 70.
8. Avery Dulles, Revelation Theology: A History (New York: Herder and Herder, 1969), p. 52.
9. *Ibid.*
10. From De Veritate, Lord Herbert's main work dealing with this subject, quoted by Basil Willey, The Seventeenth Century Background (New York: Doubleday Anchor Books, 1953), p. 129.
11. *Ibid.*

Section - C

Globalisation and Challenges to Secularism

7

Religion and Globalisation

—*Uday Mehta*

India has witnessed a massive upsurge of traditional as well as modern religio-mystical cults of God-men, Swamis, Gurus, Shastries, Bapus and Bhagats particularly during the last three decades. This period also synchronises with the acceleration and deepening of the globalisation process initiated during the Eighties under the rule of Late Mrs Indira Gandhi. Some of these cults operate at local, district or regional level, while some have established an extensive network at national as well as international levels. Along with these new cults, the hold of various traditional religious sects has acquired a new dimension in recent years. Increasing politicisation of religion in last few years has posed a serious dilemma with regard to the role of religion in modern Indian society.

It is not only in India but even in Western countries particularly in industrially advanced nations such as the United States of America (USA) that, new along with traditional religious movements have gained an unprecedented momentum in recent years. The growing influence of religion in USA and China has been widely reported. The powerful influence of church in Polish solidarity movement and Buddhist impact of Vietnamese liberation struggle has also been widely acknowledged. The dominant role of the Monastery in overthrow of the recent reactionary political upheaval in Sri Lanka could not be overstressed. The decisive influence of Islamic fundamentalism in Iranian revolution and several other Muslim countries has been sufficiently highlighted, while the emergence and significance of the liberation theology in Latin America would call for an independent appraisal.

Religion under Globalisation

P. Radhakrishnan in his excellent assessment of 'Religion under Globalisation' sums up the implications as follows:

(a) The interface between religion and globalisation is contrary to conventional sociological wisdom that as societies progress the traditional significance of religions decline.

(b) For the success of globalisation, especially in the third world, its dramatic personae have been using the major religions of the world as purveyors of their globalisation agenda, with unprecedented flow of funds for the purpose from the master world to the third world.

(c) The major consequences of globalisation have been

- The transmogrification of the traditional religions and belief systems.
- The beginning of the disintegration of the traditional social fabric and shared norms by the invasion of consumerism, cyber culture; new-fangled religions, social fads, and changing work ethics and work rhythms.
- The fast spreading anomie (in the Durkhemian sense) forcing an ever increasing number of individuals to fall back upon – for moral and social support- the easily accessible pretentious religious banalities.
- Attributing to religion the creation and acceleration of extremist, fundamentalist, and terrorist tendencies in the third world countries, which are intended to destabilise them, and strike at the root of their civilisation and multicultural and pluralist nature.
- Paradoxically, however, the resultant vicious nexus and vicious circle make these countries look to the same monster and its creators for their sustenance in a world in which they have become vulnerable. (Radhakrishnan, 2004)

Globalisation – The Recent Phase

Contemporary globalisation as brought by James Petras retains many of the key features of the earlier phases of the process: the driving forces are centred in the imperial state and the multinational corporations and banks, backed by the international financial institutions. What are significantly different are the scale, scope and speed of the circulation of capital and commodities, particularly financial hows between deregulated economies. Technological changes especially in communications (computers, fax, etc.) have been prime factors in shaping the high velocity of movements of capital.

The identification of the social, political and economic agents of globalisation is important in understanding the unequal impact of globalisation. Likewise a historical analysis of the phases of globalisation allows one to refute some of the ideological claims of its proponents. A retrospective analysis reveals that 'globalisation' has been cyclical in world historical development. There were periods of 'high' globalisation, moments of crises, and periods in which economic flows turned inward. There is no universal inevitable tendency toward globalisation. Inter-imperial wars resulting from global competition, internal crises of overproduction and more important social and political revolutions have all affected the trajectory of globalist nations and classes. The cyclical nature of globalisation allows analysts to identify the internal/external weaknesses of the globalist-imperialist project and to identify the alternative strategies that emerged from the crises of global projects in earlier times.

The very idea of 'globalisation' as a historical necessity thus is questioned by its cyclical history. The idea that technology drives globalisation, omits the point that most of the new technologies emerged prior to the current globalist phase and are compatible with expanding domestic production and popular consumption.

Rise of Globalist Ideology

The rise of globalist ideology is found originally in the business journals of the 1960s and 1970s. The major expansion and conquest of markets by the multinationals was described as 'globalisation' by business journalists, searching for an alternative to the existing Marxist vocabulary, since they sought to present the process in a favourable light. Gradually the term was taken over by the mainstream academic world and became the acceptable framework for talking about international capitalist expansion without having to deal with its origin, power relations and exploitative outcomes. (Petras, 1999)

Globalisation in its recent phase, as also widely noted is not merely an economic phenomenon. It has multiple manifestations such as social, political, cultural and religious. These manifestations are ghastly and gruesome, especially in developing nations. The political dimension is evident from the global 'Super-Cop' stalking the world and making countries of lesser might live in insecurity. The other manifestations have begun to unfold particularly in the developing countries, where societies have begun to disintegrate under the invasion of consumerism, culture and social fads. (Radhakrishnan, 2004)

Globalisation and the Rise of the Religious Fundamentalism Politicisation of Religion

The resurgence of right-wing religious movements in the 1980s and 1990s is a worldwide phenomenon. They owe allegiance to differing, often contrasting religious systems – Hinduism, Judaism, Christianity and Islam. Yet their ideas and behaviour bear striking similarities. "In India, they have burnt down churches and destroyed a historic mosque. In Palestine, they describe themselves as pioneer, desecrate Mosques and Churches, and with state support disposses the Muslim and Christian inhabitants of the ancient land. In Algeria, they are engaged in savage warfare with a praetrorian government. In Serbia, they attempted genocide and ran rape camps. In Pakistan, they have hit Christians, Ahmadi and Shia Muslims and each other. They wage holy wars and commit atrocities sanctimoniously. Yet, nothing is truly sacred to them. They spill blood in bazaars, homes, courts, mosques and churches. They believe themselves to be God's warriors, above man-made laws and the judgement of mankind". Further, "they are so called 'Fundamentalists' – an epithet reserved by the western media for the Muslim variety who are invariably referred to as 'Islamic Fundamentalists'. Others of the ilk are assigned more neutral nouns. The Jewish zealots in Palestine are called 'settlers' and occasionally 'extremists'. The Hindu militants are described as 'nationalists', while Christian militants are labelled as 'right-wing' or 'messianic'. The bias in the use of language obscures an important reality: they are reflections of a common problem, with shared roots and similar pattern of expression". (Ahmad, 1999)

Islamic Fundamentalism

The decade of 1990 particularly was marked internationally with the phenomenon of Islamic fundamentalism. As a matter of fact, a debate around the emergence of political Islam started with the success of the Iranian revolution in 1909. Nevertheless, the Iranian revolution was a far more complex phenomenon. Fundamentalism subsequently adopted a far more militant posture. It developed individual terrorism as its weapon mainly in 1980s and 1990s.

The phenomenon reached its climax in the September 11 event, by massive air attacks in New York City. However, Islamic fundamentalism should not be identified with Islam as a religion. Islamic fundamentalism is a reactionary terrorist movement aimed at returning society to a centuries-old social set-up, defying all material and historical factors. It is an attempt to roll back the wheal of history. Taliban is an ideal delineation of Islamic fundamentalism. The process, however, was initiated by the Khomenis in Iran.

Islam: Origin

Philosophically Islam implies 'surrender'. Those who surrender to the will of Allah are believers. It originates in Western Arabia around the year 610 AD, when Muhammad had his first Visitation of the Voice. The subsequent 28 years of his life he is believed to have heard the Voice hundreds of times. The Voice was a message of God brought to him by the angel Gabriel. After his death, the messages he received were collected and compiled in a scripture, now known as the Quran. The sayings of Muhammad were also recorded after his death. His sayings are known as Al-hadith. Quran and Hadith are the two main sources of interpretation of Islam.

The Rise of Political Islam

Islamic fundamentalism is a phenomenon as noted by Farooq Sulheri that finds its roots in the backwardness of society, social deprivation, a low level of consciousness, poverty and ignorance. Like Fascism and national chauvinism, Islamic fundamentalism finds its base in the petty bourgeoisie. But often it also impresses wider section of poor and lumpen elements in the third world countries with predominant Muslim population.

Farooq enlists three general causes for the contribution to the rise of Islamic fundamentalism:

1. Contradictions of Imperialism

Islam has been a political religion since the beginning. When Arabs invaded other countries, the rationale was Jihad (holy war) against infidels, although these wars had economic motives. In the nineteenth and twentieth centuries, when Muslim countries one after the other, were colonised by the imperial countries, the resistance movements used religion as well as nationalism as a launching pad for their independence struggle. In countries like Indonesia and Malaysia, the national liberation movement started in the name of religion.

Of late, as the multinationals have stepped up their super-exploitation of the Muslim world, one of the natural reactions is hatred of the headquarters, i.e. the Western nations, specifically USA where these multinationals are located.

During the Cold War, imperialism used Islamic fundamentalists against the Left. The fundamentalist parties were the closest friends of the Western nations in the Muslim World. However, in the post-cold war era advanced capitalist nations, specifically America as their leader, does not need them as in the past. The CIA has stopped funding Islamic fundamentalists. This changed the situation and brought the Islamic reactionaries into contradiction with these Western nations. At the same time, because of the experience of the centuries of colonisation and exploitation, a hatred for the West, especially for the USA is widespread in the Muslim world, as in any third world country.

In the changed situation of the post-cold war era, fundamentalists turned to anti-imperialist sloganeering and came to the fore as forces challenging imperialism. Osama Bin Laden (and similar variety operating in Iraq, Syria, Nigeria and other Muslim countries), became a symbol of anti-imperialism irrespective of their tactics and terror let loose by them on common people. The terrorist methods or fundamentalism are seen by the ranks of the fundamentalists as Jihad against the USA.

The Inability of Capitalism to Solve the Basic Problem

Islamic fundamentalism is spreading rapidly in those countries where capitalism has failed to fulfil the tasks of the bourgeoisie democratic revolution, where it has failed to eliminate poverty and ignorance and where class contradictions are sharpening. Poverty and ignorance are concomitant. A society ridden with ignorance is fertile soil for the growth of fundamentalist ideas.

On the other hand, the fundamentalists, through their massive network of social services have built alternative societies in the

Muslim countries where they are strong. They provide hospitals, orphanages, schools and many other facilities, which weak capitalist governments have failed to provide to the masses. This adds to their influence as a social force. Their schools (seminaries) are the most influential tools. These seminaries not only provide religious education but also guarantee food and shelter to the children of poor parents who cannot afford education and food.

Pakistan education sector is a striking example of such setups. Forty per cent of population is living below poverty line. The figure was 20 per cent in 1980. Pakistan spends 40 per cent of its annual budget on defence while another 40 per cent goes to IMF and World Bank in the name of debt retirement. Hardly one per cent is spent on education. The literacy rate is 30 per cent (figures are for 2003) according to the official figures. Almost 60 per cent children get no chance to go to schools. Privatisation of education is making it even difficult for the workers to send their kids to schools.

One can compare it with education networks run by the fundamentalists – According to the report by Pakistan's Interior Ministry released in May 2003, there are 6,870 seminaries. The number of seminaries in 1947 at the time Pakistan came into being was 247. There is, it means, a growth of 27 times. There are 1.5 million students enrolled at these seminaries. In comparison, there are 1.9 million students enrolled at primary level state schools. The report mentions only registered seminaries; there are reportedly over twenty thousand non-registered seminaries. According to a newspaper report, the number of seminaries is 30,000 while there are 300,000 teachers employed.

Likewise, in Palestine, Hamas and Islamic Jihad do not just send suicide bombers to Israel. The fundamentalist organisations in Palestine also run schools, hospitals and provide medicines and food.

These networks of providing facilities that are basically state responsibility help the fundamentalist to sink deep roots in the masses.

The Failure of the Left

In Iran the Islamic fundamentalists had their major victory. The Tudeh Party (Iranian Communist Party) despite having a mass base, under the pressure of Moscow dictated policy of compromise with the national bourgeois forged an alliance with fundamentalists instead of offering an alternative to the masses. The alliance with the fundamentalists proved fatal. The fundamentalists on coming to power went on to the physical liquidation of the communist, and did it successfully.

Afghanistan also witnessed a similar scenario. However, it should be noted that there is no easy, simple or even one compact explanation to understand the rise of political and militant Islam.

The extreme ideas expressed in the form of Islamic militancy can be compared with extreme ideas expressed in the form of neo-Nazism or even Hindu chauvinism when it comes to oppression of minorities. Nevertheless, the Islamic fundamentalism exhibits different form compared with other extreme right contemporary movements. With regard to its relationship with American domination, it has of late been radically anti-imperialist.

In order to understand the anti-imperialist or anti-American character of Islamic fundamentalism, one better look into the history of relationship between imperialism and Islamic fundamentalism during the Cold War.

Islamic fundamentalism provides a glaring example of imperialist hypocrisy. Now the USA and other Western nations pose as the biggest enemy of Islamic fundamentalism by presenting fundamentalism as a big challenge to world peace. But it was the same imperialism that wed these fundamentalist forces against the Left in various Muslim countries.

In the 1950s and 1960s there was a rise of populist, anti-imperialist and class movements. The USA worked out a plan to patronise the fundamentalists in order to weaken those populist movements. The CIA under the guidance of US Secretary of State John Foster Dulles established a liaison between fundamentalist parties in different countries. According to the plan, a network of Akwami Musalmaan – popularly known as Muslim Brotherhood (Egypt), Hamas (Syria), Sarakatul-Islam (Indonesia), Islamic Salutation Front (Algeria) and Jammat Islami (Pakistan) was established. These parties were given full economic and political support during this period.

The process reached its peak during the 1980s, when thousands of militants or the so-called Mujahideen were trained and sent to Afghanistan. The Jammat Islami of Pakistan provided the main force, but the above mentioned parties also sent their share.

The Islamic fundamentalists everywhere have been targeting religious minorities, women and oppressed nationalities. This is a feature they share in common with Fascists. However, it is difficult to identify Islamic fundamentalism with Fascism. The fundamentalists are even worse in some cases. They don't tolerate even art and literature. They believe in physically eliminating all their opponents. For them, Cuba and USA are both infidel state and hence enemies. (Sulehria, 2004)

New Evangelism

In USA it is not Christian fundamentalists, but 'New Evangelicalism', that has acquired deeper roots, extensive following and much greater political influence in last few decades.

World congresses of fundamentalists have enlisted distinct features of fundamentalists. We are enlisting some of the significant features.

A fundamentalist is a born again believer in the Lord Jesus Christ who-

- Maintains an immovable allegiance to the inerrant, infallible, and verbally inspired Bible.
- Believes that whatsoever the Bible says is so.
- Judges all things by the Bible and is judged only by the Bible.
- Affirms the foundational truths of the historic Christian faith. The doctrine of Trinity, the incarnation, virgin birth, substitutionary atonement, bodily resurrection and glorious ascension, and second coming of the Lord Jesus Christ; the new birth through regeneration by the Holy Spirit; the resurrection of the ungodly to final judgement and eternal death; the fellowship of the saints, who are the body of Christ.

Conventionally, 'Evangelical' generally referred to those who preached the necessity of the new birth through faith in the Blood of Jesus Christ and who stood firmly for the pure doctrine of the Scripture. Now there arose who claimed the title 'Evangelical' but who refused to obey some of the teachings of Scriptures. They are called 'New Evangelical'. Evangelicalism in the novel form is no longer a term for the stalwart defense of the word of God. A new generation of Evangelicals has emerged that is rich in all manner of worldly benefit has abandoned the spiritual zeal of their forefathers. The 'New Evangelicalism' was coined by the late Harold Ockenga. As per his observation,

> "Neo-evangelicalism was born in 1948 in connection address which I gave in the civic Auditorium in Pasadena. While reaffirming the theological view of fundamentalism, this address repudiates its eccelesocialogy and its social theory. The ringing call for a repudiation and the summons to social involvement received a hearty response from many evangelicals- it differed from fundamentalism in its repudiation of separatism and its determination to engage itself in the theological dialogue of the day. It had a new emphasis upon the application of the gospel to the sociological, political and economic areas of life." (Cloud, 1995)

According to Ockenga, Evangelicals should re-examine their idea of worldliness and not be as strict about separating from worldly evils as Bible believing Christians had been in earlier days. Further, Evangelicals should consider the possibility that modern science was right in some areas where it disagreed with the Bible. The prime example of this was in the origin of the world. He argued that Christians should not so easily ignore the teachings of evolution as separatists were accustomed to do. He taught that there could be a synthesis between modern science and the Bible, and it is this new Evangelical principle that led to such strange ideas as theistic evolution.

Now Evangelical thought has been adopted by such well-known Christian leaders as Billy Graham, Bill Bright, Harold Lindsell, D. James Kennedy and a multitude of eminent leaders. Through publications such as Christianity Today and Moody Monthly, and Publication houses such as Intervarsity Press, Zonedervan, Tyndale House Publishers, Moody Press. (Extract from David Cloud "Fundamentalism, Modernity, and New-Evangelicalism" O. Timothy Magazine, 1995)

It is quite pertinent to take of observations made by Meera Nanda in her appraisal of the extensive hold of religion in USA as well as India and increasing politicisation of religion in both these nations especially in last few decades. As she suggests, the rise of Christian theocracy in the US, and Hindu nationalism in India need careful appraisal. In both countries, there has been a slow but steady merging of the majority religion with the affairs of the State. In both countries, the secular laws on the books have proved to be incapable of stopping this creeping religionisation of the state and the public sphere. The religious right in the US wants to 'take back' the country for Jesus Christ, while Hindutva forces want to 'reclaim' India for 'Ram Rajya'.

Even though many US Presidents have invoked God in the past, the unabashedly partisan electioneering by churches and evangelical organisations for George W. Bush in the 2004 elections stunned even the most seasoned observers of politics in the US. Evangelical leaders held weekly meetings with Bush's re-election committee (which was led by none other than Ralph Reed of the Christian Coalition), and thousands of churches encouraged their congregations to 'vote their Christian values' which Bush made a great show of wearing on his sleeve. Actually, Bush did not start this trend. (He was following in the footsteps of Ronald Regan who actively wooed Jerry Falwell's Moral Majority through his two terms). Bush's re-election in 2004 was decided by a large turnout of born-again Protestants who joined hands with the most conservative elements of Catholics, Jews and other 'people of faith' to wage a war against the Islamic 'evil doers' abroad, and the godless secularist-humanists, feminists and gays at home.

Meera Nanda's observations of the extensive hold of religion in both these countries deserve careful consideration. All available data in the US and India are literally awash in faith. A recent World Values survey reported an identical proportion – 94 per cent of those surveyed in both countries professing belief in God. (Inglehart and Norris, 2004). The first thing that strikes visitors to both countries is the large number of places of worship dotting the landscapes. The recent census in India reports 2.4 million places of worship, against only 1.5 million schools and half as many hospitals (Varma, 2004). While numerical data are hard to come by, belief in miracles and supernatural powers are rife and India now has a new generation of 'tale-yogis' who can more than match American televangelists in their sales pitch for God and country. The data on American religiosity is similarly stupendous, with 55 per cent of all Americans professing the Bible to be literally true and as many as 82 per cent admitting belief in miracles and equally high proportion in the existence of heaven, hell, angels and the devil. (Phillips, 2006)

All available data shows that traditional trends have been gaining ground in the American Christianity in recent decades. The more conservative evangelical churches have been growing at the expanse of more liberal denominations. A higher proportion of believers are beginning to profess faith in the afterlife, devise judgement, possibility of miracles and the efficacy of prayer. Not only have traditional religious beliefs grown in intensity through the 1990s, the faithful also have seem to lost their earlier inhibitions about keeping faith out of the public sphere. In 1996, a significant majority (54 per cent over 43 per cent) believed that churches should take a stand on political issues, a complete reversal of the response for the same question in 1968, the new alignment in religious landscape of the US is that the religious intense in all traditional faiths against the secular culture. In that fight, the more traditionalist believers are only too keen on allowing the churches to get involved in the affairs of the State. (Kohut *et al.*, 2000; Rosen, 2000)

The growing intensity of traditional religiosity also indicates a greater sympathy for conservative social values. The Pew Foundation's trends 2005 clearly show that those who attend church more frequently tend to oppose gay marriages and stem cells research. Similarly, the polling data reported by Trends 2005 confirm greater level for support for the Iraq war and the "war on terror" among the more devoted, as compared to the less committed and liberal Christians.

Similarly referring to the equally striking case of India, Meera Nanda points out that this is another country where popular religiosity tends to merge seamlessly into nationalism, both of which are crassly exploited by the Hindu right to stoke off a blood-and-soil variety of nationalism. Hindu nationalism literally deify the landmass of 'Greater India' (which includes all of South Asia and parts of South-East Asia as well) as the homeland of 'Vedic Aryans', to whom the universal and eternal laws of cosmos were revealed. (Kaiwar, 2005). This hardcore 'Hindu Nation' ideology has appropriated and encouraged public worship of the idols and images of Bharat Mata (Mother India) in which the geographical contours of India merge into the body of a traditional Hindu goddess (McKean, 1996). It is commonplace in 'secular' India – even under the 'secular' Congress to see starkly Hindu Imagery openly and proudly displayed in government offices, police stations and even on university campuses.

Hinduisation of the public sphere is the 'operation slow poison', in everyday "indoctrination amidst bhajans (hymns), seduction in the midst of festive processions" to use Meena Kandasamy's (2004) very apt description. Bharat Mata is only a recent goddess, whose invention dates back to the early twentieth century anti-colonialism nationalism. Hindu forces have systematically targeted popular religious festivals celebrating old and popular gods like Ganesh, Ram and goddess Durga for political purposes. The agitation that led to the demolition of the mosque in Ayodhya in 1992 was given the trappings of a religious pilgrimage in the festival celebrating Ganesh, which used to be a private affair in Tamil Nadu, for example, has become a massive public spectacle. The castes and tribes long considered 'unclean' and 'uncivilised' are being induced into public worship of Ganesh, Ram and other deities and then deployed as foot soldiers in the periodic riots that break out against Muslims and Christians. (Teltumbde, 2005; Fuller, 2003)

The link between religiosity and Hindutva is not limited to idol worship and popular festivals. The more elite, 'intellectual' Hindus who prefer gurus with more eclectic mix of old and new Hindu doctrines were no less supportive of Hindutva's cultural agenda, or immune from its chauvinism. As the study by John Hariss of the Chennai industrialists shows, "interest in temple-going-following god-men and gurus, and the miraculous and ecstatic religion, as well as in the philosophical principle of what is called 'Vedic heritage' (though more properly called 'neo-vedanta')" remains strong among this class which is at the cutting edge of hi-tech led globalisation. (Harriss, 2003) For many of them- almost all of them with advanced degrees in sciences, engineering and management from Western universities – the miraculous powers of gods, godmen, planets and stars, pilgrimages and trances are real. Even the more 'philosophically inclined' followers of 'vedic Heritage' as interpreted by Swami Dayanand among Chennai's business leaders, seem to easily mix the abstractions of Upanishads, Brahma Sutra and Bhagvat Gita with a down-to-earth management ethics, a militant celebration of the superiority of Hindu ideas of Karma, ecological pantheism and goddess 'feminism,' topped with a strident opposition to religious conversion. The continuities of this 'Philosophical' crowd with the discourse of Hindu nationalism are unmistakeable. (Nanda, 2007)

Buddhist Fundamentalism

Buddhist fundamentalism has been the driving force behind Sinhala offensive against the question of the Tamil autonomy and civic and economic rights of the Tamil population as well as other minorities as Muslims and Christians democratic rights in Sri Lankan society. A Buddhist monk assassinated S.W.R.D. Bandaranaike, the leader of the Sri Lanka Freedom Party in 1959. His only crime was making "too many concessions (in fact they were too few) to the country's large Tamil minority. But the deterrent effect worked. Sinhala politicians of all stripes began to pander to the monk. Anti-Tamil discrimination was institutionalised".

As aptly brought out by Tariq Ali, "As if the anti-Tamil pogroms were not enough to satisfy the blood lust, a BBS (Bodu Bala Sena: the most active and pernicious of Buddhist fundamentalist groups) bloggers explained the 'reasoning' behind the targeting of Muslims in the Colombo Telegraph."

> "Muslims have been living in this country since seventh century and now only they want to have halal food in Sri Lanka. Population-wise they are five per cent. If we allow Halal, next time they will try to introduce circumcision on us. We have to nip these in the bud before it becomes a custom. We should never allow the Muslims and Christians to control anything in Sri Lanka. What is Halal to Muslims is Haram to Sinhala Buddhists. Slaughtering cow and eating beef should also be banned in Sri Lanka. Instead we should promote pork. We are glad that the parliament has re-introduced pork in their menu. Hijab, burqa, niqab and purdah should be banned in Sri Lanka. The law and the legislature should always be under the control of the Sinhala-Buddhists and our Nationalist Patriotic president. After all, Sri Lanka is a gift from Buddha to the Sinhalese."

It is difficult to imagine how circumcision could be 'nipped in the bud' even by a Buddhist; or how the percentage of the Muslim population could have decreased from 9.7 per cent in 2011 to 5 per cent in 2013. The decline is obviously a direct result of unchecked harassment and persecution." (Ali, 2013)

One could easily draw a close parallel between the hate-campaign, its chauvinistic and highly authoritarian spirit of the RSS, BJP and other Sangh affiliates like Viswa Hindu Parishad (VHP),

Bajrang Dal and the Buddhist fundamentalist fascist approach toward minorities in Sri Lanka.

Conclusion

The rapid rise of the religious right movements especially since 1990s, the period which coincides with the acceleration and deepening of the globalisation process at a global level raises a number of important questions.

Our common presumption that, with the advancement of science, technology and modernisation there would be sharper decline of religions, superstitions and mythology has been proved totally incorrect, as religion has increased its hold both in developed as well as developing nations particularly in the last few decades.

As a matter of fact it is also equally pertinent to note that religion in its modern guise has assumed a novel form and its content and major thrust are strikingly different from the religious beliefs and practices of ancient or even medieval period. It is no more spiritual values, it is spiritual hallo, its thrust is on simplicity, moral and spiritual values that are more dominant features now. But competitive greed, the race for pomp, publicity, material acquisition, and miracles have acquired prominence. God-men, Gurus, Gurumayisin India as well as modern Buddhist monks, Evangelical leaders in USA, or luminaries of the Islamic fundamentalist movement are known for their material acquisition, comforts and modern amenities.

In short, the modern religious heads resemble in many ways their counterpart industrial tycoons, in terms of their comforts, life style, influence and accessibility to ordinary people.

In the modern age of monopoly-finance Capital, where finance capital hold, sway over market, and which has touched all personal as well as public domain of life into marketable commodity, alienation, inner voids, inner hollowness have become such deepening phenomenon, religious appeal, supernatural world, meditation, and such techniques probably play vital role in feeling inner vacuum.

Thus, prominence acquired by religion in its multi-fold forms has to be understood in the context of the prevailing dominant form of economy governed by monopoly finance capital and its deepening crisis and especially in over last two decades.

Hence the religious appeal or the hold of religion in modern times should not necessarily be linked with everlasting, all powerful appeal of supernatural forces and happiness of the mankind before its might, but also its utilisation or exploitation for the purpose of sustaining and consolidating the hold of the prevailing rise of the monopoly-finance capital under the supremacy of the American capital.

Nevertheless for the overwhelming majority of the toiling population all over the world working hard for survival, the religion probably continues to be sigh of the oppressed, or the soul of the soulless world.

References

Ahmad, E. (1999, March). Roots of the Religious Right. *Frontline*.

Ali, T. (2013, May 5). *Sri Lanka on Buddhist Fundamentalism*. Retrieved May 09, 2015, from Colombo Telegraph: https://www.colombotelegraph.com/index.php/on-buddhist-fundamentalism/.

Cloud, D. W. (1995). Fundamentalism, Modernism and New Evangelicalism. *O. Timothy Magazine, 12*.

Fuller, C. (2003). *The Renewal of Priesthood: Modernity and Traditionalism in South Indian Temple*. New Jersey: Princeton University Press.

Harriss, J. (2003). The great tradition globalizes: reflections on two studies of "the industrial leaders" of Madras. *Modern Asian Studies*, 327-362.

Inglehart, R., and Norris, P. (2004). *Sacred and Secula: Religion and Politics Worldwide*. Cambridge University Press.

Kaiwar, V. (2005). The Aryan Model of History and the Oriental Model of Rennaisance: The Politics of Identity in the Age of Revolutions, Colonialism and Nationalism. In V. Kaiwar, and S. Majumdar, *Antinomies of Modernity: Essays on Race, Orient, Nation* (p. 24). Durham: Duke University Press.

Kohut, and Rosen. (2000). *Australian Journalism Review*.

McKean, L. (1996). *Divine Enterprise: Gurus & the Hindu Nationalist Movement*. Chicago, London: The University of Chicago Press.

Nanda, M. (2007). Secularism without Secularisation. *Economic and Political Weekly*.

Petras, J. (1999). A Socialist Perspective. *Economic and Political Weekly*.

Phillips, K. (2006). *American Theology*. Thorndike Press.

Radhakrishnan, P. (2004). Religion Under Globalisation. *Economic and Political Weekly*.

Sulehria, F. (2004). The Rise of Political Islam. *Labour Party Pakistan*.

Teltumbde, A. (2005, August 22). Edge of Reason. *Outlook*.

Varma, P. K. (2004). *Being Indian: The Truth about why the 21st Century will be India's*. Penguin Books India.

8

National Education versus Veil: Secularism and Islam in France

—*Michael Boivin*

On 18th September 1989, the principal of a secondary school in Creil near Paris, refused to let two veiled pupils into their school. This event, seemigly harmless, provoked (what the French media called): "The Islamic Foulards Affair. This paper is aimed at evaluating how this case answers the French secularism. In a broader sense, I will try to create a dialogue between French and Indian scholars on the subject of the place of minority religions in a secular state. For instance, the Creil case will have two main effects. Firstly, it will incite the Muslim community to build institutions which could be official interlocutors with the government; and secondly, it will provide feedback on the foundation of French democracy. And do not forget that French people are very proud of their Declaration of Human Rights; they call France the "Declaration of Human Rights homeland". But I know that the Indian people are not really familiar with French history. That is why I must briefly relate how secularism was born, and how a Muslim community developed in this country.

Islam and Secularism in France: An Historical Legacy

Secularism developed gradually. Its origins were in the revolutionary period. The Muslim community began to grow after the First World War. But it is important to note that when this community became a numerous one, the elaboration of secularism ended in France.

The Two Steps of Secularisation

The French Declaration of Human Rights (26th August 1789) makes reference to the Supreme Being but it was only in the tenth article that freedom of religion is upheld. But in fact, this prescription is principally for Catholics and Protestants. As a matter of fact, the Jews are forgotten; it was only on 28th September 1791 that they received equality and civic rights. The aim of the successive revolutionary governments was to destroy the powerful Catholic Church. Then a lot of discriminatory measures against the clergy were voted by the National Assembly. The dire economic conditions and the invasion of France by foreign forces incited the government to realise the first demarcation between State and Church on 21st February 1795. That means that the government took possession of numerous clerical properties. With Bonaparte, the political centralisation increased. To take definite control over all the religions, he concluded agreements with the Catholics and the Protestants (1801), and later with the Jews (1808). The result is that worship became a private affair, and religion played a social function in upholding morality. That is why, the clergies are payed by the government: the Catholic priests (1801), the Protestant ones (1804) and the Jewish ones (1830).

In 1815, the Catholics were 97.8 per cent of the population, the Protestants 2 per cent and the Jews 0.2 per cent. After the first step of secularisation, the State did not ignore religion but it did not give its control over the people. However, Bonaparte did not settle the question of education. In 1838, each local region had to maintain a school to train teachers for elementary school. In 1850, a teacher could be displaced if the priest did not like him. Important laws were adopted between 1880 and 1882. They gave a new orientation to the educational system which became free, compulsory, and secular. Upto this event, education was controlled by Catholic congregations. In 1902, a law about the constitution of associations was adopted but it excluded the religious congregations: it became impossible for the clergy to teach. In these conditions, the French Republic was able to promulgate the separation between the State and the Church, definitely, on 11th December 1905. It is important to note that religion and state are not separated in Alsace and Lorraine. These two eastern French territories were under the German rule in this period. However, even after these two territories returned to the fold of France in 1918—they were not governed by the law of 1905.

Islam and France : Birth of a Religion

According to the French Minister of National Education, the Muslims are around five million in France, viz. nine per cent of the population (*Le Monde*, 11-12 September 1994). But it is very hard to be precise because no administrative document mentions religion. Influence of Islam in France goes back to centuries. France is familiar with the date 732: Charles Martel's victorious battle against the Arabs in Poitiers. But history does not mention that the Muslims were settled in the southern half of the country at that time. In some parts, they stayed until the eleventh century. Another important period for our subject is the Crusades.

Most of the Crusaders were "Francs", viz. French. In spite of this long co-existence in the Holy Land, the war was the predominant affair. It did not change the traditional image of Islam which appears in the Roman art. The Muslims (and above all, the Prophet), were considered as devils and bad.

When a scientific interpretation of Islam was built up to sixteenth century, the Islamic culture and religion were known to the Europeans. But unfortunately, the development of orientalism in the nineteenth century shows that the comprehension of Islam is not the only goal for the scholars. Very soon, orientalism was linked to colonialism. In France, a new situation emerged with the conquest of Algiers in 1830. For the first time—except for the short Bonaparte episode of the Egypt Expedition — a French government had to administer Muslim population. One of its first measures was to create separate regulation for the Muslims and the Jews. In 1870, the latter got French nationality. The religious rights of the Muslims are theoretically guaranteed but the first act was to transform the Great Mosque of Algiers into a Cathedral. The Muslims had to abandon their Personal Law if they wished to become French. The colonial administration wanted to destroy Islam as a social power.

The Muslim Community of France: Its Origins and Aspects

The first Maghrebian Muslims came to France during the First World War. Thousands of them fought against the Germans and when peace was achieved, the government and the City of Paris gave financial assistance to build a mosque and a Muslim Institute which was inaugurated in 1926. Later, the Muslim population increased, especially after the Second World War, when France needed workers for the reconstruction of the country. Today, about two million Muslims are French: 800,000 form the "second generation". They are the children of Maghrebian people, who were born in France and as a result, they automatically got French nationality; 800,000 are *harkis.* They are Algerian people who wished to become French after the independence of Algeria in 1962. Among these French Muslims, I must indicate a Muslim community of 30,000 from Indian origin — Gujarat and Tamil Nadu. They come mainly from East-African territories (Madagascar, Rwanda, Reunion Island) and ancient French territories in India (Pondicherry, Yanaon, Karikal, etc). Some of them are Ismaili Shi'is. Except for several thousand Ithna ashri Shi'is of Iranian or Lebanese origins, the Muslim community in France is Sunni. Among the French Muslims, the last group was formed of "ne@-Muslims", which means French people converted to Islam accounting for 50,000 to 100,000. Some of them are famous (in France) and others — scholars, who have specialised in Islam (Michel Chodkiewicz, Denis Gril, etc.).

The other Muslims are not French: they are Algerians (900,000), Moroccans (600,000), Tunisians (300,000), Turks (200,000), Africans (150,000) and ex-Yugoslavians (100,000). Till the seventies, this Muslim community was insignificant. They were treated as the *Wretched* of the earth. They had no demands and their mosques were miserable dwellings. All of a sudden, around the end of the eighties, the French realised that France *had* a significant section of Muslim community. One of the reason for this discovery was the publication of a book by Gil-les Kepel, a French scholar, called *Suburbs of Islam: Birth of a New Religion.* Unfortunately, his thesis stated that Islam was infiltrated by terrorism, fundamentalism — and that the growth of a Muslim population was very dangerous for the country.

At the same period, the Muslims wished to build institutions which were officially recognised, and to be treated on a equal footing with other religions. Today, three main poles exist: each of them try to be the only representative of Muslims in France. The older one is the Mosque of Paris; the Rector, Dr Dalil Boubakeur, won the challenge when the Minister of Religious Affairs, C Pasqua, acknowledged him as the leader of Muslims in France on 10th January 1995. But the two other associations which are important, refused this nomination. They are; the National Federation of the Muslims in France (FNMF in French), created in 1985 and which brought within its fold 150 associations, around 40 per cent of Islamic organisations in France. Then there is the Union of Islamic Organisations in France (UOIF in French), created in 1983, which enrolled 30,000 members in their December 1994 meeting. But other independant organisations exist such as Faith and Worship, which depends on the well-known Indian Jama'at al-Tabligh.

Renewal of the Debate About Secularism: The Islamic Foulards Case

Since 1905, the school has always been the scene of dispute between the two poles in France: the secularist and the religious one. In 1959, a new law compelled the government to pay the teachers of the private schools, but the private schools had to respect the programmes and methods of the public one. Today, private schools represent 13 per cent of which 90 per cent are Catholic. After the election of President Mitterrand, (a socialist), in 1981, a reform was announced. In 1984, A Savary, then head of the Ministry of National Education, proposed to standardise education, including the private one. It provoked people to organise a big rally of about one million, (population of France was 53 M).

The Case and the Institutions

Before the fateful date of 18th September 1989, what was the situation of the Foulard, or the veil, in France? It is a very difficult question. I do not really remember but probably some old Algerian women wore what they called *haik,* a piece of cloth to hide their hair. But the same tradition existed among old Sicilian women, and also Spanish, Portuguese and sometimes French women, from the southern part of the country. Of course, none of them were Muslims. They were all firm believers of Catholicism. When I travelled in Maghreb or in Mashrek, I noticed that the veil was worn especially in the bourgeois class of the cities: it was a kind of status symbol. It is also important to know the environment which prevailed in France at the end of the eighties. The population suffered the consequences of the world economic crisis. Some radical political parties (above all the National Front), began to explain that the immigrants were responsible for the situation. Most immigrants were Muslims. Equally important; terrorrist acts committed by extremist groups from the Middle East not only killed people but created a negative attitude towards Muslims.

Very quickly, the case in the city of Creil set off a mechanism: similar problems happened in other places (Avignon, Montfermeil, Orleans, Lyon...) All of a sudden, the French became suspicious of anything which was not part of the status quo. In Savoy, a member of a major council accused a Jewish fundamentalist group of being different as if it were a crime! (Le *Monde,* 17 November 1989). On the other hand, the Freemasons gathered to look for the defence of secularism which was threatened by the Creil case. On the institutional level, the Minister of Religious Affairs decided to form a Representative Council for Islam in France in November 1989: it was created in March 1990. As for the Minister of National Education, he confessed that the problem was too complex; he asked the Council of State for its judgement. It gave its judgement on 27th November 1989: the final decision, after a lot of historical research, was that the veil was authorised in the schools but the final decision was the principal's. It is important to note that the text did not mention the Islamic Foulards but "religious signs". However, it is a Christian pupil of Portuguese origin who declared to the newspaper *Le Monde:* "Our teachers have crosses, why we can't we have a veil?" (4 June 1994). Some principals forbade the veil, others forbade even the crosses. Sometimes, the situation became absurd: a French Muslim teacher was not authorised to work because she wore the veil!

The Intervention of Intelligentsia

It is impossible to analyse the multiplicity of discourses which followed the affair: political people, religious dignitaries from the main religions, all of them wanted to talk. But a very important event was the manifesto written by five intellectuals in November 1989 in the pro-socialist *Nouvel Observateur.* The title was: "Teachers, do not surrender!". The first words were significant: "The future will tell us if the year of the bicentenary (of French Revolution) would be the year of the Munich of the Republican School". The authors — who were very close to the government: one of them was the Minister of Justice's wife — then said that the foundation of school was Reason and that the traditions were not of their concern if they were contrary to Human Rights. That means that traditions should not have authority in cases of violations of Human Rights. For the authors, the veil was the symbol of the submission of women, created by the "harshest patriarchy of the planet". For them, the so-called "new secularism" was a danger which would leave a school open to all lobbies.

This manifesto represented only a part of French intelligentsia. The dramatic tone was amplified by the striking historical reference (Munich, 1938). This fear emphasised a recent affair which affected French intelligentsia. It was the death-sentence proclaimed by Ayatollah Khomeyni, on 14th February 1989, against Salman Rushdie for his book *The Satanic Verses.* Various intellectuals discovered at the same time, an aggressive Islamic discourse and the existence of a Muslim community on the French territory. Some answers to the manifesto are published but very few indeed; One of them was a brief statement by the famous sociologist Alain Touraine, who asked: "Why must we oppose the absolute of Reason to the particularity of belief?" (Nouvel Obser-vateur, 19-22 November 1989).

It is important to note the reactions of the Muslim intelligentsia in France, The French intellectuals, appendixed a brief paper written by Muslims to the manifesto. One of the most remarkable reaction is by Mohamed Arkoun, the professor of History of Islamic Thought at the University of the Sorbonne (Paris). He stated that Rushdie touched "that country of the sacred which is essential for all human existence" *(Le Monde,* 15 March 1989). For him, it was clear that the discourse on the Human Rights is based upon a western value system — which is based upon an unacceptable postulate and his value system accompanied the process of colonisation. Arkoun became virulent when he affirmed that the Reason of the Enlightenment had substituted the dogma of its sovereignty to theological reason, without creating the conditions to understand other cultures. Another intellectual, from the same Algerian origin, professor of Arabic Literature in another Parisian University, answered that the eternal principles of 1789 were the only possible foundations of democracy *(Le Monde,* 4 April 1989).

Perspectives on Belief and the Future of Secularisation

An epiphenomena gave birth to a debate as important as the Dreyfus affair, a century ago. This case touched the question of the tolerance of different communities, and of their place in French society. In 1894, question was raised about the Jews. It is difficult to know the impact of the Dreyfus affair on the evolution of secularism. The Creil case was created in a specific historical context, but above all, this event revealed to France; a transformation of their belief. The French learned that French secularism was created in precise historical conditions, and that its form was not at all an eternal shape.

The Islamic Foulards Case: An Endless Story

From 1990 to 1994 — several such cases occured. Five of them have been brought before the judiciary. Each time, the principal of a school refused to accept veiled children; the judge gave an reverse judgement. Meanwhile, the principal of Creil became deputy in a conservative party and was trying to impose a law in the National Assembly to prohibit the Islamic veil. This was because, there was no law existing regarding this problem. Thus, the newly elected minister of National Education, Alain Bayrou, told a newspaper that "ostentatious Islam" increased in France: he counted tens of veiled pupils and the principal of Creil, seven hundred.

The minister decided to publish a note to help the principals to find solutions on 29th September. It was known as: "Wearing of ostentatious signs in schools". The minister said that it was no longer possible to accept "the multiplication of signs so ostentatious that their signification is precisely to separate some pupils from the rules of the common life in school". Consequently, the minister asked the principals to note in the regulation the interdiction of these ostentatious signs, but not to prohibit the more discreet presence of them, which signified only a personal conviction.

Prejudices and Secularist Injustice

The problem became worse because of the ancient prejudices against Islam and Muslims. In the political and economic context, a major part of the French media abandoned an objective point of view. For instance, an article was published on 24-30 November 1994 in the *Nouvel Observateur.* The title was: *The Loubavitch of the Gospel.* The Gospel is a little district in Paris. It proposed to bring this radical Jewish community nearer to Christianity. The author described the coexistence between the Jews and other people. But in this case, the fanatics were those who did not accept the Loubavitch way of life. The author quoted a graffiti which used the term "reactionary fundamentalist" and accused its author of being racist. The Loubavitch did not authorise the children of the two communities to play together. It is clear that if this Jewish community were a Muslim one, the word "reactionary fundamentalist" — a pejorative one — would have been used by the author.

French secularism is not equitable because five million Muslims do not have the fundamental right to worship. Until today, nobody could open a private Muslim school. One should not forget that in France, you are in the Human Rights homeland. Concerning the mosques, several books would have to be written to state the vicissitudes of the different Islamic projects in the main cities of France. In Lyon, the second largest city, it lasted for many years. Several hundred thousand Muslims live in Lyon, but they have no rights to pray in a mosque. The project was presented in 1979 and the mosque was inaugurated by the Minister of Religious Affairs in October 1994. The same situation prevails in Marseilles, Lille, and so on. But the divisions among the Muslims was an impediment.

The indifference of the government which is based on the law of 1905 — is dangerous because the different Muslim organisations must look for some assistance - mostly financial. They receive financial support from the political parties as a barter for votes. They also acquire finance from Muslim States. For instance, Algeria is the only country which provides financial aid to the Mosque of Paris. Saudi Arabia finances the National Federation of the Muslims in France (FNMF), etc. And so, the detractors of Islam say that these countries use the Muslim associations to control the Muslim population, or even to create terrorist groups on national territory. It is necessary to clarify that there is no Islamic Institute to train *Imams* and other *Ulamas.* In this field, the statute of the Muslim Institute of the Paris Mosque is not precise. A few years ago, the Union of Islamic Organisations in France (UOIF) tried to create an Islamic Institute to train *Imams* in Europe (because for many millions of Muslims in this continent, even in countries like Bosnia and Albania — very ancient Muslim countries — there is no Islamic Institute!). But the government obviously wants to suppress the institution which no longer functions.

Multiplicity of the Sacred and Intolerance

All these considerations lead to a new question: what is the statute of the sacred in the French contemporary society? Firstly, it is important to remember that the modem France was built by destroying the old religious sacred and by instaurating a new one based on secularism. This new France was built by the eradication of regional particularisms: the unity of the nation was on a uniform basis — based on the destruction of cultural identities. On the other hand, the aim of the fathers of this secularism was to annihilate the still powerful clergy consequently anti-clericalism was the real dynamic of this process. Today, the context is quite different and that is why French secularism has to be adapted to these new conditions

In France, the secularisation of the society is only understood through the separation between political and religious spheres. But indeed the main effect was to give birth to a new sacred which never affirmed its real nature. However, like every sacred, it evolves. What was sacred at the beginning of the century is not sacred anymore. The contemporary sacred in France is marked by its plasticity. For instance, when an author writes a cynical book about the death of a policeman — without using the right names — it is forbidden by the authorities. And when Muslims say that a book is blasphemous against their religion, they are fanatics. Where does the sacred begin? Where does it end? In France, a school of historians deny the Shoah (Jewish genocide) of the Second World War. Some of them - who publish books and reviews - find places in French universities: but where is the sacred? I am convinced that excessive individualism in France (and in the West) generally instigate the dispersion of the sacred which sometimes takes refuge in very strange places.

The Search for Universality and the Plurality of the Beliefs

It is impossible to elaborate a new secularism without a reflection on the contemporary forms of the sacred and the beliefs in the East and in the West, in the South and in the North. As is the rector of the Muslim institute of the Paris Mosque, I am convinced that one of the first steps must be an increasing knowledge of the other. It is a very old reality that incomprehension comes from ignorance. In this field, the task of the school is very essential. The inquiry published in *Le Monde* (10 November 1994) showed that communication is actually impossible between the French population and the Muslim one. Though 55 per cent are not against the creation of Muslim private schools helped by the government, here are the words chosen to represent Islam: fanaticism (37 per cent), submission (24 per cent) and rejection of the West (12 per cent); among the Muslims, there are democracy (21 per cent), justice (17 per cent) and liberty (17 per cent). What else? I think that the task of scholars and other research fellows is vast. Unfortunately, most of them have been fascinated by the more spectacular development of Islam in

France: what about the hundreds of thousands of Muslims who wish to live in peace in France?

It is important to note that the French radical secularism eradicate all religious references from education at the school level. The pages of books which study other civilisations than the West represent between 10 per cent and 15 per cent of the total in the different specialised books prescribed for the schools. Nevertheless, another enquiry published in *Le Monde* (10 November, 1988) showed that 65 per cent of the French wanted the history of religions to be taught in schools. A few days ago, a young student told me: "I tried many times to read the Bible, but I do not understand anything because I have no references in this matter". And she is a student of history, second level in the university. Which is why, I am convinced that this mutual knowledge must be promoted by individuals and Indian scholars that could create an Historical Anthropology of Beliefs. The first task is to elaborate a programme of research.

Conclusion

Every nation possesses its own history. The contemporary world tries to build a universal conception of these Human Rights. One of the most difficult tasks is to teach these universal principles as liberty and equality in the context of specific cultural traditions. In France, the Islamic Foulards Case awakened ancient fears. Some people shouted that barbarism was threatening the country. They said that if the veil was accepted, other savage customs will invade France, especially the horrible African practice of excision. Intellectuals thought that the Islamic challenge was as dangerous as the Nazi danger. This fear was created by what has been the greatest horror of the century and may be of history: The great German author Bertolt Brecht called it "the unclean beast". And this beast was in Europe, not so long ago.

In the enquiry of *Le Monde* (13 October, 1994), 59 per cent of the French accepted their children marrying Muslims. This result indicates that Islam as a private religion is not rejected. Consequently, it is important that the community create an official Islamic organisation to be helped, like other religions, by the government. The rector of the Muslim Institute of Paris gave a constitution for such an organisation to the Minister of Religious Affairs recently. In this *Chart of the Muslim Religion in France,* it is said that secularism signifies that the neutrality of the government implies equal treatment of all religions.

Section - D

Nehru and Practice of Indian Secularism

9

Pandit Nehru on Communalism and Nationalism in India

— DR ASHOK S. CHAUSALKAR

Pandit Nehru was a great supporter of secular nationalism in India and throughout his life he tried to spread the ideas of democracy and secularism. He was a keen student of world history with deep historical insight which enabled him to understand the complex social reality clearly. He was of the view that concept of religious nationalism was outdated and backward. He developed the concept of secular nationalism in the light of concrete historical reality.

Personally, Nehru was not influenced by any religious fervour or faith. He was a "born Brahmin" but his family background represented the best of composite culture of north India. Hence Persian culture and Islam were not alien to him and he didn't look at them with antagonism. His father, Motilal Nehru, was a tolerant liberal who didn't join the movements which had religious background. Nehru wrote, "Motilal did not look back to revival in India of ancient times. He disliked old customs, castes like which he considered reactionary."[1]

Nehru joined Indian politics in the second decade of this century. He was of the view that the moderates were more advanced in their social outlook and they advocated petty reforms. The religious nationalism of the extremists was reactionary in nature. He hastened to add that inevitably new nationalism in India and the East was religious nationalism.[2] He was of the opinion that the outlook of khilafat movement was religious and ultimately the Maulavis got a lot of prestige at the cost of educated Muslims.

He did not like conventional form of religion but its ethical and moral aspects attracted him. Hence, he favourably viewed the concept of spiritualisation of politics and the idea that the worthy ends should have worthy means. An organised religion was largerly an empty form devoid of any real content; though it may satisfy deep inner craving of human being. But for a large number of people and nations, the external revolution was necessary, before inner revolution could take place.

Thus, emphasising the ethical aspect of religion, Nehru argued that in the attempt to get this outer freedom and to change the environment so as to remove all hindrances to inner development it was desirable to employ fair means.[3]

After the end of Khilafat movement, Nehru was witness to growth of communal politics in India. It was a direct result of failure of Non-Co-operation movement. He held that there were three factors which encouraged growth of communalism in India. First, there was a British policy of divide and rule. Secondly, there were communal leaders in both the communities who played upon their feeling of insecurity and thirdly, the communal leaders were social reactionaries who played the politics of upper classes and feudal lords.

Nehru blamed the alien government for fanning the communal passions and for playing one group against another. He wrote, "Divide and rule has always been the way of empires and the measure of their success in this policy has always been measure of their superiority over those whom they thus exploit. We cann't complain of this at any rate, We ought not to be surprised at it. To ignore it and not to provide against it is itself a mistake in one's thought."[4] Therefore, he held that the communal problem could not be solved by marketing and bargaining because "whatever offer we make, however high our bid might be, there is always a third party which can bid higher and what is more give substance to its word. If there is no common national or social outlook, there will not be common action against adversary if we think in terms of temper of existing political structure and merely wish to temper with it here and there to reform it, to Indianise it, then all real inducement for joint action is lacking. Then object becomes one of sharing in the spoils and the third and controlling party inevitably plays the dominant role and hands out its gifts to the prize boys of choice.

Only thinking in terms of a different political framework and even more so a different social structure, can we build up a stable foundation for a joint action."[5]

Nehru was of the view that the communal leaders from both religions represented social reaction and fanned communal passions with the help of newspapers to secure political benefits. The communal temper, raised by the communal elements affected the Congress and many a Congressman was communal under a national cloak but the Congress normally remained secular.[6] He held that communalism was largely an urban phenomenon and it struck roots in urban middle classes. Rural masses were not influenced by them. But after the formation of the Swaraj Party, the communal tempers increased and both Hindu and Muslim groups grew as a reaction to each other. It was based on mutual fear and sense of insecurity of middle class job seekers as each group was afraid of being ousted by the other group. Electoral politics gave fill up to communal feelings."[7]

Nehru was of the opinion that the communal groups represented interests of vested interests. They used the fair name of religion to get mass support for demands and programmes which had nothing to do with masses or even more with lower middle classes. Every one of the communal demands put forward by communal leaders was in the final analysis demand for job and these jobs and additional seats in legislature could go to a handful of the upper middle classes. These narrow political demands benefitted at the most a small number of upper middle classes and often created barrier in the way of national unity and progress. They were cleverly made to appear the demands of the masses of that particular group. The Muslim communal leaders put forward these demands as if they had nothing to do with Indian nationalism and Indian freedom. The Hindu communal leaders always claimed that they spoke on behalf of Indian nationalism, but in practice they had nothing to do with it. Hindu communal leaders humbled themselves before the government and they did it in vain.[8]

Nehru lamented the fall of Muslim nationalist leaders because he was of the view that they were of upper class background and had a little touch with the masses. On the other hand, the communal leaders had better contacts and they were adept at exploiting every opportunity. They exploited class antagonisms between Hindu land lords and Muslim peasants in Bengal and Hindu traders and Muslim peasants in Punjab, though they had nothing to do with the betterment of peasants. But because of these antagonisms, the Muslim communal leaders did represent some mass elements and gained thereby; Hindu communal leaders in economic sense, represented rich banker and professional classes and they had a little backing among the Hindu masses.[9]

Nehru took historical review of Hindu-Muslim problem and held that most of the Muslim insecurity came from their relative backwardness. Sir Sayed opposed the Congress because Muslims then were not in a position, historically and ideologically to benefit from bourgeois nationalist revolution as they had developed no bourgeoisie as the Hindus had done. Politics at that time was upper class affair and lower middle classes and masses on either side were not in a picture at all. Sir Sayed's reformist legacy was not progressively carried out and it was possible that had he lived a generation later, he could have given new orientation. The Aligarh school encouraged students to plump for government jobs and a student was happy if he got deputy collectorship. His pride was being soothed by his being reminded that he was a unit of great democracy of Islam. Having assured himself of his inalienable right to democracy, which enabled him to feed and pray with his brother Muslims, he did not worry about the existence of political democracy in India. Muslim feudal elements dominated their politics, Hindu youth were also after government jobs but circumstances forced them to join national movement. Both communalists quarrelled for jobs, the Hindus in defensive because they had most of existing jobs and the Muslims always wanting more and more.[10]

Nehru was critical of so called nationalism of Hindu Mahasabha because he said, "The Hindu Mahasabha is always laying stress on its own irreproachable nationalism when it criticises Muslim Communalism. That the Muslim organisations have shown themselves to be quite extra, ordinarily communal has been patent to everyone. The Mahasabha's Communalism hasn't been so obvious, as it masquerades under a nationalist cloak. The test comes when a national and democratic solution happens to injure upper class Hindu interests and in this test the Mahasabha has repeatedly failed."[11] Their anti-national outlook got expressed in the round table conferences.

The Britishers deliberately encouraged Muslim Communalists stating the utter incompatibility between Hindu and Muslim cultures. The inevitable deduction from this was that the Britishers must remain in India for ever to hold scale and to mediate between the two. "To talk of Muslim nation meant there was no nation at all but a religious bond. It meant that no nation in modern sense must be allowed to grow, modern civilisation discarded and autocratic foreign government allowed to exist."[12]

Nehru criticised the concept of two nation theory and argued that the Indian Muslims were culturally and racially integral part of India. Muslim culture didn't necessarily mean the racial memory of great deeds of Arabs, Persians and Turks because the Persian influences had come to India for 2000 years and it had nothing to do with religion. In fact, great achievements of Islam were common heritage of all Asiatics and both Hindus and Muslims should prize them. Secondly, the vast Muslim masses in India were not necessarily different from Hindus because there was a great cultural similarity between the two. Nehru disliked backward attitude of Hindus and Muslims and praised modernist project of Kemal Pasha. Hence he argued that in most of the Islamic nations like Turkey, Egypt and Iran, religion was taking back seat and nationalism was emerging. Thus, there was no 'Muslim nation' as such and progress demanded broader viewpoint.[13]

He was of the view that the Muslim invaders were Afgans who could be called a border Indian group and subsequently they got completely Indianised. Most of the Muslim converts were local people. Due to impact of the Islam, popular regional languages emerged and great synthesis between two religions began. Therefore, conversion in those days didn't arouse opposition except when force was applied. There was cultural commonness in Hindus and Muslims and only upper class Muslims opposed local influence and tried to find their own roots in West Asia. Hindus looked upon Mughals as their national rulers.[14] He held that India did not have racial and national minorities as in Europe. Racially, India was a patch work and curious mixture, hence no racial questions had arisen here. Religious barriers were obviously not permanent as conversion could change it. There was common cultural and linguistic inheritance. He argued that there was nothing in Indian history to compare with the bitter religious feuds and persecution that prevailed in Europe. "When Muslims came to India they had already exhausted themselves and the Turks who came to India did not have tolerance and culture of Arabs. The open creative and rational current of Islam did not come to India.[15]

Thus, from historical viewpoints there was no inherent conflict between Hindus and Muslims because due to the impact of Islam there was great synthesis and reform in India. The problem emerged when early movements of nationalism in India were religious and Hindu idea of nationalism was definitely that of Hindu nationalism and not that of true nationalism and it was difficult to draw clear line between the two. These got overlapped because India was only land of Hindus and they formed majority in India. It was thus easier for Hindus to appear as full blooded nationalists than the Muslims although both stood for their own respective brands of nationalism. The Muslim nationalism looked to the community rather than to the country. Emergence of group nationalism was unfortunate yet it was natural because it was the result of group awakening and each group looked at it from its own interests. A group or a community was always selfish although individuals in community might take an unselfish view. Each group wanted more than its share and the conflict grew.[16] In India, Britishers encouraged extreme communal leaders and added fuel to fire. Communal question in India was largely a middle class question and peasants and working class were largely unaffected by it.

Nehru was of the opinion that religion could not become the basis of modern nation. There was rising tide of nationalism in Asia and it represented awakening of its energy and creative urge of the people. The communal forces represented forces of reaction and backwardness. The communal elements could become fascist because fascism was a perverted form of nationalism. Though it talked in the name of socialism and deified the state, it was in fact rule by the property owners and reactionaries. It was imperialism in its worst form and gave support to religious and racial conflicts.[17]

Nehru argued that progressive and forward looking composite culture of India was the basis of Indian nationalism. In his famous book 'The Discovery of India', he tried to argue that the cultural basis of Indian Nation was strong and resilient enough to absorb all the changes that took place in last hundreds of years. Nationalism in its healthy and natural growth was necessary for subject country like India and it was one of the powerful urges that moved the people and round it developed, a cluster of sentiments and traditions and a sense of common living and common purpose. He wrote, "Traditions have to be accepted, to a large extent adapted and transformed to meet new conditions and ways of thought and at the time new traditions have to be built up."[18]

He knew that there were many weaknesses in India but there was always a visible attempt to understand, adapt and harmonise it with the old. Some times the old retained its outer form only as a kind of symbol and changed its inner content. Some thing living and vital continued. There was diversity, infinite variety among Indian people but there was tremendous impress of oneness which held all of them together for ages and no amount of misfortune or political divisions had been able to overcome it. There was a long cultural tradition and common outlook which held fast despite bewildering variety and diversity in India. There was essential unity between the Pathan and a Tamil or between Hindus, Muslims, Parsees and Christians. Therefore, Indian Muslim in Arabia was looked as an Indian where Islam was a dominant religion.[19]

He held that the inner unity of India was clearly understood by great teacher like Adi Shankara who was a practical reformer and able organiser. The difference of languages between north and south didn't prove formidable barrier to him and he encouraged unity and common consciousness.[20] Cultural pluralism, tolerance of dissent, the capacity to accommodate new ideas and trends and ability to absorb change while maintaining the continuity of tradition was essence of Indian culture.

During the independence movement, Nehru constantly fought against wrong tendencies and held that both Hindu and Muslim communalisms were dangerous. He was of the view that a majority couldn't injure huge minority like Muslims and the latter should realise that separate electorate or excess representation could not convert a minority into majority. Separate electorate made matters worse because majority lost interest in it and there was little occasion for mutual consideration.[21] He fought against Muslim separatism by launching mass contact programme but due to complex political situation, inadequate communication, imperfect political mobilisation, limited franchise and vicious communal propaganda of the League proved too powerful to avoid partition. But partition did not dim his faith in secularism and democracy.

After independence Nehru tried to build new state in India. According to him, nationalism was group memory of the past achievements, traditions and experience. At present there was a strange contradiction between nationalism and internationalism. There was growing international atmosphere due to international capital but at the time of crisis men turned to nationalism. They sought comfort and strength in their old traditions. National progress could therefore lie neither in repetition of past nor in its denial. The new patterns must be adopted but they should be integrated with the old. In India, there was a proper blending of change and continuity; freedom, flexibility of mind and tolerance of spirit.[22] New culture should be continuation and development of past trends and it must also represent their new urges and creative trends. The spirit of India was that of tolerance and synthesis but it was not synthesis with backwardness. Hence, he wrote, "As far as India is concerned, we shall proceed on a secular and national lines, in keeping with powerful trends towards internationalism. India will be a land as in the past of many faiths, equally honoured and respected but of one national outlook, not, I hope, narrow nationalism living in its shell, but rather the tolerant and creative nationalism, which believing in itself and the genius of people, takes full part in the establishment of international order."[23]

He was of the opinion that the nation could not be formed on the basis of religion. In India, there was no village where no Muslim existed. India was a secular state in the sense that she had given freedom of religion and conscience, including freedom for those who did not have religion. She had given free play to all religions subject to the law of land. Both minorities and majorities should understand it. The latter should not use its advantageous position which might prejudice India's secular ideals. Secularism stood for progressive outlook and caste ridden society was not properly secular. Nehru said that the state must honour all the faiths and give equality of opportunities to all the religions. Though India had a tradition of tolerance but we must not be complacent. The very fact that one religious community formed overwhelming majority of the people, might colour, to some extent, the cultural climate of the state. In India, there was always danger of emergence of communalism, hence we must make secularism, part of our thinking and living.[24]

After independence, Nehru faced the challenge of Hindu communalism and fought it with determination. He thought that it was based on fear and hatred and these sentiments would destroy unity of the country. There was lot of misunderstanding about Islam in India. He pointed out that Chengiz Khan was not a Muslim, Timur killed thousand of Muslims and Mehamood of Gazni threatened Baghdad Khalifa. In fact, many Muslim kings were tyrants and they had nothing to do with tolerance of Islam.[25] Hindus should understand that they formed overwhelming majority and nobody was going to push them from their position. Therefore, he held that minorities should be given full freedom and opportunities.

Nehru discounted the talk of appeasement of Muslims as nonsense and wrote.[26] We have a Muslim minority who are so large in numbers that they can't, even if they want to, go anywhere else. They have got to live here. That is a basic fact about which there can be no argument. We have got to deal with minorities in a civilised manner. We must give them security and rights of citizens in a democratic state."[27] Nehru was opposed to two nation theory as well as tendency among some people to demand loyalty from Muslims in India and to condemn pro-Pakistani sympathies among them which were wrong. He wrote, "I think it is wrong to stress on loyalty on behalf of Muslims in India. Loyalty is not produced to order or by fear. It comes as a natural growth from circumstances. We have to produce conditions which lead to this sentiment being produced."[28]

Nehru opposed Hindu communalism and held that the R.S.S. was the fascist organisation that grew on hatred and fear. It drew support from the lower middle classes and what they said in private was entirely opposed to what they did in public. It should not be allowed to poison our nation. Hence, there should be no compromise with it. It had developed narrow and unscrupulous mentality, it was essentially a secret organisation with a public facade, having no rule of membership, no register of membership and no account, although a large sum was collected; it did not believe in peaceful methods and satyagraha. They spoke in soft language but acted otherwise. The R.S.S. should not talk about *Satyagraha* because they were far removed from the spirit of *Satyagraha.* The Hindutva cry was reactionary, disruptive and against national unity.

Nehru supported secular nationalism and argued that there could be no equation between religion, nationalism and state and

Indian nationalism was based on tolerance of each others faith. He wrote, "we have to build a mighty structure free and the republican India. Let us remember all these innumberable faces that India has and provide for them. Let us not try to remould any of them forcibly do conform to our particular conception of what is India. We can't regiment whole of India in a single pattern, neglecting its variety and rich traditions. Each culture should be allowed to grow and should not be coerced into a single pattern. New methods of transportation and communication inevitably tend to produce certain uniformity and regimentation, whether it is good or bad I can't say, but no deliberate attempt should be made to accelerate the process because it may deaden something that is bright and make lacklusture what has been vital in our national life."[29] Hence, he argued that the country should not be made rootless. Cultures nourished deep roots in nation's soil and to uproot a nation was to destroy its soul which made it living entity through the ages.[30] Hence, Nehru pleaded for development and blossoming of different cultures in India which could be properly strung together with the help of democracy, secularism and nationalism.

Pandit Nehru relentlessly attacked narrow and sectarian view-point of nationalism and advocated progressive, forward looking and secular nationalism. He correctly understood the social and economic bases of communalism and argued that the communal leaders represented narrow vested interests in society. He did not think that nations could be based on the principle of religion. He welcomed the new awakening in Asia which was essentially anti-imperial and nationalistic. In India, he favoured development of cultural pluralism and held that plural and composite Indian culture was the Indian nationalism. But this nationalism was secular and democratic. It wanted to strengthen the unity of Indian people by solving their problems and respecting their cultural diversity. Thus, he sought to encourage the process of national integration but at the same time he did not want to uproot people from their moorings. He exhorted the people to move out of their narrow considerations and adopt modern attitude so that they could progress along with other nations. He was confident that with the help of principles of democracy, secular and tolerant nationalism and socialism, we will be able to defeat forces of reaction and build a strong and resilient India.

References

1. Nehru, J. An autobiography (Seventh impression) Oxford University Press, Delhi, p. 23.
2. *Ibid.*, p. 24.
3. *Ibid.*, p. 379.
4. *Ibid.*, p. 136.
5. *Ibid.*, p. 137.
6. *Ibid.*, pp. 135-136.
7. *Ibid.*, p. 159.
8. *Ibid.*, p. 138.
9. *Ibid.*, p. 140.
10. *Ibid.*, p. 464.
11. *Ibid.*, p. 467.
12. *Ibid.*, p. 469.
13. *Ibid.*, pp. 471-72.
14. Nehru, J. The Discovery of India (11th impression) Oxford University Press, New Delhi, 1991. p. 344.
15. *Ibid.*, p. 382.
16. Nehru, J. Glimpses of World History (Seventh impression) Oxford University Press, New Delhi, 1989, p. 181.
17. *Ibid.*, pp. 720-721.
18. *Ibid.*, p. 825.
19. Nehru, J. The Discovery, pp. 52-53.
20. *Ibid.*, p. 62.
21. *Ibid.*, p. 191.
22. *Ibid.*, p. 383.
23. *Ibid.*, pp. 515-17.
24. Nehru, J. An Anthology, Oxford University Press, New Delhi, 1983. p. 208.
25. *Ibid.*, p. 328.
26. *Ibid.*, p. 471.
27. Nehru, J. Letters to Chief Ministers Vol. I. Publication Division, Government of India, New Delhi, 1983, p. 2.
28. Nehru, J. Letters to Chief Ministers Vol. III. Publication Division, Government of India, New Delhi, 1988, p. 41.
29. Nehru, J. Speeches of Pandit Jawaharlal Nehru, Publication Division, Government of India, New Delhi, pp. 405-06.
30. Nehru, J. Speeches of Pandit Jawaharlal Nehru, Vol. III, Publication Division, Government of India, Delhi, 1964, p. 170.

10

Nehruvian Secularism and the Minority Problem

—MADHVI YASIN

After the partition of India in 1947, India opted for a secular State, which was a difficult decision, as the Partition was the result of the two nation theory, based on the principle of religion. Pakistan, Burma and afterwards Sri Lanka declared themselves theocratic States, and a large section of the Hindu population also wanted this pattern for themselves, but Jawaharlal Nehru laboured hard to make India a secular State. It may be noted that the 'Objective Resolution', which was the foundation of the Constitution of India was formulated by Nehru.[1] The Indian Constitution which was framed under the chairmanship of B R Ambedkar retained the essence of the Objective Resolution, which is the cornerstone of secularism and its points are enshrined in the Constitution. Besides, the Constitution incorporated all the features of a secular State, e.g., freedom of religion, equality of citizenship, and separation of State and religion, i.e., no special taxes for promotion of religion and no religious instruction in State educational institutions.[2] According to Nehru, democracy is the breath of secularism, and he regarded it as a sine qua non of modern democratic practice.[3] 'He weathered the storm of the Hindu opposition to make India a Hindu nation with determination and resolution. Even the Congressites supported him in this endeavour, taking inspiration from ancient Hindu ideals of Sarva Dharma Sambhava[4] and Vasudhav Kutumbkam.[5] Nehru took these ideals in another light. He knew that India has a fine tradition of eclectic and composite culture, which is forcefully reflected in Ashoka's toleration towards non-Buddhists and Akbar's peace with all (Sulah-Kul), thus there was 'Some inner urge toward synthesis'.[6] In 1963, he said: 'A secular State does not mean an irreligious State, it only means that we respect and honour all religions, giving them freedom to function. This has been the basic attitude of India throughout the ages.[7] Nehruvian secularism differed from the dictionary meaning of secularism, and was liberal in interpretation, which was not irreligion or atheism, but, on the contrary, it recognised the relevance of religion to human life and meant that all the religions practiced in India were entitled to equal freedom and practice.[8] His secularism had no place for communalism.[9]

Nehruvian secularism was different from the materialistic philosophy based secularism of the USSR (now Russia)[10] or Mustafa Kemal Pasha's Turkey, which declared the right of 'freedom from religion',[11] but drew inspiration from USA.[12] In some respects it became more broadbased keeping in view the pluralistic nature of Indian socio-religious system.[13]

With all its ideals and constitutional safeguards, Nehruvian secularism is not foolproof. It has got detractors. One section says that Nehru was opposed to religion due to his alleged ignorance and abhorrence of the past history and culture of India. His writings *The Discovery of India* and *Glimpses of India* bely this allegation. The books have captured the best of the Indian tradition and this reality would be hard to deny. He had a historical mind and learnt from history 'of growth and possibility of an infinite advance for man'. Being a thinker and intellectual he fully understood the importance of roots of the people and the country's history and culture. He fully realised the value of history and the past, but advised to look ahead. He condemned the tendency to look backwards and think only of the roots. While resus citating the past, one should not blindly eulogise it, and reject what is superfluous. He was opposed to 'organised religion' which invariabry be came a vested interest and thus inevitably a reactionary force opposing change and progress.[14]

Another snag was the question of the Uniform Civil Code, which was not implemented in accordance with Article 44 of the Constitution. Interference with the Hindu personal law by enacting the Hindu Code Bill brought severe resentment.[15] The Hindu Maha Sabha leader, Chatterjee, warned that the Act would encourage the conversion of Hindus to Islam, as those Hindus who wanted to have more than one wife would convert to Islam, as its personal law permitted polygamy.[16] Acharya Kripalani sarcastically remarked: 'If monogamy and divorce are good and desirable features of a marriage law, why favour the Hindus and withhold monogamy from the Muslims and divorce from the Catholics? If, on the other hand, these reforms are not so good and desirable, why punish the Hindus alone?'[17] The Muslim League leader, Mohammad Ismail, objected, strongly to any interference in their personal law.[18] The government could not enact the Uniform Civil Law and thus yielded to the pressure of the Muslims. Nehru was evasive in his reply when pressurised for the failure in enacting Uniform Civil Code: 'I confess I do not think that at the present moment the time is ripe in India for me to push it through'.[19]

Though Nehru was critical of the caste system in his statements he had neither suggested nor took any concrete steps to abolish it and to make the society open and free. In fact, the reservations made in employment and admission to schools and colleges on a community basis made the people more caste conscious than help them to get out of their caste shells.

The right to religious propaganda was another point of criticism, as it had been abused widely by foreign Christian missionaries. These missionaries engaged in converting tribal people to Christianity were very active in Madhya Pradesh and Assam. Dr Katju was right when he said in 1953 that the right to propagate religion guaranteed in the Constitution applied only to Indian nationals and not to foreigners.[20] Nehru did not adhere to the advice of Dr Katju. One strong step in cancelling the visas of the foreign missionaries would have checked the proselytising mission, and would be in accordance with the spirit of the Constitution. It would have saved the Government of India from many troubles, like the Mizo rebellion. Some of the missionaries were the active agents of CIA. "Nehru did not justify the cause and concepts of his secularism but endangered the unity and peace of those areas."[21]

Nehru strongly disapproved of imparting religious instructions in the institutions run by the State. Thus, according to his wishes, the Constitution of India under Article 28 (1) declares; "No religious instructions shall be provided in any educational institution wholly maintained out of State funds." But Nehru was not opposed to religious instructions, and he said in Parliament and outside that secularism did not mean insensitiveness to the deeper values of life.[22] During the last few months of his life, he circulated a message to the educational institutions of India, asking them to include religious instructions in their routine courses.[23] So Nehru's concept of secularism included imparting religious education to students.

Nehruvian Secularism and the Minority Problem

In modern political terminology, the term minority "is restricted to distinct 'racial or national' groups in minority in terms of numerical strength within a Sovereign State."[24] This means that there are two types of minorities, viz., racial and national. The members of the minority groups, like the members of the majority community, are linked to one another by common ties of religion or language or by national or cultural consciousness. The problem of the minorities is created when it comes into conflict with the majority with regard to its peculiar cultural features, social institutions, and religion. In medieval times also the minority problem existed on the ground of the sovereign's religion, i.e., the majority was formed by those who believed in the sovereign's religion. It did not matter whether numerically they were in minority or majority. Islamic State in India charged from the non-Muslim minorities (they were numerically in majority) a tax known as *Jezia,* which allowed them religious freedom, retention of their lands and property.[25] In Europe, after the Reformation the different nation states were divided into Protestant and Catholic States. In the long run, the Protestant revolt led to greater toleration, and in Catholic France the Huguenots secured toleration by the Edict of Nantes in 1598, which signalised the commencement of the principle of civic equality in a secular State, irrespective of religious differences.[26] After the First World War, the League of Nations provided for the protection of Minorities, and the Council of the League received petitions from representatives of racial and religious minorities.[27]

Nehru thought that the whole question of minorities and majorities in India was tied up with foreign and third party rule. The British government however, sought shelter in communal difficulties and made the agreement of certain reactionary communal groups and minorities a prerequisite for any further consideration of the political problem.[28] Under the Government of India Act the definition of the minorities was so stretched by Sir Samuel Hoarse as to include every minority which the governor thought fit to consider a minority. Acharya Kripalani pertinently attacked the British government when he said' "As a matter of fact the British Government have left no majority in India. According to it, Muslims are a minority; Sikhs, Europeans, and the princes are minorities; nay even the women are a minority. The non-Brahmins and Marathas are minorities. The only majority left are the Brahmins bereft of their women folk."[29] The Muslims consider themselves a racial minority, but barely ten per cent of the Muslims had any ancestral bearing of foreign origin. This proves to the hilt that barring their faith, they are as much Indians as the Hindus.[30]

According to Nehru the first priority of a minority is to safeguard its culture, i.e., language, education and schools. There are certainly many differences between the traditional Hindu and Muslim philosophies of life. But these differences are hardly noticeable when both of them are compared to the modern scientific and industrial outlook of life. The real struggle today in India is not between Hindu culture and Muslim culture, but between these two and the conquering scientific culture of modern civilisation.[31] These views were of an idealist, who wrote them in the backdrop of 1946 India.

After becoming the first Prime Minister of Independent India, while inaugurating the Indian Council of Cultural Relations, he said: "No culture in the world which is absolutely pristine, pure and unaffected by any other culture — culture is bound to get a little mixed up, even though the basic element of a particular national culture remains dominant."[32]

Language is the first contentious issue between the minorities and the Government of India.[33] The problem is double pronged — that of national language and safeguarding the languages of the minority groups. The first arose because of introducing Hindi as the national language in Devanagari script under Article 343 (1). Non-Hindi speaking population demands English to be made the national language in India. Muslims were always a vocal minority. They wanted under the colonial rule Urdu to be declared as the national language.[34] Even after independence they demanded Urdu to be declared the second language in UP and Bihar, which was conceded. Even a national Urdu University is to be found at Hyderabad. They vociferously objected to the Uniform Civil Code. It is said that Nehru had a soft corner for the Muslims. After the Partition when religious frenzy was at the zenith, he saved the lives and properties of Muslims at the risk of his life.[35] He was against granting specific privileges to the minorities in the Constitution but at the same time he argued that some privileges should be given the backward classes, as they had suffered discrimination for ages.

The Christian minority posed no problems for the Government of India. Being educated their economic condition was better off than the Muslims. The Christians were mainly converts from the downtrodden Hindu community. They took casteism from the Hindu religion along with them. Thus, the Indian Christians are first castemen, afterwards Christians.[36] Even when they celebrate their festivals, they perform *arti* in the Hindu way. The Christians, therefore, have not felt alien to the Indian Culture. Consequently, as regards culture, language etc., the Christians had neither conflicts nor divergence.[37]

With regard to the Sikhs, the relations between the Hindus and the former were intimate and cordial. There were intermarriages between them. The Hindus generally gave their eldest son to Gurudwaras. In the Freedom Struggle the Sikh sacrifices were unparalleled. During the partition of India, the Sikhs were the worst sufferers. The Sikh politics is connected with the *Gurudwaras*[38], which are managed by an elected Board for a five years term, known as the Shiromani Gurudwara Prabandhak Committee. Master Tara Singh, leader of the Shiromani Akali Dal and other Sikh leaders became disgruntled with the Nehru Government. They got the impression that in spite of their sacrifices[39] in not going the way the Muslims had gone and got Pakistan in reward, the Government of India and the Congress had gone back on their promises. They had a feeling that their identity, language and culture in due course would get absorbed in the encompassing Hinduism.[40] The Sikhs also toned down their demand from the Sikh State to a Punjabi-speaking State not without grouse. Chandigarh has become a bone of contention, as the Sikhs demand it as the capital of Punjab. Their resentment - after Nehru was gone - grew in geometrical progression, and led to terrorist activities aiming at separation from the Indian Union. With the prevalence of saner voices and reaction against violence, Punjab is marching towards normalcy through democratic means.

Nehruvian Secularism Analysed

Nehru's contention is that a synthesis between the Hindus and the Muslims in India would have taken place, had the British not stepped in. One dissenting voice charges Nehru for skirting inconvenient issues: "He, for instance does not tell us why the Christian Muslim encounter did not lead to a synthesis despite the common Semitic origins of the two faiths."[41] Further being educated in western style and unfamiliar with Sanskrit, the source of Indian culture, he could not grasp the essence of Indian culture.[42] Another detractor says that there had never been such a thing as a secular tradition in India.[43] Yet, another comment is that Nehruvian secularism was an anti-Hindu policy designed as a device for capturing minority votes. A Jan Sangh (non Bharatiya Janata Party) document states: 'What passes as secularism today, however, is only a euphemism for the policy of Muslim appeasement. It is neither nationalism nor secularism but only a compromise with communalism which demands a high price for its lip loyalty to this country".[44] S Gopal is also of the view that Nehru pampered Muslims. Even the Congressites held the same view. Patel was reported to have said: "There is only one genuinely nationalist Muslim in India - Jawaharlal".[45] The Marxist-atheists attack communalism among the Congressites and the failure to promote secular thinking and the public display and practice of religion. T N Madan,[46] Ashis Nandi[47] and others of their credo are of the opinion that the time has come 'to reject secularism as a failure and as irrelevant, unworkable and unsuitable to India.' Balsubramanian says that the secularism as propagated by Nehru was 'minority oriented' minority by which Nehru meant Muslims in India. Hence, it has not done full justice to its principles and policies.

Whatever criticism may be levelled against Nehruvian secularism, but it is the only solution to the Indian problem. It might not be flawless, but for a plural society like India there is no other outlet than this. To Nehru religion is a personal affair and it should not be brought into political affairs. The citizens are given full freedom to practice and propagate their religion. Though India was declared a secular State, a direct reference to secularism was made only in 1976 when it was introduced into the Preamble of the Constitution by the forty-fourth amendment. With all the religious fanaticism and violence specially in Punjab and Jammu and Kashmir, Ram Janam Bhumi episode, destruction of Babri Masjid and bomb blasts in Bombay, secularism is not dead. Even in USA there is a disenchantment against the secular policies of the State. In a theocratic State — Pakistan — a film actress is contesting against a religious leader Maulana Faz-ul Rahman. Her plank is development - net religion. During the recent tragic air disaster at Charkhi Dadri, a Saudi correspondent has praised RSS volunteers for their remarkable role which rendered all possible help to the relatives of the victims mainly Muslims as well as to the media people 'while, except for a small presence of Jamat-e-Islami Hind workers, there were no government or Muslim workers to take care of the relatives of the victims or visitors. This is the triumph of the Nehruvian Secularism, founded on democracy, humanitarianism, justice and rationalism. "Unlike the secularism of Lenin or Attaturk, Nehruvian secularism is inseparable from a liberal and democratic society and is fully accommodative of religious freedom. A *leit motif* of the separation of religion from other institutional spheres is the preservation of India's ethnic - religious pluralism." Nehru had laid a foundation for secularism, superstructure on it could be raised by the coming generations. No system is perfect, change is the law of nature. Nehru knew it, believing in the dictum of Frost: "The woods are lovely dark and deep, but I have promises to keep and males to go before I sleep and miles to go before I sleep."

References

1. Constituent Assembly Debate, Vol. I, pp. 55-57. Nehru explained his point: "The resolution that I am placing before you defines our aims, describes an outline, of the plan and points. It has ever been and shall always be our ardent desire to see the people of India united together so that we may frame a Constitution which will be acceptable to the masses of the Indian people."
2. D E Smith, *India as Secular State,* Princetion University Press, 1963, p. 155.
3. SL Verma, *Towards Theory of Positive Secularism,* Jaipur, Rawat Publications, 1986, p. 92.
4. All Religions can co-exist.
5. Whole world is one family.
6. Jawaharlal Nehru, *The Discovery of India,* Calcutta 1946, pp. 64-65.
7. Jawaharlal Nehru, *Speeches,* Vol. V, March 1963- May 1964, New Delhi, 1968, p. 59.
8. Jawaharlal Nehru, *Speeches,* Vol. III, March 1953 - August 1957, New Delhi, 1958, p. 333.
9. *Ibid.,* p. 60, We have said repeatedly that we will not tolerate any communalism in this country and that we are building a free, Secular State, where every religion and belief has full freedom and equal honour.

10. M Balasubramaniam, *Nehru: A Study in Secularism,* New Delhi, 1980, p. 83.
11. *Ibid.*
12. Nehru during his visit to USA, as the first Prime Minister of India, said: "It may interest you to know that in drafting the Constitution of the Republic of India we have been greatly influenced by your own Constitution." Jawaharlal Nehru, *Visit to America,* New York, 1950, p. 5.
13. In 1950, in one of his speeches he said: 'The Government of India, with many religions that have secured great and devoted followings for generations, can never function satisfactorily in the modern age except on a secular basis', *The Hindu,* September 13, 1950.
14. D R Goyal, *Communalism vs Nationalism: The Nehru Approach,* New Delhi, n.d., pp. 10-11.
15. D E Smith, *op. cit.,* "The enactment of Civil Laws for one community only is discriminatory, it does represent a communal approach, it does undermine the basic principle of equality before the law, it does place the State in a position where it is either persecuting Hinduism or promoting it, depending on one's point of view. Looking at the total picture quite objectively it is true that the principles of secularism are not being adhered to."
16. *Ibid.,* pp. 237-38.
17. *Ibid.,* p. 288.
18. *Ibid.,* p. A21.
19. *Ibid.,* p. 290.
20. *Ibid.,* p. 203.
21. M Balasubramaniam, *op.cit.,* p. 95.
22. T M P Mahadevan, *Problems of Teaching Religion in Indian Universities,* A Pamphlet, n.d., p. 2.
23. *Ibid.*
24. M N Dalal, *Whither Minorities.,* Bombay, 1940, p. 1.
25. Ishwari Prasad, *History of Medieval India,* Allahabad, 1945, pp. 59-60.
26. M N Dalal, *op.cit.,* p. 42.
27. William Rose, *An Outline of Modern Knowledge,* London, 1937, p. 755.
28. *Hamara Hindustan Special,* No.2, Mumbai, 1943, p. 84.
29. *The Hindu,* January 16, 1940, p. 5.
30. WC Smith, *Modern Islam in India,* London, 1946, p. 189.
31. Jawaharlal Nehru, *An Autobiography,* London, 1953, pp. 169-70.
32. *Ibid.*
33. Jawaharlal Nehru, *Speeches,* Vol. 11: 1949-1953, New Delhi, 1958, p. 356.
34. *The Hindu,* January 1, 1940, p. 3.
35. D R Goyal, *op.cit.* Appendix I. Norman Cousins wrote: 'The fact that Nehru risked his life to save a single Moslem had a profound effect far beyond New Delhi. Thousands of Moslems who had intended to flee to

Pakistan now stayed in India staking their lives on Nehru's ability to protect them and assure them justice. In years to come, this confidence of India's Moslems in Nehru was to become a major factor in building a nation and holding it together.'

36. Mare Galanter, 'The Problem of Group Membership: Some Reflections on the Judicial view of Indian Society', *The Journal of the Indian Law Institute,* Vol. 4. No. 3, July-September, 1962, p. 353. "Is an individual convert's acceptance of Christianity invariably evidence of a loss of membership in the caste group to which he belonged at the time of conversion. There is evidence that in some cases, atleast the convert continues to regard himself and to be regarded by others as a member of the old caste."
37. M Balasubramaniam, *op.cit.,* p. 59.
38. D E Smith, *op.cit,* pp. 443-446.
39. Devinder Singh Duggal, *The Truth About Sikhs,* Amritsar, n.d., 'In 1932, at the time of 2nd Round Table Conference, the British Government through Sardar Bahadur Shivdev Singh, then a member of the Indian Secretary of State's Council, made an informal proposal to the Sikhs that if they dissociate themselves from the Congress they would be given such a decisive political weightage in the Punjab as would lead to their emerging as a third independent element in India after the British transfer power to the inhabitants of the sub-continent. Master Tara Singh is reported to have said at that time that he cannot blacken his face by agreeing to this suggestion. '......in April 1947, Mr Jinnah, with the concurrence of the British cabinet offered to the Sikhs, first through Master Tara Singh and then through Maharaja of Patiala a sovereign Sikh State comprising of areas lying in the west of Panipat and east of the left bank of the river Ravi on the understanding that this State confederates with Pakistan on the following terms......'
40. D E Smith, *op.cit.,* p. 454.
41. *The Times of India,* New Delhi, November 14, 1991, An article by Girilal Jain, 'Nehruvian Secularism.'
42. *Ibid.*
43. A B Shah, *Jawaharlal Nehru: A Critical Tribute,* Bombay, 1965, pp. 85-86. 'It may be chat the upper echelon of Indian leadership was itself too much attached to nationalism as its source of inspiration; that it had too many emotional investments in such non-secular themes as the flag, the language, Indian spirituality — whatever that means — and that they were eventually barred from evolving a completely rational, i.e., secular matrix in national affairs, and devolving it in administrative and political training to the coming generations.'
44. D E Smith, *op.cit.,* p. 471.
45. Michael Brecher, *Nehru: A Political Biography,* London, 1959, p. 315.
46. T N Madan, 'Secularism in its place', *Journal of Asian Studies,* Vol. 46, No. 4, 1987, p. 751, South Asian religions are 'totalising in character, claiming

all of a follower's life so that religion is constitutive of society', and thus out of tune with modern secularism.

47. Ashis Nandi, 'An Anti-Secularist Manifesto', *Seminar,* October, 1985, 'The Politics of Secularism and the Recovery of Religious Toleration', paper presented at the Workshop on Theology and Liberation organised by Pipal Tree, April 28 - May 2, 1986, Bangalore.

11

Manava Dharma and Pt. Nehru's Concept of Secularism

—DR S.H. PATIL

The concept of Dharma constitutes the central thinking of Indian people from the ancient period to the modern period. Etymologically, the Sanskrit word. Dharma is derived from the root, *dhar*, which means to hold or to maintain. But the philosophical meaning of Dharma is interpreted differently by different sages through Srutis and Smritis. However, it has generally come to mean observance of principles and prescriptions as laid down in the holy books. The word, Dharma, has some prefixes like Rajdharma, Manavdharma, etc. Manavadharma covers certain cardinal virtues like respect and concern for humanity.

Though Pt. Jawaharlal Nehru did not believe in any religion, yet he believed in and practised Manavdharma on secular basis. He had the greatest concern for humanity and wanted to lift it from poverty, ignorance, superstition, communal passions, etc. and planned to make men and women prosperous, rational, scientific, humane, secular, etc. The means that he adopted for these goals in India were democracy, socialism and secularism. The last one runs through the former two means. His concepts of democracy and socialism were coloured by secularism.

The present paper intends to explain how Pt. Jawaharlal Nehru's concern for Manavadharma shaped his concept of secularism. Pt. Nehru's concept of secularism is rooted in his ideological foundations and practices which were developed/cultivated from his early days.

Nehru's Ideological Sources of Secularism

Pt. Nehru had faith in indivisibility of humanity and was known for his concern for human dignity, equality and freedom. He was an international humanist and used to react to every wrong in any part of the world. His concept of Manavdharma transcended all barriers of nations, nationalities, races, religions, castes, etc. Though he did not believe in any religion, yet he had greatest regard for innate spirituality of human beings. Thus, his concept of secularism springs from his belief in indivisibility of humanity.

As Pt. Nehru had developed rational and scientific mind, his general outlook was not coloured by religious beliefs and practices and he was totally opposed to superstitions and dogmas. As a rationalist, he looked at problems from secular angle rather than from communal angle. His was objective approach to the problems of the country. He was critical of those who looked at politics through religion and he was more concerned about human life on earth rather than life after death. As Indian society was bound by tradition, orthodoxy, communalism and scientific backwardness, he wanted to build a new India on the basis of modernity, secularism and scientific spirit. Thus, his concept of secularism is the outcome of his rational and scientific outlook.

Pt. Nehru was totally opposed to oppressive tendencies of organised religion but believed in moral and ethical development of individuals and society even without reference to religion. His concept of social religion is one which leads to inner change and development of individuals which in turn influences outer environment.[1] Though he was opposed to religion, yet he had belief in the innate spirituality of human beings.[2] He did not attack religion for the sake of criticism. His concept of secularism was not directed against the internal contents of religion but was directed against purposeless and outmoded external manifestations of religion. He wanted both man and state to be free from such religion which puts restrictions on change and progress which are inherent in both individual and society. In this respect he was very much influenced by Kemal Pasha of Turkey who was non-religious, abolished the Sultanate and Khilafat and built a secular state. Pt. Nehru thus admired Kemal: "This very policy, however, made him more popular among the younger generation of both Hindus and Muslims."[3] Thus, Pt. Nehru welcomed and appreciated the progressive forces/movements in any part of the world. As an opposition to the oppressive nature of organised religion and as a believer in scientific training and spirit, he developed liberal and progressive concept of secularism.

Pt. Jawaharlal Nehru was very much influenced by scientific socialism of Karl Marx. Though he modified scientific socialism in his own way at both ideological and operational levels, yet he continued to be under the influence of scientific spirit of socialism. He declared himself as a socialist at the Lahore session of the Indian National Congress (1929) in his presidential address and believed in all pervading philosophy of socialism: "I must frankly confess that I am a socialist and republican.......But we must realise that the philosophy of socialism has gradually permeated the entire structure of society the world over...... India will have to go that way too."[4] Scientific socialism had profoundly influenced Pt. Nehru's concept of secularism. Scientific socialism and communalism not go together because they are diametrically opposed to each other.

As a socialist, Pt. Nehru considered both the Hindu Mahasabha and the Muslim League as reactionary forces which stood for vested interests. Addressing students of the Banaras Hindu University, Pt. Nehru said, "Under the cover of seeming nationalism, the (Hindu) Mahasabha not only hides the rankest and narrowest communalism but also desires to preserve the vested interests of a group of Hindu landlords and princes."[5] On some other occasion, Pt. Nehru said that the Muslim League was a reactionary organisation and stood for vested interests as against the general and national intersts.[6] He opined that the communal forces were not only anti-secular but also reactionary. Thus, he believed that such communal and reactionary forces could be eliminated only through secularism and socialism.

Communal unity, tolerance and peace which are some of the elements of secularism had tremendous influence on Pt. Nehru's outlook towards communal harmony. In this connection, he was influenced by Buddha, Asoka and Gandhiji. In his broadcast to the nation at Delhi on 26th March 1964, he emphasised tolerance and communal harmony: "Ever since the distant past, it has been the proud privilege of the people of India to live in harmony with one another. That has been the basis of India's culture. Long ago, the Buddha taught us this lesson. From the days of Asoka, 2300 years ago, this aspect of our thought has been repeatedly declared and practised. In our own day, Mahatma Gandhi laid great stress on it and indeed lost his life because he laid great stress on communal goodwill and harmony. We have, therefore, a precious heritage to keep up, and we cannot allow ourselves to act contrary to it."[7] Thus, Pt. Nehru's concept of secularism has been influenced by India's legacy of social harmony.

Nehru's Two Concepts of Secularism

Pt. Jawaharlal Nehru's concept of secularism can be explained at two levels – ideal and practical.

Ideal concept of secularism of Pt. Nehru which exists at his free thinking level is free from existing conditions and compulsions and is based on the highest concept of Manavadharma and scientific spirit. As Pt. Nehru was influenced by scientific rationality and socialism, his concept of secularism was totally free from the control of religions. Religion is personal and private. State has nothing to do with religion and religion has nothing to do with state. Under such free condition the individuals are free thinkers and grow with their creative abilities. They interact with one another as fellow human beings and are held together by common secular ideals. They are humane and are guided by concept of Manavadharma in their social interactions and in the pursuit of common goals.

Pt. Nehru's another concept of secularism is a compromised concept which is a mixture of his free thinking and compulsions of existing conditions in India. This second best concept of secularism is influenced by concern for unity of India. He believed that territorial unity of India should be based on a unity of mind and heart.[8]

The following are the features of Pt. Nehru's operational secularism (second best concept of secularism): (i) In his concept of secular state all religions have equal status. "India will be a land, as in the past, of many faiths equally honoured and respected,"[9] said Pt. Nehru. (ii) All religions shall have freedom to perform religious ceremonies. (iii) No religion shall have any special privilege. (iv) No community shall be deprived of its legitimate rights on the basis of religion. (v) There shall be equal opportunities for followers of all religions. Pt. Nehru proclaimed: "We have laid down in our constitution that India is a secular state. That does not mean irreligious. It means equal respect for all faiths and equal opportunities for those who profess any faith."[10] (vi) Pt. Nehru had respect for composite culture of India which is a multi-religious country and has been home to all those who have come and settled here. In such composite society majority and minority communities should learn to believe in peaceful co-existence. However, the majority religion has a major role in maintaining communal harmony and secularism. Pt. Nehru as the president of the Indian National Congress used to write letters to the presidents of the Pradesh Congress Committees about need for communal harmony and responsibility of major community in preserving and promoting secularism. In one of his letters he emphasised that the Hindus must always remember that the interests and the well-being of the minorities were their sacred trust. (vii) Every citizen has the same rights, duties and privileges and has full freedom to profess and practise his religion. No citizen is subject to any social inequalities imposed by religious sanctions. (viii) The state shall follow the policy of neutrality in religious matter and the government shall not directly associate itself with any religion. Pt. Nehru's concept of national state is not a theocratic state but a secular state in which citizens of different religions live peacefully. In his address to the students of Aligarh Muslim University in 1948, Pt. Nehru opposed the concept of theocratic state and opined that such state was outdated. The modern state should be essentially a secular system. (ix) As a modern state is a secular institution, it has nothing to do with religion. *Pt. Nehru did not accept the relevance of religion to national identity.*

Nehru : Symbol of Secularism

Pt. Nehru's early association with Muslims, cosmopolitan atmosphere in the home, early exposure to Western influence in England, his love for science, etc., shaped his concept of secularism.

Pt. Nehru set an example of secular spirit and practice. He has been described as an Englishman by training and education, Muslim by culture and Hindu by accident of birth. Though description is satirical, yet it represents secular and universal character of Pt. Nehru. As he was brought up in such composite environment, his views and practices were secular and universal.

As a visionary and revolutionary, Pt. Nehru preached and practised secularism which was an article of faith with him. Secularism was a part of his inner self. Even if one studies Pt. Nehru from psychological angle, one finds secular dimensions of his inner self. This part of his inner self was projected through his writings, speeches and actions. Thus, there was no gap between his private life and public life with regard to secularism. He set an example in this regard and wanted his countrymen to be secular in thought and action. As a charismatic leader, he had an emotional hold over the people of India. He was able to convince the masses about potentialities of secularism from various angles.

Two Models of Secularism

Secularism was developed by the Indian National Congress during the freedom movement as means to bring about unity and harmony among the various religious groups in India. Among the Congress leaders, Mahatma Gandhi and Pt. Nehru immensely continued to the concept and practice of Indian secularism.

Gandhian secularism is based on oneness of God, one mankind, religious tolerance and mutual respect. It has religious touch and is in tune with the traditional Indian ideal of Sarvadharma Sambhava.

Pt. Nehru's concept of secularism is influenced by humanism, rationalism, scientific spirit and socialism. It comes nearer to the Western liberal concept of secularism.

In course of time these two models of secularism (Gandhian and Nehruvian) came to be developed informally. Indian secularists are influenced by either of these two models depending upon their upbringing and ideals. The Indian constitution has tried to provide synthesis of Gandhian and Nehruvian models of secularism to some extent.

Challenges to Secularism

Pt. Jawaharlal Nehru considered the religious passions, organised religions, communalism, alliance between religion and politics, etc., as serious challenges to the Indian secularism.

He was totally opposed to religious passions, which blunt reason. He said, "But religious passions have little to do with reason or consideration of adjustments."[11] Such irrational passions are hurdles to bring about tolerance and adjustment among different religious groups.

Pt. Nehru was against organised religion, which develops vested interest in course of time and becomes reactionary force opposing progress and change. He was a continuous and unending war between religion and science. Religion imposes restrictions on mind while science encourages open mind. Secularism flourishes only in open and rational societies. Thus, organised religion which is a closed religion cannot sustain and encourage scientific secularism.

Communalism not only divides the people but also puts back the state to the medieval period. It exploits and encourages hatredness against another religious group in the name of religion. According to Pt. Nehru, the conflict is not between the Hindus and the Muslims in India but it is between communalism and secularism and between reactionary forces and progressive forces. Thus, he condemns communalism : "Communalism is the badge of a backward nation, not of the modern age."[12]

According to Pt. Nehru, alliance between religion and politics is unholy. Such alliance leads to disintegration of plural societies and such politicised communal groups are always at war with one another and are enemies of India. Such communal forces "have, therefore, taken advantage of the cloak of religion to cover up their reactionary policies, have exploited the name of religion in politics and have excited people's passions in that name."[13] Speaking in the Constituent Assembly on 3rd April 1948, Pt. Nehru condemned alliance between politics and religion: "We must have it clearly in our minds and in the minds of the country that the alliance of religion and politics in the shape of communalism is a most dangerous alliance, and it yields the most abnormal kind of illegitimate brood."[14]

Nehru's Measures to Secularise India

Pt. Nehru suggested among others two important measures to establish secularism in India. These are secular social life and secular education.

Though Pt. Nehru was fully aware of hold of religions in India on social codes, social rules, marriage, inheritance, civil and criminal law, social organisation, etc., he wanted to secularise all walks of life of Indian people. He introduced many social legislations to secularise the life of people. He was not merely interested in a secular *state* but was very keen in establishing a secular *society*. According to him, it is only secular society which can sustain and promote secular state.

As education is a means to bring about pre-determined socio-economic and political changes in society, Pt. Nehru emphasised scientific, rational and secular education with concern for society and individuals. He believed that such modern education alone could create secular citizens who in turn could build a secular state. On several occasions he laid greater stress on modern and secular education and made attempts to restructure educational system in that direction.

Relevance of Nehru's Concept of Secularism

Pt. Nehru's concept of secularism is not only relevant to India but also to the whole world because it is progressive and is in tune with evolution of human civilisation and scientific development.

If India has to come out from the clutches of communalism, ethnicism, casteism, etc., it has to adopt Pt. Nehru's concept of scientific secularism. Communal conflicts, communal hatred and communal violence which have assumed structural dimensions and have become autonomous in recent years can be removed by implementing Pt. Nehru's measures meant for establishing secularism based on Manavadharma.

Though the framers of Indian constitution had given secular state structure to great extent, in recent years attempts have been made by the various political parties and pressure groups to restructure Indian political system and subsystems on communal/ caste basis in order to win over votes. It is Nehruvian secularism which can provide antidote to these attempts to communalise Indian politics and can keep Indian political structure and Indian citizens secular. It is only secular citizens who can create secular political process.

When Nehruvian secularism is relevant today, *its contents should form a part of syllabi of textbooks in schools and colleges.*

Mass media like T.V., Radio and Newspapers should periodically carry features on Nehruvian concept of secularism.

Mass movements should be carried on in the various parts of India to convey the message of Pt. Nehru's concept of secularism to the people.

Pt. Nehru's secular practices should be model to the leaders and the masses of India.

Pt. Nehru firmly believed that the Indian nationalism is to be built on secularism rather than on communalism. As a student of

Indian and world history, he was convinced that Indian nationalism is to be built on secularism. He was totally opposed to the concept of Hindu nationalism, Muslim nationalism and Sikh nationalism. He was in favour of secular nationalism. Today Nehruvian concept of secular nationalism is to be developed vigorously to meet the communal challenges from the various parts of the country to the unity of India.

Secularism based on Manavadharma, socialism and scientific temper is one of the greatest contributions made by Pt. Nehru to the nation-building process in India.

Pt. Nehru maintained and promoted secular nature of sub-system like the party system. Under his leadership, the Congress never lost its secular character and outlook. It had become a vehicle for secular expression and a secular agent for political socialisation.

As Pt. Nehru was an internationalist, he believed in peaceful co-existence different nations based on different religious, social and economic ideologies. According to him, India should be a model in peaceful co-existence and should demonstrate it from its own experience of peaceful co-existence on secular basis. He was very confident that India would be a model in this respect and would become a part of 'one world order' in future. Thus, he expressed his hope: "As far as India is concerned, I can speak with some certainty. We shall proceed on secular and national lines in keeping with the powerful trends towards internationalism. Whatever confusion the present may contain, in the future, India will be a land, as in the past, of many faiths equally honoured and respected, but of one national outlook, not I hope, a narrow nationalism living in its own shell, but rather the tolerant creative nationalism which, belief in itself and the genius of its people, takes full part in the establishment of an international order. The only ultimate aim we can have is that of one world."[15] Thus, Pt. Nehru's concept of secularism which is based on enlightened Manavadharma and rationality is not only relevant to India but also to the whole world. Essentially it is a unifying ideology and force for the whole mankind. In Nehruvian concept of one world, peace, prosperity, freedom and secularism are indivisible.

References

1. Nehru, Jawaharlal, *An Autobiography* (Bombay: Allied Publishers Private Ltd., 1962), p. 379.
2. The Hindu, March 28, 1960, quoted by Neeraj, *Nehru and Democracy in India* (Delhi: Metropolitan Book Co. Pvt. Ltd., 1972), p. 74.
3. Nehru, Jawaharlal, *The Discovery of India* (Delhi: Oxford University Press, 1989), p. 350.
4. Nehru, Jawaharlal, *India's Freedom* (London: Unwin Books, 1962), p. 14.
5. Nehru, Jawaharlal, *Recent Essays and Writing* (Allahabad: Kitabistan, 1937), pp. 45-46.
6. *Ibid.*, pp. 49-51.
7. Nehru, Jawaharlal, *Jawaharlal Nehru's Speeches*, Vol. V, March 1963 – May 1964 (New Delhi: Publication Division, Ministry of Information and Broadcasting, Government of India, 1968), p. 12.
8. Nehru, Jawaharlal, *Jawaharlal Nehru's Speeches*, Vol. II (Delhi: Publication Division, Ministry of Information and Broadcasting, Government of India, 1967), p. 93.
9. Sen, N.B. (ed.), *Glorious Thoughts of Nehru* (New Delhi: New Book Society of India, 1964), p. 62.
10. Saxena, A.P. (ed.), *Jawaharlal Nehru and Indian Administration* (New Delhi: Uppal Publishing House, 1991), p. 171.
11. Nehru, Jawaharlal, *An Autobiography* (Bombay: Allied Publishers Private Limited, 1962), p. 135.
12. Nehru, Jawaharlal, *Jawharlal Nehru's Speeches*, Vol. IV, September 1957 – 1963 (New Delhi: Publication Divisions, Ministry of Information and Broadcasting, Government of India, 1964), p. 12.
13. Nehru, Jawaharlal, *Jawaharlal Nehru's Speeches*, Vol. II, (Delhi: Publication, Ministry of Information and Broadcasting, Government of India, 1954), p. 351.
14. Nehru, Jawaharlal, *Independence and After* (A Collection of the More Important Speeches of Jawaharlal Nehru from September 1946 to May 1949) (Delhi: Publication Division, Ministry of Information and Broadcasting, Government of India, 1949), p. 47.
15. Sen, N.B. (ed.), *Glorious Thoughts of Nehru* (New Delhi: New Book Society of India, 1964), p. 262.

12

Secularising the Literary Space: Problems and Possibilities

—SUDHIR KUMAR

The present essay is an attempt to read some works of fiction[1] written by the contemporary Muslim writer's in the context of the growing need to connect the literary space with the secular space in India. In other words, how the literature written by the so-called minority (Muslim) - writers addresses the question of secularism in the Indian context? Since the reconstruction of a nation primarily depends on its cultural civilisational matrix which also influences the production of its literature and arts, the agency of literature in the nation-building process assumes a critical significance. This essay also analyses how literature becomes the site of a union between the sacred and the secular. The "nation-space" in the present-day India seems to be almost suffocated with the mutually combative and competitive theories of secularism. The first part of the paper is an attempt to critique the highly intellectualised, ultra-sophisticated, hypersanitised and hypertextual constructions of secularism that, true to its western epistemology, emphasises the separation of politics from religion in the Indian context. In other words, the oppressive burden of secular theory makes an Indian citizen proudly proclaim his adherence to secularism whereas he (or she) is sure to be charged with lese majesfe if he tries to fearlessly articulate his faith in dharma or mazhab in the public sphere, the constitutional provisions notwithstanding. The second part of the essay is an attempt to read a few recent provocative novels written by the Muslim writers to analyse how they discuss the discourse of secularism in their fictional works. Do they discount and denigrate religion altogether in their works and are they all for a secular, civil society? Or, do their works point to a possibility of creating a constructive dialogue between the spirit of true religion and that of "true" secularism ? Or are there some avowed followers of the West sponsored theory who use their "secularism" as a weapon to maim the body of "faith or religion". The essay is also concerned, with the majority-minority-syndrome and its reflection or refraction in the literary space. What emerges out of the discussion is that there are some alarming as well as constructive alliances or affiliations between the theories of secularism and the practice of writing fiction at the present time. The writers whose works I intend to read in this essay (i.e., Salman Rushdie, Intezar Husain, Manzoor Ehtesham and Taslima Nasrin) are, inspite of their different locations intimately connected with the Indian subcontinent and their works betray the different and differing paradigms of "acceptance/co-option" and "resistance/reconstruction".

I

Secularism as Theory: Tyranny of Reason

The question of secularism, in the so-called "global-space" of present times, is, in many ways, largely related to the vexing issues of "modernity", "Economic liberalisation", and the fast growing but almost globally cherished need to create "a new kind of hyper-rational human being" - genetically cloned to be well-disposed to science and technology and a nay-sayer to the ways of God to men (or women). "I reason, therefore, I am secular, and therefore, I am" - seems to be the highly exclusivist parodic motto of the so-called secular West. Parodied further, it implies - "you believe (in any faith other than Christianity!, therefore, you are a fundamentalist, and therefore, you are not!" I must confess at the outset that I can't write a history of secularism as an objective onlooker only to clinically apply its findings to the peculiar Indian conditions to win some national or international critical attention and applause. As a citizen of India, at the same time, I witness an avalanche of "theory" (in its new hegemonic *avatars* of secular reason as postmodernisn, postcolonialism, subalternism etc) to re-package almost every item of knowledge in the technologically manufactured languages. To cut these controversial matters related to the strategies of neo-imperialism short, these "languages" come from the West and brazenly attempt to engineer "knowledges" for the rest of the world.

It is, therefore, no coincidence that after the 80's, the impact of this imported (or imposed) theory on the national debate on "secularism" became more and more obvious in India. Even the so-called "secularists" are now busy in outsmarting one another through the cunning of language, giving rise, so to say a flourishing publishing industry of secularism. Their preoccupation is not with the condition of the people of India, (most of them are still illiterate and deprived of the basic amenities of life) their world-views, their faiths and their dreams - instead these critics or academics have hegemonised the entire space (or the "nation-space") of debate, discussion and interpretation in which their sole concern is the manufacturing of "theories" of secularism and their imposition on the Indian academia.

Let me, in brief, substantiate my preceding argument by commenting on some of the jargon-infested post-modern propositions on secularism published in *Economic and Political Weekly* (July 9, 1994) - viz. Akeel Bilgrami's *"Two concepts of Secularism : Reason, Modernity and Archimedean Ideal"* (pp. 1749-1761), Partha Chatterjee's *"Secularism and Toleration"* (pp. 1768-1777) and Rajeev Bhargava's *"Giving Secularism Its Due"* (pp. 1784-1791). These three essays are self-consciously couched in ultra-sophisticated languages - and (pre)-tend to be a discourse on "the nation" (or the people of India) but not for "the nation". Take, for example, Bilgrami's essay which starts off well by asserting the significance of "the dialectic between the concept of nation and that of religious community" (p. 1749), but the writer seems to be itching to marshal his discursive superiority over the likes of Partha Chatterjee, Ashis Nandy, Aijaz Ahmed and others, by co-opting Lenin and Nehru in a Gramscian or Derridian mode. It's a triumph of the non-committed academic trivialisation of a serious, people-civilisation-centred debate. To prove his grounding in the "postmodernist theory" it is sufficient to cite his own interpretation of the concept of religious community which is, according to him, non-existent in India or Pakistan!! To him, the Muslims or the Hindus in India and Pakistan are neither religious nor a community (p. 1760)!! Similarly, Partha Chatterjee's attempts to upset the logic of the so-called Hindu right in his above-mentioned essay is yet another abortive effort to relate his Faucauldian text (i.e. his essay) to the native Indian context which, at times, defies the "majority-minority" stereotypes so fondly circulated in the academic discourse on secularism.

Similarly Rajeev Bhargava's "Giving Secularism Its Due" is also concerned with the need for promoting secularism in the various institutions of the nation state. What makes his otherwise well-written piece a bit skewed is his preoccupation with the anxiety of influence. It is this burden of information that makes such "Postmodernistic pieces on secularism" full of sound and fury signifying nothing.[2] To understand the Indian experiment with nation-building, it is worthwhile to use, to a considerable extent, the available native thinking on such issues as secularism, the minority-majority problems, religion and modernity etc. What is disconcerting to note is that most of the circulating treatises on secularism and nation-building betray the elitist bias of speaking on India and its people in oblivion of its civilisational living traditions. Secularism has to be re-defined as a living experience constantly in dialogue with the cultural context of India, not as mere collation of contesting theories. Unfortunately, "Secularism" as theory has almost become an orthodox institution which is engaged in a sort of war not so much against religious fundamentalism but against religion as such. The tradition of Indian civilisation, which constantly flows through its past and present and will considerably influence its future - has conveniently been obliterated or erased in these postmodernistic attempts to theorise secularism in India. But, had these theories of "subversions" and "ruptures" been the only tools to gain knowledge about India as a nation, it would have been considered a nation of "floating", "liberated" and "fragmented" dehumanised beings. Since India is a living organism, - constantly adapting herself to new challenges posed to her unique ways of living in togetherness and harmony, it is worthwhile to focus on some of the other voices of secularism that are addressed to the people of India cutting across the demographic profiles of population.

Religion and Secularism : The Great Indian Experiment

It is a peculiar feature of the Indian civilisation that it upsets the apple cart of secularism based on the primacy of reason and logic. The Upanishads, the Sufism and the Bhakti Movement may easily be cited as counter-movements to re-define and re-construct "faith" or "religion" in the context of the Indian civilisation or nation. India seems to profess a kind of "secularism" or "pluralism" which comes, not from the sphere of modern reason or science, but from its age-old spiritual traditions. The sacred is, thus, the secular. If secularism means a mere seclusion of religion from politics, no thinking Indian ought to doubt its relevance to our civilisation. The Indian state has to be secular in order to be viable and just. If it further embodies a kind of symbiotic relationship among the various religious faiths practised in India, it is in keeping with the tradition of India which has always been pluralistic. Since the measure of all social, political, cultural, economic institutions is a thinking, imaginative human being, it is unjustified and uncalled for to lay him or her on the proverbial Procrustean bed of secularism where he is always supposed to shout - "God is dead!!" It is here that I wish to record some other voices in Indian tradition that have tried to reconcile secularism with religiosity in the process of nation-building. A kind of secularism which threatens the Indian Muslims (or Hindus or any other religious community) to lose their identity in the state-sponsored processes of development and progress (read modernity) has had its detractors. The rhetoric of a secular India, ironically, poses itself as, or becomes, an instrument of anti-religion-propaganda. This position is untenable to the people of India-who are, in one way or the other, the believers tied to some sacred spiritual tradition. Professor Mushir-ul-Haq aptly condemns the role of the so-called Indian secularists thus:

> *"Indian secularists, Muslim or Hindu, committed the mistake of undervaluing the Muslims' religious sentiments, and thus created a situation where the tradition-bound Muslim community took secularism to be an anti-religious force. This explains in part the Muslims' obstinate resistance to change".*[3]

The Secularists ought to know that the Muslims (read Hindus/ Sikhs/and other communities also) are all for a secular state which the constitution of India guarantees to them but they must not be sold to the dogma of secularism *(la diniyat* or *ghair mazhabiyat* or *dharma-nirapekshata).* Even the neutralising but highly politicised discourses of universalism and humanism are offered in support of "secularism" as if the religions of the world are inimical and antithetical to humanism and humane progress. Professor Haq warns that secularism in the context of making a modern India "became a vague objective and everyone was free to define it according to his educational, religious and communal background. In fact, the relationship between secularism and religion was seen in terms of hostility or indifference, determined largely by the background of the person using the term."[4]

In fact, it is impossible to compartmentalise the secular and the religious (non-secular) spheres of human activities. How else can we account for a Bill Clinton, a Boris Yeltsin, a Shankar Dayal Sharma attending the church or supplicating to a Sai Baba during their political campings? They say that religion is a private affair!! Or will it be politically correct if a surgeon offers prayers to his God before he performs surgery on a serious patient? Isn't Mother Teresa, a paragon of human virtues, a devout Christian? Can the Muslims (or the people of India) stripped of their faith, ever be secular in their world-view? Is the spiritual goal of religion (say Islam or Hinduism) anti-people and anti-progress? If the abuse of religion results in communal violence and riots, the abuse of science produces mass-scale destruction and environment?.! disasters. These are some of the disturbing questions challenging the academic discourses of secularism today.

Secondly, let us focus our attention to the kind of questions the Muslims in India seems to be asking today in their effort to re-define secularism even as they question the secular image of the state. The so-called primacy of secularism rests largely on the belief that it helps to build an environment of peace and harmony in which the majority and the minorities live in togetherness. Imtiaz Ahmed makes a valid case for re-defining the term "minorities" in the social context of India.[5] To him. "every social community in India is a minority at some level of social segmentation or another. In other words, it is problematic in the Indian context to speak of some social communities as minorities and to contrast them with the majority or to assume that the minorities are any more disadvantaged and deprived than other social communities."[6] Prof. Imtiaz's important and timely intervention is symptomatic of a revelatory trend in the thinking of the present-day Muslim intellectuals who refuse to be ghettoised and pampered as mere "minority". It is important to recall that even Javed Akhtar lamented the general tendency among the intellectuals to view the problems of Muslims in India as the problems of a typical religious minority. Instead of focusing on the sign of their religious identity, he suggests that we should study the so-called minority communities as people of India.[7] Religious identity cannot be pitted against the national identity. Maulana Wahiduddin Khan stresses the role of Islam in making the Muslims better human beings in a civil society. According to him, success does not make a Muslim proud and power "does not make him haughtly. No bad treatment by others drives him to seek vengeance in anger. At all events, he remains serene. It is such a man who is called a peaceful soul in the Quran. And it is this man, who, according to the Quran, has achieved the highest spiritual state."[8] Is this "man" following the path of the Prophet antagonistic to the creeds of secularism? Does a democratic secular state have no place for the ideal and honest citizens who derive their spiritual-progress from some faith?

These new trends in the secularism-religion debate compel me to bring Mahatma Gandhi's views on the significance of religion even in his politics:

To see the universal and all pervading spirit of Truth face to face one must be able to love the meanest of creation as oneself. And a man who aspires after that cannot afford to keep out of any field of life. That is why my devotion to Truth has drawn me into the field, of politics, and I can say without the slightest hesitation, and yet in all humility, that those who say that religion has nothing to do with politics do not know what religion means.[9]

Gandhiji is not here talking of some esoteric *"shastric"* or *"sanskritic"* form of faith. Gandhiji was not, for some selfish ends, mixing religion with politics. Rather he was aiming at purifying the political domain by spiritualising it. Yet he was against any doctrinaire form of religion- "I decline to be bound by any interpretation however learned it may be, if it is repugnant to reason or moral sense."[10] Faith, to him, is tested on the touch stone of reason. The Gandhian project was to use the latent spiritual energy in human beings into making them ideal human beings. Elsewhere he also cautioned the members of the Indian National Congress that "we must cease to be exclusive Hindus or Musalmans or Sikhs, Parsis, Christians or Jains. While we may staunchly adhere to our respective faiths, we must be in the Congress, Indians first and Indians last. A good Hindu or a good Musalman should be a better Hindu or a better Musalman for being a lover of his country."[11] For the so-called minorities of India, in his vision of the free nation, there was no possibility of losing their identities or viewing the state as an agent of the majority community. Thus, like some of the present-day Muslim thinkers, Gandhiji was also aware of the inherent contradictions in the much-hailed majority-minority-discourse. Even much before Gandhiji entered the scene of Indian politics, Sir Sayyed Ahmad Khan (1817-1898) re-defined the term *"qawm"* meaning "one nation for all communities in India'' -an important historical reconstruction that has conveniently been ignored by the present-day growing tribe of secularists:

In short the word qawm refers to the inhabitants of a country. O Hindus and Muslims! are you the residents of any other country than India?...If you do live and die in this land then remember that the words 'Hindu' and 'Muslim' are used in the religious sense, and otherwise the Hindus and the Muslims and the Christians who live in this country are one qawm.[12]

Sir Sayyed Ahmed Khan was, perhaps, much ahead of his times as, at the fag end of the twentieth century, we are in deep need to rejuvenate his revolutionary ideas to understand the true import of secularism. In his opinion, "the word Hindu does not denote any religion. Every Indian can call himself Hindu".[13] "Both Hindus and Muslims who live in India are to be considered as 'Hindu', that is, the nation of India (Hindustani qawm)".[14] This also reminds us of the latter-day thinkers such as Gandhiji and Abul Kalam Azad as they insisted on the significance of the national identity which takes precedence over the religious identity in the process of national reconstruction.[15] But we, the people of India, are not for a theocratic (Hindu-Muslim-nation) state as it goes against the basic nature of our ancient civilisation. That is why Sultan Shaheen in his article "Mindless Violence, not Jihad" (See *The Hindustan Times* dated 15/3/1997 p. 13), asks the Muslims of India to be proud of their Indian heritage: "Our ancient civilisation, humanity, secularism, decency, morality and democracy are the strongest cards we have that distinguish us from, say, Pakistan." In the same article, he cautions the Muslims not to misinterpret the Babri-mosque demolition: "Even the seemingly religious problem of Babri-Masjid was essentially a political problem. Our religion is safe in India. It is certainly safer than in Pakistan." Thus, this "Indian civilisation-called nation" which draws its sustenance from the spiritual traditions is the best guarantee for the promotion of secularism "as a living experience" not as an acrid and arid academic debate.

It is in these troubling contexts of secularism as theory, Secularisation as a social process and the task of the national reconstruction that I intend to read some works of fiction written by the Muslim writers. My attempt is to analyse how these writers write "secularism" in their fiction with reference to their approach to Indian civilisation.

II

The Sacred, The Secular and The Text

If there is one recent text that grossly slandered "religion" on the altar of "postmodernistic secularism", that must be Salman Rushdie's much-cited, little read, *The Satanic Verses*.[16] The reasons for choosing *The Satanic Verses* for analysis here are obvious. Salman Rushdie, *a la,* a postmodernist version of the mythical Sulaiman attempts to slaughter the great, eternal spirit of Islam with the help of a "secular theory". Would that he were true to his name - Rushdie (meaning "one who shows the path of righteousness")!! I prefer to call this "theory" (read Euro-Americo-centric postmodernism) secular as it secedes literature or arts from "meaning" - rendering literature as a mere "game" or "play". The Indian notion of art (or literature here) as Kala comes closer to the much hailed postmodernist/deconstructionist theory; but Kala or art in our tradition is ever allied to a "sacred meaning" which is the meaning of meaning - *paramartha.* The seemingly secular is the sacred. Interestingly enough, the term secular cornes from *sikle* (to cut). Hence Rushdie's intimacy with the West that inspires him to use the ideological weapon of "theory" to attack a holy faith - Islam and protects him under the guise of such platitudes as "freedom of expression" or "fundamental rights". Let alone the *Fatwa* issued by Ayatulla Khomeini of Iran, the Muslims all over the world condemned the book. This does not mean that if his novel *The Satanic Verses* displeased a certain fundamentalist group, it stands to condemnation by all. The truth is that it is an instance of sheer blasphemy perpetrated at the behest of a self-styled secular West!! The text created a clash over its "meanings" between a modern (or postmodern/secular/predominantly Christian??) West and a so-called conservative, reactionary Muslim ("the other" of Christianity) community.

The secular theorists of the West while defending Rushdie's sacrilegious act, say that Rushdie in the writing of *The Satanic Verses* is only concerned with "newsness" or "novelty" of form which "tries to put new questions in novel (new) forms."[17] Gayatri Spivak defends the content of the narrative while she contests its form - even as she locates the writer and his text in a Europe of secular reason. By this analogy, since religion lies in the realm of "unreason", it easily exposes itself to all kinds of rationalistic derisions. Yet another Western critic Easterman seems to applaud Rushdie for exposing the "fears of Muslim culture" in *The Satanic Verses.*[18] In yet another attempt to absolve Rushdie of his *"unrushdian"* conduct (path of untruth), some criticised Khomeini for misinforming the poor and illiterate Muslim masses and recruiting his most dedicated "volunteers for martyrdom."[19] The question still hangs, "Did Khomeini really misinform the masses about the content of the novel?" while the West is not tired of demonising Khomeini for his issuing a medieval *fatwa* against Rushdie, it protects Rushdie from the charge of blaspheming Islam under the shield of the secular reason."

Let me quote a few textual instances to show how far Rushdie has gone to win friends and influence people in the West by sacrileging the sacred space of Islam. The Prophet becomes Mahound (a derogatory term reserved for the Muslims), a messenger and a businessman rolled into one-whose identity is conflated with Gibreel, his *alter ego.* Mahound (or the Prophet) is transformed into a sex-maniac who gets "God's permission to f... as many women as he liked (TSV, p. 386)", and identifies writers with whores (TSV, p. 392). Rushdie mentions the twelve wives of the Prophet and makes Ayesha (prophet's wife) full of bestial lust (p. 210). The list of blasphemous references to Islam may easily run into pages. This patent profanation of the domain of spirituality (Islam) with the tools of "secular" reason proves my argument that secularism becomes religion's "other". Moreover, Rushdie seems to use literature to replace religion with secular reason. Such strategies of constructing secularism as these are as dangerous as the menace of religious fundamentalism. I would not like to comment on the latest controversy about M.F. Husain's *"Saraswati"* for want of space here.

It is worthwhile to read Taslima Nasrin's *Lajja*[20] in conjunction with Rushdie's *The Satanic Verses.* It is ironical indeed that Taslima and Rushdie are often clubbed together because of their (much-craved-for !!) writer-in-exile status. The fact is that their ideological stances are quite different. Taslima's discourse in *Lajja,* on the one hand, calls for adopting a more humanitarian and egalitarian approach to the task of nation-making, while, on the other, it also underlines the need for a thorough questioning of the causes of the religious fundamentalism. She suggests the Bengali (i.e., national) identity as an antidote to the poison of majority fundamentalism. To Rushdie, the notion of nation is an outdated fancy, an essentialism, a hegemonic ideology in the context of growing globalisation (read Americanisation). He therefore, makes the sacred, profane and the profane, sacred with aplomb in his fiction catering to the desires and designs of his Western allies (masters!) - and pretends to be utterly oblivious of the religio-cultural sensibilities of the people of the Indian subcontinent. He does stuff the Indian subcontinent, its civilisational characteristics and realities into the alien and alienating Western ideological/theoretical grids and the outcome is his much-lauded postmodern-fiction about the people of the subcontinent. Taslima, to the contrary, is seriously concerned about her nation-her people - the enormity of communal violence and uses her fiction to send the much-needed warning signals to the ruling elites in Bangladesh (and by extension, to the ruling elites in India too) to relate the agenda of secularism to that of nation-building.

Lajja opens with a revealing motto, "Let Another Name for Religion be Humanism" - which serves as a kind of reminder to the followers of majority fundamentalism in Bangladesh and India both. Even if the signifiers are reversed, the message does not change - Let another Name for Humanism be Religion." But the latter statement implies that if the people of Bengladesh or India are the true followers of their respective faiths - the gory incidents of communal violence will never take place there.

Lajja, may be considered a badly-structured novel but it makes a bold protest against the forces that want to perpetuate a tyranny of the majority over the minority on the pretext of religion *(majhab or dharma).* Taslima makes it clear that she detests "fundamentalism and communalism" and that is why she "wrote *Lajja* soon after the demolition of the Babri Masjid in Ayodhya on 6 December 1992" (L, p. ix). As a matter of fact, the same pattern of communal frenzy was witnessed in Bangladesh also - the Muslims ruthlessly killing and persecuting the Hindus. *Lajja,* apart from being a catalogue of the incidents of communal violence, is a discourse of the nation as well. It has a powerful subtext that the nation cannot be reconstructed by setting the demographic profile of population in order - in other words, by making the minorities non-existent in the country. The condition of the Duttas inspite of their sacrifices in the freedom struggle, their patriotism, their liberal attitude to religion, their secularism, reminds us of the horrors of communal violence in Bangladesh. Inspite of the widespread loot and plunder, Sudhamoy, Suranjan's father cooly analyses this situation: "Actually, do you know what the truth is? Those who are causing these riots are not doing so for the love of any particular religion. Their main aim is to loot and plunder" (L, p. 61).

But this is mere wishful thinking as the events unfolded in the narrative tell us. The loot and the violence was not directed at the majority community. The common "Bangla Identity" that sustained the entire freedom-struggle and promoted democracy and peace was thrown to the winds. The Duttas, unfortunately, suffer as they cling to their "Bangla identity". That is why Sudhamoy curses the "migrating Hindus for being cowards" as they have not 'stayed back and fought for their rights in their own country" (L., p. 68). Taslima's message is loud and clear - "let us forget our religious differences and come together to build a new nation under the environment of Bengali culture." It is this commonality, this thread of Bengali cultural identity that binds the majority and the minorities together in an indissoluble bond. By extension, it is this Indian cultural tradition, of harmony, of synthesis, of plurality that binds the majority and the minorities together in India. In her recent address (on April 28, 1996), Taslima reiterated this position - "It was Bengali culture which unified the Muslims and the Hindus of the land and gave them their real identity."[21] Her agenda is that it is the Bengalis who are said to be a "majority" and again, it is the Bengalis who comprise "minorities". A plea for sanity in the insane times! She attempts to relate the discourse of secularism to the Bengali culture without banishing religion from the realm of secularism.

It is in this context of revising the agenda of secularism that I want to discuss two other texts - Intezar Husain's *Basti*[22] and Manzoor Ehtesham's *Dastan E Lapata.*[23] It is surpirising to know how Intezar Husain, a noted Urdu writer of Pakistan uses, perhaps, most of the ingredients of the postmodern fiction (such as intertextuality, fabuiation, magical realism, self-reflexivity etc) in *Basti* - a *Katha* (a tale told in the Indian tradition of narration) of partition and post-partition situations in the Indian subcontinent. Through the tale of Zakir, the protagonist, his parents, his relatives and friends, the writer mourns the decline of a civilisation in which the old *bastis,* full of mutual love and cooperation among the different communities are dying to pave the way for the so-called "progressive", "developing" new *bastis* - full of greed, hatred, violence and bloodshed. *Basti* is a dirge, in this sense, lamenting the decline and fall of the Indian civilisation in which Islam, Hinduism, Buddhism and other faiths lived in a symbiotic existence. There are many references to the *Upanishads,* the *Ramayana,* the *Mahabharata* and the Buddhist *Jataka* tales which are deftly interwoven in the fictional matrix of the narrative. Zakir's Rupnagar (or Dibai in Bulandshahar distt. in UP in India) is the archetypical Indian subcontinent ever-ready to receive - even willing to give - and ever eager to assimilate the other. This archetypal *Basti* which does refer to the Indian concept of nation, is endangered when selfishness, greed, distrust and hatred and violence dictate the politics of the state - during pre- as well as post-partition days. Irfan, Zakir, Salamat, Ajmal and Afzai are the modern Pakistani intellectuals who, in the present-day Pakistan, are unable to do anything, with their notions of communism, secularism and revolutionary terrorism, to reform the nation. Intezar ends the novel on a desquieting note which seems to ask a question: "who will be a Prophet of Peace and Love now, amidst so much of violence and anarchy? When will a new Buddha or Gandhi come to re-create the new *bastis* (nations/civilisations) of truth, love and peace?

Similarly, Manzoor Ehtesham's novel *Dastan-E-Lapata* raises several uneasy questions about the discourse of secularism in the Indian context. Zamir Ahmed Khan is a hypersensitive middle-aged business man who longs only for love and "humanity" around him and is not ready to be an active participant in the so-called "progress" and "development" of the country. He, ironically, becomes one of the *"Lapatas"* (lost people) who are unwanted in the present-day socio-political system. To him, the inner (spiritual) progress must precede the external progress. Zamir wants to rule over his "self first and that turns out of be his greatest flaw in the present times. It is an experimental kind of Hindi novel in which external domain of history and politics is shown to have been in conflict with the inner domain of the protagonist. In the inner domain lie spirituality and truth-which to Zamir, are and must be "the essential ingredients of real progress and happiness" (DL, p. 26). This also implies Gandhiji's Swaraj (i.e. control over one's senses and desires) - a precondition for spiritualising the inner as well as the outer domain to bring about a national *swaraj* in which the discourses of communalism (majority / minority) are dissolved into nothingness. It critiques the excesses of faith only to highlight the need to follow the true religion which is present in all the faiths of the world - the religion of truth, humanity and love. In *Dastan-E-Lapata,* Ehtesham doesn't have to beat the tom-tom of secularism in order to represent his anxieties and doubts about the condition of nation question. To him the inner space (the spiritual or the sacred space) is very much related to the nation-space which has to be secular in the context of India.

Thus, we can say that secularism as a Western ideology co-opts some of the modern/postmodern critics, writers/artists who valorise the secular reason over the true spirit of religion or *dharma.* And they come in marauding hoardes armed with deadly "theory" to frighten people into submission. But there are resisters also like Intezar Husain, Rahi Masoom Raza, Manzoor Ehtesham, Taslima Nasrin etc. who are constantly interrogating, and to a great extent, subverting the Western model of secularism and trying to reconstruct a new *samvad* (dialogue) between the true spirit of religion and secularism.[24] True religion, whatever may be its external form, implies and subsumes secularism if it connotes a policy of peaceful co-existence. It is in this sense that the writers writing the nation in the Indian subcontinent have to make a conscious choice of creating the sacred spaces in process of secularising the literacy spaces. The peculiar Indian civilisational situation cancels the binary of the sacred and the secular, or shouldn't we go back to the writings of Kabir, Nanak, Tukaram, Tulasi, Bulle Shaha and others in order to cleanse the sacred space of communalism and politicisation which is a *sine qua non* for building a truly secular nation that the Indian civilisation ever was and is. If literature promotes the principles of truth, goodness and beauty, it is bound to be sacred and hence secular.

References

1. In order to perspectivise the various challenges to Indian experiment with "secularism", I have selected for analysis some provocative novels written by Muslim writers such as *The Satanic Verses* by Salman Rushdie, *Lajja* by Taslima Nasrin, *Basti* by Interzar Hussain and *Dastan-E-Lapata* by Manzoor Ehtesham.
2. To see the alliance between "theory" and the discourse of secularism, please refer to Homi Bhabha's "Unpacking My Library.. Again" (pp. 199-211), *The Post-Colonial Question - Common Skies: Divided Horizons* (Eds, Iain Chambers and Lidia Curti) London, Routledge, 1996. In this essay, Homi K Bhabha makes a case for a subaltern secularism!!. Mention can

be made of such tracts of secularism as *Khaki Shorts, Saffron Flags* (New Delhi; Orient Longman, 1993) written by five secularists, Amartya Sen's *The Threat to Secular India* (Calcutta, Socio-Economic Research Institute, 1990) and K.N. Panikkar's *Communalism in India: a Perspective for Intervention* (New Delhi, People's Publishing House 1991). Rustam Bharucha's *The Question of Faith* (New Delhi, Orient Longman, 1993) is a bold attempt to re-define secularism in the context of Indian civilisation where "faith" reigns over the minds of the people. Even Asghar Ali Engineer's latest project, *Towards Secular India,* aims at reconstructing the Indian society "in the context of growing communalism, regionalism and related issues", not at the cost of religion. Also mentionable are Rizwan Salim's *"Slave mentality in Indian artists"* (The Hind Times, 16/3/97, p. 13) and Bhai Mahavir's, *"The Prophet and the other Religion"* (The Hind Times 16/3/97, p. 13).

3. Mushir-Ul-Haq, Islam in Secular India, Shimla, Indian Institute of Advanced Study, 1972, p. 4, *ibid*, p. 2.
4. *Ibid.*
5. Imtiaz Ahmed, "Defining minorities in India", The Hindustan Times dt. 17/10/96, p. 13, and "The Problems of Indian Muslims", *Bharatiya Musalman : Mithak Aur Yathartha* (Ed. Raj Kishore), New Delhi, Vani Prakashan, pp. 24-37.
6. Imtiaz Ahmed, "Defining minorityism in India", The Hindustan Times, 17/10/96, p. 13.
7. Javed Akhtar, "The Muslims and The Hindus Have Similar Problems", *Samchetana,* 135-36, No. 1-2, 1995, p. 20.
8. Maulana Wahiduddin Khan, "Spiritual Goal of Islam" The Hindustan Times, dt, 26/9/95, p. 13. Also see his article, *'Mussalmano Ka Rajanitik Darbhagya"* (Political Misfortune of the Muslims). Dainik Jagran, dt. 22/2/97, p. 6. Also see Z.A. Nizami's "Gandhi and Islam", Journal of Gandhi Smriti and Darshan Samiti, Vol. 1, No. 1 and 2, July, 1996, pp. 89-95.
9. M.K. Gandhi, *An Autobiography* or *The Story of My Experiments with Truth,* Ahmedabad, Navjivan, 1995, First published, 1927, p. 420.
10. M.K. Gandhi, "Hinduism" in *Young India,* 6 October, 1921, quoted in Mahatma Gandhi, *What is Hinduism?,* New Delhi, National Book Trust, 1995, p. 7.
11. M.K. Gandhi, *Young India,* 9 January, 1930, pp. 13-14 cited in M.K. Gandhi. *The Way to Communal Harmony,* Ahmedabad, Navijivan, 1994, First published in 1963, p. 116.
12. Sayyid Iqbal Ali, *Sayyid Ahmad Khan Ka Safaranamah-i-Punjab,* Aligarh, 1884, p. 94. cited in Mushir-Ul-Haq, *Muslim Politics in Modern India* (1857-1947), Meerut, Meenakshi Prakashan, 1970, p. 30.
13. Cited in Mushir-Ul-Haq's *Muslim Politics in Modern India* (1857-1947), p. 31.
14. *Ibid.,* p. 31.

15. See Anwar Moazzam, "Religious Aspects of Abul Kalam Azad's Thought"? *Towards Secular India,* Vol. 2, No. 4, Oct-Dec. 1996, pp. 98-116.
16. Salman Rushdie, *The Satanic Verses,* London, Viking, 1988. Hereafter referred to as *SV* with page numbers in parentheses. Rushdie working under the spell of West-sponsored "secular theory" - blasphemes Islam with the convenient postmodernist tools such as magical realism, metafiction, parody and self-reflexivity. Will the West ever allow a Virgin Mary to be portrayed as a slut under the camouflage of "magic realism" or "freedom of expression" or "secularism"?
17. Nigel Wheale, (Ed.), *The Postmodern Arts: In Introductory Reader,* London, Routledge, 1996, p. 193. See also pp. 193-203 for Nigel Wheale's spirited defence of Rushdie's *The Satanic Verses.* This anthology includes yet another entry on *The Satanic Verses* by the noted deconstructionist scholar Gayatri Chakravarti Spivak who justifies Rushdie's controversial book by relating it to the forces of secular reason in Europe!! (see her article *"Reading The Satanic Verses"* pp. 221- 242 in the same anthology).
18. Daniel Easterman, *'Still Lives'* pp. 210-22 in *New Jerusalems: Reflections on Islam, Fundamentalism and The Rushdie Affair,* London, Grafton. 1993, p. 219.
19. Lisa Appignanesi and Sara Maitland (eds), *The Rushdie File,* London, Fourth Estate, 1989, p. 95.
20. Taslima Nasrin, *Lajja (Shame)* Tr. Tutul Gupta, New Delhi, Penguin Books, 1994, first Published in 1993. Hereafter referred to as L with page nos. in parentheses.
21. Taslima Nasrin, "On Islamic Fundamentalism" (Taslima Nasrin's speech delivered at Harvard University on 28 April, 1996) *New Quest,* Vol. 119, Sept-Oct. 1996, p. 292.
22. Intezar Husain, *Basti* (Hindi Tr. Namrata Burman and Abdul Mughani), New Delhi, Radhakrishna, 1982. The subsequent references are to this text with page nos. in parentheses.
23. Manzoor Ehtesham, *Dastan-E-Lapata,* New Delhi, Rajkamal Prakashan, 1995, Hereafter cited in the paper as DL with page nos in parentheses.
24. For further analysis, please refer to my "Writing Nation - The Nation-Question In Muslim Writers" *"Towards Secular India"* Vol. 2, No. 3, July-Sept. 1996, pp. 11-32.

13

Secularism Betrayed

—*Justice Hosbet Suresh*

The Supreme Court (Varma J) in the case of Dr Ramesh Yeshwant Prabhoo (1995 (7) SCALE 1) held Dr Prabhoo and Bal Thackeray guilty of corrupt practice having appealed for votes on the ground of religion (Hindu religion) u/s. 123 (3) of the Representation of People Act, 1951. However, in the next judgement (1995 (7) SCALE 30) Manohar Joshi was exonerated. The Supreme Court did not change the law, but in the process made observations which have the effect of virtually giving licence to communal parties to invoke religion in electoral battle. Now for a detailed analysis of the judgements.

Dr Ramesh Prabhoo had been held guilty of corrupt practice u/s. 123 sub-section (3) and (3A) of the Act, by the Bombay High Court in Election Petition No. l of 1988 (pertaining to election held on 13th December, 1987). In that case, Bal Thackeray was held to be his agent and as such with his consent had appealed for votes on the ground of Dr Prabhoo's religion and that the said appeal had promoted or tended to promote feelings of enmity and hatred between different communities. Prabhoo's election was declared to be void on the ground u/s. 100 (1) (b) of the Act. Bal Thackeray was named u/s. 99 of the Act. Justice Varma dismissed both the appeals by Prabhoo and Bal Thackeray.

Manohar Joshi's election was also declared void u/s 100 (1) (b) of the Act in Election Petition No. 24 of 1990 (pertaining to election held in February 1990), by the Bombay High Court. In the election rally held on 24th February, 1990, Bal Thackeray, Pramod Mahajan (BJP) and others including Manohar Joshi had addressed the meeting appealing for votes. Bal Thackeray's speech on that occasion (and on earlier occasions) was not different from the speeches delivered in Ramesh Prabhoo's campaign. However, Varma J held that Bal Thackeray was not the agent of Manohar Joshi so as to attract the provisions of S. 100 (1) (b) of the Act and that Manohar Joshi's appeal was not an appeal on the basis of his religion. Varma J thus allowed the appeal of Manohar Joshi. In both these matters it was made known to the Supreme Court that Bal Thackeray was the leader of Shiv Sena.

In Prabhoo's case, Varma J construing the manner of appeal for votes in the name of religion (u/s.123 (3) of the Act) held that the words used need not be direct, and if indirect but lead to an inference that the appeal is on the basis of religion would be sufficient to invoke the prohibition u/s. 123 (3) of the Act. In terms he said: "The substance of the speech and the manner in which it is meant to be understood by the audience determines its nature, and not the camouflage by an artistic use of the language. For understanding the meaning and effect of the speech, the context has to be found in the speech itself and not outside it with reference to any other background unless the speech itself imports any earlier fact in the context of that speech. The speech has also not to be construed in the abstract or in the manner in which it would be construed in the debate. Care must be taken to remember that the public speeches during election campaign ordinarily are addressed to audience comprised of common men and, therefore, the manner in which it would be understood by such an audience has to be kept in view."

However, in Manohar Joshi's case, the speech which was held to have been proved was the speech delivered by him on 24th February, 1990 which he had, *inter-alia,* stated that the first Hindu State will be established in Maharashtra. Varma J held that "*however despicable be such a statement* it cannot be said to amount to an appeal for votes on the ground of his religion." He further observed that was at best the "expression" of "such a hope", though "we would express our *disdain at the entertaining of such a thought of such a stance in a political leader* of any shade in the country." Though the statement was "despicable" and to be looked at with "disdain", in Varma J's opinion it was not a corrupt practice "to permit negation of the electoral verdict." What was overlooked in this case, is his own observations in Prabhoo's case, as set out above. We are made to believe that in Manohar Joshi's case, we have to ignore that he was addressing an election rally in which Bal Thackeray and Pramod Mahajan had given the most provocative speeches. We have to overlook the manner in which it was meant to be understood, and the manner in which it would be understood by such an audience. We have to forget the surrounding circumstances and that was the final rally before closing of election campaign 48 hours before the date of election. We have to imagine that in such a rally the audience had only gathered to hear Manohar Joshi (in isolation) expressing a pious — but *disdani-fiil, despicable* — hope that a Hindu State would be established!

Why disdainful ? Why despicable ? The Learned Judge has not explained. But coming from a Judge from the Apex Court, it is legitimate to presume that the Judge had *S R Bommai* Vs. *Union of India* (1994 Vol. 3 SCC 1) in mind. For, it is in that case a nine judges Bench of the Supreme Court has clearly spelt out that our Constitution prohibits the establishment of a theocratic State. Yet a political leader could be permitted to express in public — in an election rally — a hope that he would establish a Hindu State, though such a desire was opposed to the unalterable basic feature of the Constitution!

In Prabhoo's case, it was argued that the appeal for votes on the basis of religion, in order to make it prohibitive u/s. 123(3) of the Act, should necessarily be related to the religion of the candidate himself. Accordingly, it was contended that it did not prohibit the candidate from seeking vote in the name of a religion to which the candidate did not belong. Thus, a Muslim candidate contesting on behalf of BJP/Shiv Sena could appeal for votes in the name of Hindu religion, as the appeal is not on the basis of "his" religion. Similarly, it was argued that appeal to refrain from voting must also be on the basis of the religion of that other candidate, and then only it could be said that such an appeal fails within S.123 (3) of the Act. That is to say, a BJP candidate contesting against any one who happens to be a Hindu, could say that "Islam (or for that matter Christianity) is no good for us" and therefore vote for BJP, and such an appeal would not be a corrupt practice u/s. 123 (3) of the Act. Varma J seems to have accepted these contentions when he says: "There can be no doubt that the word "his" used in sub-section (3) must have significance and it cannot be ignored or equated with the word "any" to bring within the net of sub-section (3) any appeal in which there is any reference to religion. The religion forming the basis of the appeal to vote or refrain from voting for any person, must be of that candidate for whom the appeal to vote or refrain from voting is made. This is clear from the plain language of sub-section (3) and this is the only manner in which the word "his" used therein can be construed". He further says: "It is thus clear that for soliciting votes for a candidate, the appeal prohibited is that which is made on the ground of religion of the candidate for whom the votes are sought; and when the appeal is to refrain from voting for any candidate, the prohibition is against an appeal on the ground of the religion of that other candidate. The first is a positive appeal and the second a negative appeal. There is no ambiguity in subsection (3) and it clearly indicates the particular religion on the basis of which an appeal to vote or refrain from voting for any person is prohibited under sub-section (3)".

These observations are directly contrary to what is stated in *S R Bommai (Supra)* at Para 149:

> *"With respect, we are unable to accept this contention. Reading subsections (3) and (3A) of Sections 123 together, it is clear that appealing to any religion or seeking votes in the name of any religion is prohibited by the two provisions. To read otherwise is to subvert the intent and purpose of the said provisions. What is more, assuming that the interpretation placed by the learned counsel is correct, it cannot control the content of secularism which is accepted by and is implicit in our Constitution."*

Again in R Prabhoo's case, it was argued that in order to sustain the charge of corrupt practice u/sub-section (3), mere appeal is not enough, but there should be a further element of prejudicial effect on public order. Varma J has rightly negated this contention. So also he has held that the appeal need not be a direct appeal. Further, after 20.9.61, since the Act stood amended, even one appeal could be sufficient to bring home the charge. Yet Manohar Joshi's appeal was not held to be impermissible.

It was argued that S. 123 (3) of the Act was *ultra vires* Art. 25 of the Constitution of India which guarantees freedom of conscience and propagation of religion. This contention was not accepted. But the Learned Judge takes into account certain statements made by A K Sen in the Parliamentary Debates. *Inter-alia,* the following statements were relied on i.e. *"But in the guise of framing an electoral law, no fundamental right of the citizen can be taken away. That is what*

I am saying. The right to preserve one's language cannot be taken away by an election law. That is as clear as daylight"......But we are not debating here - on the aesthetics of language or the philosophy of language; nor are we here to debate the fundamental rights of a citizen to preserve his own language and culture. Fortunately, that is guaranteed to every man and woman in this country as it is not elsewhere..."

From this, Varma J infers, "The clarification given in the speech of the Law Minister clearly shows that a speech for the protection of fundamental rights, preservation of own language, religion and culture, etc. are not forbidden by sub-section (3) of Section 123, and the limit is narrow to the extent indicated". Thereafter, he proceeds further to say that *"mention of religion as such in an election speech is not forbidden by subsection (3)"* so long as it does not amount to an appeal to vote for a candidate on the ground of his religion or refrain from voting on the ground of other candidate's religion.

He then says:

"It cannot be doubted that an election speech made in conformity with the fundamental right to freedom of religion guaranteed under Articles 25 to 30 of the Constitution, cannot be treated as anti-secular to be prohibited by sub-section (3) of Section 123, unless it falls within the narrow net of the prohibition indicated earlier. It is obvious that a speech referring to religion during election campaign with a secular stance in conformity with the fundamental right to freedom of religion can be made without being hit by the prohibition contained in sub-section (30), if it does not contain an appeal to vote for any candidate because of his religion or to refrain from voting for any candidate because of his religion. When it is said that politics and religion do not mix, it obviously does not mean that even such permissible political speeches are forbidden. This is the meaning and true scope of sub-section (3) of Section 123 of the Act".

I do not understand how on an election platform, a candidate can told of religion and call them "permissible speeches". Why should anyone talk of religion in an election rally? What is election? or electoral process? Is it a matter of politics? Or is it a matter of religion? Why do people attend an election meeting? Not for a religious discourse ! What is the meaning of the word "propagate" in Art. 25? "Propagate", for what purpose? How does anyone "propagate" religion without an element of persuasion? Is persuasion not an appeal? Varma J's opinion does not answer any of these questions. It only assumes that just because a candidate has a fundamental right under Art. 25, he could legitimately exercise the same in an election rally.

In fact, the scope of secularism and in particular Article 25 has been elaborately dealt with in S R *Bommai* and those observations should have the binding effect on Varma J, sitting in a bench of three judges. It is said *in S R Bommai:* (Per Sawant J) (Para 148)

"One thing which prominently emerges from the above discussion on secularism under our Constitution is that whatever the attitude of the State towards the religion, religious sects and denominations - cannot be mixed with any secular activity of the State. In fact, the encroachment of religion into secular activities is strictly prohibited. This is evident from the provisions of the Constitution to which we have made reference above. The State's tolerance of religion or religions does not make it either a religious or a theocratic State. When the State allows citizens to practise and profess their religions, it does not either explicity or implicity allow them to introduce religion into non-religious and secular activities of the State. The freedom and tolerance of religion is only to the extent of permitting pursuit of spiritual life which is different from the secular life. The latter falls in the exclusive domain of the affairs of the State. This is also clear from sub-section (3) of section 123 of the Representation of the People Act, 1951 which prohibits an appeal by "a candidate or his agent or by any other person with the consent of the candidate or his election agent to vote or refrain from voting for any person on the ground of his religion, race, caste, community or language or the use of or appeal to religious symbols.

More elaborately, (Per Ramaswamy J) after explaining that political activities include matters relating to the management of affairs of State and activities pertaining to parties to control those who manage the affairs of a State, it was observed: (Para 187)

"Politics in positively secular State is to get over their religion, in other words', in politics a political party should neither invoke religion nor be dependent on it for support or sustenance. Constitution ensures to the individual to protect religion, right to belief or propagate teachings conducive for secular living, later to be controlled by the State for betterment of human life and progress. Positive secularism concerns with such aspects of human life."

Again (at Para 190):

"Article 25 inhibits the Government to patronise a particular religion as State religion overtly or covertly. Political party is, therefore, positively

enjoined to maintain neutrality in religious beliefs and prohibit practices derogatory to the Constitution and the laws. Introduction of religion into politics is not merely a negation of the constitutional mandates but also a positive is not merely in negation of the constitutional mandates but also positive violation of the constitution obligation, duty, responsibility and positive prescription of prohibition specifically enjoyed by the Constitution and the R P Act. A political party that seeks to secure power through a religious policy or caste orientation policy - disintegrates the people on grounds of religion and caste. It divides the people and disrupts the social structure on grounds of religion and caste which is obnoxious and anathema to the constitutional culture and basic features. Appeal on grounds of religion offends secular democracy."

In other words, it should have been clear to anyone that under our Constitution, there shall be no religion in politics just as there shall be no politics in religion. (Para 196)

"In a secular democracy, in other words a flagrant breach of constitutional features of secular democracy. It is, therefore, imperative that the religion and caste should not be introduced into politics by any political party, association or an individual and it is imperative to prevent religious and caste pollution of politics". A religious talk, may be a dissertation or a discourse or even hoping for a religious State, on the basis of any so-called exercise of fundamental right u/Article 25, in an election meeting which is a political activity, would undoubtedly pollute politics, and can only be construed as an appeal to vote on the basis of religion.

Varma J, thereafter sought to lay down the meaning of "Hindutva" and Hinduism", all because he wanted to convey that reference to "Hindutva" or "Hinduism" or "mention of any other religion" in an election speech does not bring it within the net of S. 123 (3) or (3A) of the Act. As pointed out above, this proposition itself is contrary to the dictum laid down in *S R Bommai.*

Even otherwise there was no justification for going into this exercise for he himself has said that what is relevant is the speech, *"the* manner in which it was likely to be understood by the audience to which *the speech was addressed"* and the words are not to be construed in the abstract. If that is so, whatever be the meaning which the speaker wanted to convey would be meaningless inasmuch as no one could say with certainty that the speech would be understood the way the speaker wanted it to be understood.

Varma J thereafter summarises "Hindutva", "Hinduism" in about four pages (printed), alrnost reminding me of Namboodripad's case (AIR 1970 SC 2015) in which C J Hidayatullah performed a similar exercise of summarising Communism and dialectical materialism in about four pages — needless to say, both being an exercise in futility. Neither "Hinduism" nor "Communism" or for that matter any philosophy or religion can be confined to a few paragraphs in a legal judgement, for setting out its true meaning and content. After considering one or two judgements of the Constitutional Bench (not any matter arising in an election petition) Varma J observes:

"These Constitution Bench decisions, after a detailed discussion, indicate that no precise meaning can be ascribed to the terms "Hindu", "Hindutva" and "Hinduism"; and no meaning in the abstract can confine it to the narrow limits of religion alone, excluding the content of Indian culture and heritage. It is also indicated that the term "Hindutva" is related more to the way of life of the people in the sub-continent. It is difficult to appreciate how in the face of these decisions the term "Hindutva" or "Hinduism" per se, in the abstract can be assumed to mean and be equated with narrow fundamentalist Hindu religious bigotry, or to be construed to fall within the prohibition in sub-sections (3) and (3A) of Section l23 of the R.P. Act".

What are the implications of these observations? According to the Learned Judge, what is prohibited u/s. 123(3) and (3A) of the Act is "Hindu Fundamentalism" and not Hindutva as a way of life. The Learned Judge himself has seen the text of the speeches given by Bal Thackeray, in respect of which he could not help *"recording our distress at this kind of speeches given by a top leader of a political party."......"The offending speeches in the present case discarded the cherished values of our rich cultural heritage and tended to erode the secular polity."*

But the question is, how would the Judge categorise the speeches given by Bal Thackeray? He has held that the speeches would fall within the scope of S.123 (3) of the Act. Therefore, can it be regarded as speeches delivered by a Hindu fundamentalist? What fundamentalism of the Hindu religion did these speeches sought to convey? If one analyses these speeches made by Bal Thackeray, there is no mention of any fundamental concepts of Hindu state of mind. Neither BJP nor Shiv-Sena can be considered as a party of fundamentalists. On the other hand, in every religious group, there are fundamentalists. They are opposed to any reform in their own religion. But they may not be interested in any election. They may not even bother about the other religious groups. When BJP or Shiv Sena appealed for votes, they did so not on the basis of Hindu fundamentalism, but on the basis of Hindus v/s. Muslims and that this shall be a Hindu State and Muslims and other groups shall only stay here as subordinate citizens. The idea is to maintain a permanent divide so that the majority community shall always have the right to rule over the minority communities, the communities being divided not on the basis of political or economic ideologies, but on the basis of religion.

The Learned Judge concludes:

"It is, therefore, a fallacy and an error of law to proceed on the assumption that any reference to Hindutva or Hinduism in a speech makes it automatically a speech based on the Hindu religion as opposed to the ether religions or that the use of words "Hindutva" or "Hinduism" per se depict an attitude hostile to all persons practising any religion other than the Hindu religion. It is the kind of use made of these words and the meaning sought to be conveyed in the speech which has to be seen and unless such a construction leads to the conclusion that these words were used to appeal for votes for a Hindu candidate on the ground that he is a Hindu or not to vote for a candidate because he is not a Hindu, the mere fact that these words are used in the speech would not bring it within the prohibition of sub-section (3) or (3A) or Section 123. It may well be, that these words are used in a speech to promote secularism or to emphasise the way of life of the Indian people and the Indian culture or ethos, or to criticise the policy of any political party as discriminatory or intolerant".

The moot question is why should a candidate speak of Hindutva in an election rally? Why should anyone speak in any election meeting, if not for seeking votes? So also for what purpose does the audience attend an election rally? Is it for learning Hindu way of life? Or to knew what a candidate stands for and on what basis he is seeking votes in his favour? If a Hindu candidate says: *"I am a Hindu, please vote for me"* it becomes an appeal for "a *way of life of the Indian people and the Indian Culture*". What about Christianity? Is it a way of life of the Indian people or not? What about Islamic way of life? Is it a part of Indian culture or not? So if what the Learned Judge says is right, candidates belonging to each of these religious denominations can speak of their way of life, necessarily based on their respective religious faiths, beliefs, and texts and seeks votes and that is permissible!

The Learned Judge says:

"The fallacy is in the assumption that a speech in which reference is made to Hindutva or Hinduism must be a speech on the ground of Hindu religion so that if the candidate for whom the speech is made happens to be a Hindu, it must necessarily amount to a corrupt practice under subsection (3) and/or sub-section (3A) of Section 123 of the R P Act".

With respect, the fallacy is in assuming that in an election rally the candidate and the audience would be interested in preaching and learning Indian way of life or Indian Culture or Indian ethos!

In Manohar Joshi's Case, the High Court had indicated its perception of the nature of trial of the election petition as under:

"It must be noted that this Election Petition is not based upon individual acts of Respondent or his Election Agent or any other person with his consent. This petition is based upon the above-mentioned plank and/or policy decision of the Shiv Sena and BJP and the campaigning by the party and the Respondent on the basis of that plank......" Varma J brushed aside this as *"an erroneous impression of the High Court which had led to serious errors..."* In other words, the plank theory did not appeal to Varma J. The only meaning of this is that whatever be the plank or policy of a party, even if it contains religious appeal, the High Court cannot go into it and the corrupt practice required to be established should be of the candidate, and not of the party to which he belongs. In other words, the party can indulge in any corrupt practice and that cannot be attributed to the candidate. The Learned Judge thinks that such allegations have *"no relevance for the pleading and proof of corrupt practice u/sub-section (3) and (3A) of S. 123 of the Act."*

If what the learned Judge says is right, it will lead to an absurd situation wherein the political parties can carry on the most vicious campaign and the candidate has just to keep his mouth shut. Neither the party nor the candidate can be held liable for corrupt practice! Ours is a parliamentary democracy and must necessarily function through political parties having distinct policies and programmes. If a policy and programme of a political party is anti-secular, it cannot be said that its candidate will have a different policy and programme.

Either he survives by the party or he fails. It is here what the Supreme Court says in *S R Bommai* becomes relevant: (Para 188)

"For a political party or an organisation that seeks to influence the electorates to promote or accomplishing success at an election for governance of parliamentary form of Government, the principles are those embedded in the Directive Principles of the Constitution vis-à-vis the Fundamental Rights and the Fundamental Duties in Part IV A and should abide by the Constitution and promote tolerance, harmony and the spirit of commonness amongst all the people of India transcending religious, linguistic, regional or sectional diversities and to preserve the rich heritage of our composite culture, to develop humanism, spirit of reformation and to abstain from violence. Therefore, the manifesto of a political party should be consistent with these fundamental and basic features of the Constitution, secularism, socio-economic and political justice, fraternity, unity and national integrity".

Referring to S. 123(3) and (3A) of the Act, the Court said: (Para 189)

"Apolitical party, therefore, should not ignore the fundamental features of the Constitution and the laws. Even its manifesto with all sophistication or felicity of its language, a political party cannot escape constitutional mandate and negates the abiding faith and solemn responsibility and duty undertaken to uphold the Constitution and laws after it was registered under Section 29-A. Equally it/they/should not sabotage the same basic features of the Constitution either influencing the electoral process or working the Constitution or the law. The political party or the political executive securing the governance of the State by securing majority in the legislature through the battle of ballot throughout its tenure by its actions and programmes, it is required to abide by the Constitution and the laws in letter and spirit".

Further, (para 252)

"Political parties, group of persons or individuals who would seek to influence electoral process with a view to come to political power, should abide by the Constitution and the laws including secularism, sovereignty, integrity of the nation. They/he should not mix religion with politics. Religious tolerance and fraternity are basic features and postulates of the Constitution as a scheme for national integration and sectional or religious unity. Programmes or principles evolved by political parties based on religion amounts to recognising religion as a part of the political governance

which the Constitution expressly prohibited. It violates the basic features of the Constitution."

Dealing with political parties indulging in anti-secular activities, the Court said: (Per Jeevan Reddy J Para 310)

"Given the above position, it is clear that if any party or organisation seeks to fight the elections on the basis of a plank which has the proximate effect of eroding the secular philosophy of the Constitution it would certainly be guilty of following an unconstitutional course of action. Political parties are formed and exist to capture or share State power. That is their aim. They may be associations of individuals but one cannot ignore the functional relevance. An association of individuals may be devoted to propagation of religion; it would be a cultural organisation. They are not aimed at acquiring State power, whereas a political party does. That is one of its main objectives. That is what we mean by saying "functional relevance". One cannot conceive of a democratic form of Government without the political parties. They are a part of the political system and constitutional scheme. May, they are integral to the governance of a democratic society. If the Constitution does not recognise, it does not permit, mixing religion and State power. Both must be kept apart, that is the constitutional injunction. None can say otherwise so long as this Constitution governs this country. Introducing religion into politics is to introduce an impermissible element into body politic and an imbalance in our constitutional system. If a political party espousing a particular religion comes to power, that religion tends to become, in practice, the official religion. All other religions come to acquire a secondary status, at any rate, a less favourable position. This would be plainly antithetical to Articles 14 to 16, 25 and the entire constitutional scheme adumbrated hereinabove. Under our Constitution, no party or organisation can simultaneously be a political and a religious party. It has to be either. Same would be the position, if a party or organisation acts and/or behaves by word of mouth, print or in any other manner to bring about the said effect, it would equally be guilty of an act of unconstitutionality. It would have no right to function as a political party. The fact that a party may be entitled to go to people seeking a mandate for a drastic amendment of the Constitution or its replacement by another Constitution is wholly irrelevant in the context. We do not know how the Constitution can be amended so as to remove secularism from the basic structure of the Constitution. Nor do we know how the present Constitution can be replaced by another; it is enough for us to know that the Constitution does not provide for such a course — that it does not provide for its own demise".

In Manohar Joshi's case, the Learned Judge did not accept the submission that Bal Thackeray was his agent, because Bal Thackeray was his leader. He said that agency *"implies a subservient role of the person to whom consent is given and the authority of the given of the consent to control the actions of the agent. It is difficult to ascribe to an acknowledged leader of the party a role subservient to the candidate set up by that party in as much as the candidate is ordinarily in no position to control the actions of his leader".*

It is difficult to appreciate the notion of agency being construed as in a commercial transaction. An agent is the one who acts for another. The leader of a party canvasses for his party candidate, and in law he should be considered as an agent of his candidate. The Learned Judge thinks that the candidate must be able to control the actions of the agent, and then only the notion of agency would apply. But why? If the candidate acts and if someone else acts for him and on his behalf, where the consent is express or implied, the latter becomes an agent of the former. If the candidate is unable to control the act of the agent because the agent is the leader, the consent does not stand vitiated. He is still his agent and not a stranger.

The Learned Judge was construing S.100(1)(b) and 100(1)(d) of the Act: The relevant provisions are as under:

"(1) Grounds for declaring election to be void — (1) Subject to the provisions of sub-section (2) if the High Court is of the opinion —

(a) ...

(b) that any corrupt practice has been committed by a returned candidate or his election agent or by any other person with the consent of a returned candidate or his election agent.

(c) ...

(d) that the result of the election, in so far as it concerns a returned candidate has been materially affected —

(i) ...

(ii) by any corrupt practice committed in the interests of the returned candidate by an agent other than his election agent.

(iii) ...

(iv) ...

(2) If in the opinion of the High Court, a returned candidate has been guilty by an agent, other than his election agent, of any corrupt practice but the High Court is satisfied —

(a) *that no such corrupt practice was committed at the election by the candidate or his election agent, and every such corrupt practice was committed contrary to the orders, and without the consent, of the candidate or his election agent;*

(b) *omitted;*

(c) *that the candidate and his election agent took all reasonable means for preventing the commission of corrupt practices at the election; and*

(d) *that in all other respects the election was free from any corrupt practice on the part of the candidate or any of his agents, then the High Court may decide that the election of the returned candidate is not void.*

If one analyses the above, it would show that there could be four categories of persons who could be committing corrupt practice: Under Cl. (b),

(1) The candidate:

(2) his election agent;

(3) any other person with the consent of a returned candidate or his election agent; and, under Cl. (d)(ii),

(4) and agent other than his election agent.

Significantly, under Cl.(b), the third category of person has not been referred to as "agent". But he has been referred to as a person who has the consent of the candidate or of his election agent. If any corrupt practice is committed by any of these category of persons under Cl.(b), the liability is absolute and the election is liable to be set aside.

However, under Cl. (d) one more category of persons has been mentioned. He has been referred to as an agent, but not the election agent. If this person commits any corrupt practice, and the candidate or his election agent is not guilty of corrupt practice, the candidate gets a chance to say that this agent committed corrupt practice without his consent and contrary to his order and that he took all reasonable steps for preventing the commission of corrupt practice. Further under Cl.(d), the election petitioner has to prove that the result of the election has been materially affected by the act of such an agent.

What the learned Judge did was that Bal Thackeray at best would fall within the scope of Cl.(d)(ii), but the petitioner has not pleaded or proved that the result was materially affected by the speech of Bal Thackeray.

Therefore, the question is, in which category, the leader of a political party could be placed under these provisions. Certainly, he would not come under Cl.(d)(ii) because the candidate would not be able to order him not to commit corrupt practice nor would be able to take any step reasonable or otherwise, to prevent the leader from committing any corrupt practice. Similarly, when a leader himself canvasses for a candidate or for his party, there can be no question of pleading and proving that the results were materially affected by the presence of such a leader. That is the natural consequence of any campaign when the leader himself comes to the field for canvassing.

Clause (d)(ii) applies to such an agent who is not a regular campaigner. He could be a person from amongst the audience who is requested to speak and if he transgresses his limits, he can be asked to stop and all steps can be taken to see that he does not indulge in any corrupt practice. Such a person could be someone who is influential in the locality and his help is sought, but who can always be controlled from going beyond certain limits. That is why in such a situation, the candidate gets a chance to prove that he was not responsible for the corrupt practice and that he had done his best to prevent such acts. It is natural that in such a situation, the petitioner knows that even if the returned candidate has not committed corrupt practice, it was that other agent who has committed corrupt practice, and because of the acts of that other agent, the returned candidate could win and the results were materially affected. Such a situation would not arise where the leader himself canvasses for his party candidate.

Analysed this way, which appears to be the natural meaning of Cl.(d)(ii) and sub-clause (2), Bal Thackeray would fall within the scope of the third category of persons mentioned under Cl.(b). He is that other person, not an agent, and the consent is express or implied. If he indulges in corrupt practice for getting his candidate elected, and the candidate is unseated, he has to thank himself for the same.

Any other construction of these provisions would result in such an illogical and irrational situation, that the leader of a political party can indulge in all sorts of corrupt practice for and on behalf of his party candidate while the candidate himself remains a silent approver of what his leader does, and the election remains valid. In other words, according to Varma J, the party plank and the party leader remain above the law. The Learned Judge says:

"Thus even if the acknowledged leaders of a party have committed any corrupt practice which results in benefit to the returned candidate then on proof of the benefit having materially affected the election result in favour of the candidate, his election would be set aside on the ground under Section 100(l)(d)(ii) of the R P Act".

Where is the question of proving that a leader's action has materially benefited his party candidate? In every election that is the natural consequence of a leader supporting his candidate. He is there to see that his candidate wins. With respect, a leader of a political party would fall, not under Cl.(d)(ii), but under Cl.(b).

It is unfortunate that, in effect, the two judgements tend to side-track all that has been said on secularism in *S R Bommai.* Secularism betrayed is democracy denied, and rule of religion is no substitute for rule of law.

Section - E

Struggle for Secularism

14

The Struggle Against Communalism: Defining a Positive Alternative

—ROHINI HENSMAN

Introduction

On 26 January 2015, the Bharatiya Janata Party-led National Democratic Alliance (NDA), Government of India marked Republic Day by publishing in newspapers across the country an advertisement which quoted the Preamble of the Constitution as saying, 'We, the people of India, having solemnly resolved to constitute India into a SOVEREIGN DEMOCRATIC REPUBLIC...' (*India Today,* 2015). The omission of the words 'SOCIALIST SECULAR' after 'Sovereign' was at first viewed by some as a faux pas, but after the Shiv Sena demanded that the words 'socialist' and 'secular' should be dropped from the preamble, and Union Telecommunications Minister Ravi Shankar Prasad indicated that the government wanted a debate on whether the words should be included, it became clear that this was not a faux pas but a very deliberate attempt to move towards an elimination of these words from the constitution. According to Sanjay Raut of the Shiv Sena, India had never been secular because 'Shiv Sena Chief Balasaheb Thackeray and before him Savarkar always said that if Pakistan was carved out after Partition for Muslims, then the rest of the country is a Hindu Rashtra'; and Prasad observed that the words were introduced in a constitutional amendment in 1976 during the Emergency, and remarked, 'What is wrong if there is a debate on these two words? Let us see what the nation wants' (*The Hindu,* 2015).

Opposition to secularism from these quarters is entirely predictable. What is more unexpected is the ammunition provided to them by high-profile liberals. For example, Ashish Nandy declared, 'I call myself an anti-secularist because I feel that the ideology and politics of secularism have more or less exhausted their possibilities'; he identified two meanings of the word, a dictionary definition which chalks out an area in public life where religion is not admitted, and a distinctively Indian definition, revolving around equal respect for all religions, which is what Gandhi had in mind (Nandy, 1998: 326-327). And in May 2014, after Narendra Modi's election victory, Shiv Visvanathan wrote, 'What secularism did was it enforced oppositions in a way that the middle class felt apologetic and unconfident about its beliefs, its perspectives. Secularism was portrayed as an upwardly mobile, drawing room discourse they were inept at. Secularism thus became a repression of the middle class. For the secularist, religion per se was taboo' (Visvanathan, 2015). If the publication of the Constitution without the words 'secular' and 'socialist' was pre-planned, it is almost certain that it was undertaken in the belief that such public intellectuals would endorse the omission.

There was indeed a vigorous debate on the two words in the days that followed the newspaper advertisements. Gopalkrishna Gandhi pointed out that while the original omission of 'secular' and 'socialist' in a constitution that was clearly secular and socialist did not matter, *deleting* the words once they had been included would be highly significant. 'The focus today is on the word; tomorrow it will be on the concept. "We do not have to be "secular" to be a democracy" can well be the next line. And who knows, "We do not have to be a democracy as long as we have good government" can follow. "Let us debate secularism" is part of the tablet which contains the following edicts: "Gita for National Book", "Good Governance Day instead of Christmas", "Sanskrit as a compulsory language in schools", "Shaurya Divas for Shahid Divas". It fuels the "Ram vs Haram polarisation" and "We want Godse mandirs and statues" demand' (Gandhi, 2015). Others, too, argued strongly that the words must stay.

Confusion over the meaning of secularism and its relevance in the Indian context is one factor hampering the struggle against communalism; the lack of a positive alternative to the communal vision of society, one which is not simply an absence of communalism but a goal which the vast majority finds attractive enough to fight for, is another. What is attempted here is to address these two problems. But before examining the meaning of secularism, it is necessary to clarify what we mean by religion and democracy.

Religion

Religion attempts to answer questions which cannot be answered by science – especially about the moral and ethical bases of human and social relationships – and communities grow around shared beliefs about these questions. However, beliefs and practices may differ widely amongst those claiming to follow the same religion; indeed, the same religion or sect can be interpreted in diametrically opposite ways by different adherents. To some adherents of all religions, their own religion demands a recognition of the importance of the spiritual dimension inherent in every human being, which makes human life of infinite value and implies that human needs – and therefore rights – are not simply physical, material ones. Recognition of the common, universal spirit shared by all implies recognition of the rights of all human beings not only to life and the means of life but also to freedom, dignity and autonomy. It means desiring for all human beings the respect and consideration that one desires for oneself. This progressive notion of religion is based on values of respect, solidarity and love which are not confined to those who share the same faith. It is incompatible with the urge to exercise power over others, and can therefore never seek to capture state power.

However, for many people – both those who practise religion and those who do not – the universal, spiritual dimension is completely absent. For them, religion is a hierarchical, authoritarian, male-dominated institution, which inculcates a sense of difference from and superiority to anyone who does not share their own beliefs. This kind of religion is the breeding-ground of communalism. Indifference to the suffering of those outside the community, abdication of the responsibility to think for oneself and make moral judgments, and the hierarchical, authoritarian structure and ideology, make it possible for those at the top to manipulate large masses of people to commit unspeakable atrocities in its name.

The resurgence of this kind of reactionary religion today, at a time of rapid social change and capitalist expansion, plays more than one role. Apart from the leaders, who see it as a means of bolstering their own power or capturing state power, wide strata of the population suffer a deep sense of alienation and insecurity as 'all that is solid melts into air,' and they are easily persuaded to cling to the illusory security promised by returning to a mythical past. For others, communalism offers a means of getting ahead in an increasingly competitive environment, obtaining everything from employment to school places for their children to physical elimination of their business rivals. Finally, for the lumpen cadres of organisations like the Bajrang Dal and Shiv Sena, the sense of power derived from the ability to loot, burn, rape and kill with impunity must be quite irresistible.

It is evident that followers of the progressive versions of different religions are much closer to one another, as well as to non-religious humanists, than they are to practitioners of the reactionary versions of their own religions. They have no problems relating to each other even in the closest ways, for example in the same family, and there is no question of violence between them. On the other hand, although the reactionary versions of all religions have much in common – for example, they are all sexist and homophobic, and all discourage independent thinking, in some cases even punishing dissenters with exclusion or worse – they also erect barriers against one other, each regarding the others as inferior and unworthy of the same rights. These are the sections which engage in so-called religious violence, but politically they have hardly anything in common with the progressives, and it is a serious mistake to lump them all together as 'religious' people.

Democracy

For most people in India, the meaning of 'democracy' is very simple: it means majority rule by means of representatives who are elected once every four or five years and are then more or less free to do as they wish. According to this conception, if the government elected by the majority then proceeds to allow or practise discrimination against, persecution of, or even extermination of various sections of the population, this behaviour is not in conflict with the norms of democratic government because they do, after all, represent the majority of the electorate.

This kind of majoritarian 'democracy' can go along with the violation of human rights and civil liberties, and is quite compatible with communalism, casteism and sexism. While the holding of elections may distinguish it from a more thoroughly authoritarian state, it is no guarantee of either liberty or equality. If this is what most people understand us to be advocating when we advocate 'democracy', they might well say, 'What's so great about it? We've had it since independence, and look at our condition today!' Alternatively, they might feel that a rabidly communal government is perfectly democratic provided it comes to power through an election.

Very different is the conception of constitutional democracy as the protection of certain basic human and democratic rights: the right to life, freedom from torture and arbitrary detention, the right to information, freedom of association, expression and peaceful assembly, the right to unionise and go on strike, and so on. Central to this conception of democracy are equality before the law and equal protection of the law, equal rights and opportunities, and freedom from discrimination. In order to qualify as a constitutional democracy, a state must be able to guarantee these rights, freedoms and equality to all, irrespective of differences: it has to be democracy for everyone, or it is not democracy at all.

In a capitalist society, of course, this is still far from being an ideal state of affairs. There is no guarantee, for example, that everyone will receive basic necessities like food, clothing, shelter, healthcare and education; poverty and deprivation are not ruled out, and there is little or no democracy within the workplace. However, liberal democracy does provide the conditions in which people can organise and take collective action to obtain these necessities for themselves; it provides conditions where people have sufficient control over their own lives to enable them to live with dignity. Equally importantly, it limits the power which some people have over others: the power to deny to others the rights and liberties which they claim for themselves.

This kind of democracy, which includes women's, children's, workers' and minority rights, trade union rights as well as the right to choose your own marriage partner, hardly exists on a mass scale in India today, except as a dream. It is incompatible with communalism, casteism, sexism or racism, all of which endow people of one group with rights and privileges denied to others. If democracy is to be a positive value, we have to make it clear it is this kind of democracy we are arguing for and not the other. And this meaning of democracy is inseparable from secularism.

Secularism

It should be obvious that if equality is a condition of democracy, then a state that is linked to any particular religious group cannot be democratic, because the very fact that it is thus linked will mean that it favours members of that group and discriminates against others. Moreover, not only citizens who do not follow that religion, but even those who do, will be denied basic democratic rights; as we have seen, the same religion can be interpreted in innumerable ways, but the freedom to do so is denied by theocratic states, which in all cases have their own doctrinal definition of their faith and discriminate against or persecute those whose interpretation is different. So no matter what claims are made for them, Islamic, Christian, Jewish, Buddhist, Hindu or other theocratic states cannot be democracies. However, there are at least four definitions of a secular state, not all of them compatible with democracy.

The first is a state that does not intervene in religion under any circumstances. This would be neither practicable nor desirable. It would mean, for example, that the state would not be able to intervene to prevent practices such as human sacrifice, so long as it is claimed that these are undertaken for religious reasons. A democratic state implies freedom of religious belief, but religious practices should be restricted to those that do not violate the human rights and civil liberties of any individual. In this sense, religious rights are subordinate to fundamental human rights in a democratic state.

The second is a state that actively clamps down on all forms of religious expression and association. This, too, is undemocratic because it interferes with the democratic rights to freedom of expression and association. It can result in actions similar to those of a theocratic state – destruction of places of worship and religious monuments, persecution of followers of various religions, and so on – except that these will be directed against followers of *all* religions without exception.

The third is the Indian variant of the secular state: equal respect for all religions, or *sarva dharma samabhav.* The biggest problem with this definition is that it fails to acknowledge that the same religion can have numerous variants, some of which are in conflict with each other. It simply assumes that each religion is monolithic; and since the progressive variants of religions do not want to be linked to state power, it is in every case the most conservative or reactionary variants that are accorded respect by the state. For example, for most Hindus in India, the entire string of events leading up to and following the demolition of the Babri Masjid, including the widespread bloodshed, are a matter of regret and shame. For the Hindutva brigade, however, demolishing the mosque and building a Ram temple in its place has been at the top of their agenda for decades. The fact that the mosque was, in fact, demolished, and that no one has been punished for that act of vandalism or the murder and mayhem that accompanied it, is a clear indication of which variant of Hinduism the state endorses.

This example also illustrates another drawback of the Indian version of secularism: as pointed out by Irfan Habib (Ashraf, 2015) and Romila Thapar (Shankar, 2015), it is biased towards the religion of the majority. This should be obvious: if state personnel are allowed to bring their religion into their official duties, the right-wing variant of the religion of the majority will dominate. None of the major players in the demolition of the Babri Masjid and the carnage surrounding it was ever prosecuted for those crimes; on the contrary, one of them (Bal Thackeray) was given a state funeral with all the accompanying honours. Even the judiciary succumbed to the majoritarian bias around the event. The Allahabad High Court in 2010 gave a verdict in the Ayodhya case which was more in accordance with the myth that the mosque was built on the precise spot of Ram's birthplace, despite the fact that a mosque had stood there for more than four centuries, which, as Justice Rajindar Sachar pointed out, made 'a suit for declaration by Hindus claiming that it was a temple..hopelessly barred by time,' and the legal title for the land should have been awarded to the Sunni Waqf Board (Hensman, 2010).

However, this majoritarian bias does not mean that members of minority religions are uniformly disempowered. For example, a large number of Muslims, both women and men, agreed with the judgment in the Shah Bano case that a Muslim woman divorced by her husband is entitled to maintenance beyond the iddat period; yet it was those Muslims who raised an outcry against the judgment who got what they wanted. By insisting that Muslim women could not obtain relief by appealing to Section 125 of the Criminal Procedure Code, the All-India Muslim Personal Law Board

(AIMPLB) established the principle that the secular laws of the land do not apply to Muslims. (That this particular provision is completely inadequate for protecting the rights of women is irrelevant in this context.)

The latter case brings us to the issue of religious personal laws versus a Uniform Civil Code. Since the Shah Bano controversy, feminists have correctly moved away from the demand for uniformity. Uniform laws need not be either gender-just or secular; indeed, patriarchal theocracies have extremely uniform family laws! What is needed are family laws which satisfy the democratic requirements of equality before the law and equal protection of the law, and which must therefore be secular and gender-just. There are women and men of all religions who believe that their faith demands that family laws should be gender-just, yet there is no equality between men and women under religious family laws. Hindu nationalists allege that these laws constitute 'appeasement of minorities', yet the real losers are women and progressives of all religions.

Indeed, it is possible to argue that far from being a condition for freedom of religion, religious family laws actually *violate* freedom of religion. In enacting religious personal laws, the state takes sides in theological disputes and forces those who disagree to submit to its interpretation. This is the very opposite of freedom of religion and conscience, which should allow people to practise their own religion in their own way. Thus, the so-called Indian version of secularism guarantees neither equality nor freedom of religion, and therefore is incompatible with democracy. *Once religion is allowed to enter the state, the resulting free-for-all allows the most powerful – i.e. right-wingers of the majority religion (Hinduism in India and Nepal, Islam in Pakistan and Bangladesh, Buddhism in Sri Lanka and Myanmar, etc.) – to rule the roost, while the least powerful (i.e. the progressives of all the religions) have little or no say.*

The only remedy is to go back to the standard definition of a secular state, namely a state which is not linked to any religion, but which upholds the right to believe in, practise or propagate any religion so long as the secular laws are not broken and human rights are not violated. This definition is quite compatible with most of the Indian Constitution; for example, the right to freedom of religion is upheld, but untouchability, which violates the human rights of

Dalits, is banned (that it is still practised is testimony to the disarray of the law enforcement system rather than the law itself).

Does this mean that state personnel are barred from practising any religion? Not at all. It only means that they are barred from practising any religion in their *official* capacity, whereas they are free to practise it in their *private and personal* capacity. The distinction is easy to understand for followers of the progressive versions of all religions, but not for those who follow the right-wing versions. Thus, Narendra Modi's performance of Hindu rituals described by Visvanathan (2014) was a blow against secularism, because he engaged in them not in his personal capacity but as a politician. Later, when he declared Christmas to be 'Good Governance Day', cancelling a public holiday which had been in force since Independence (Indo-Asian News Service, 2014), it was another blow against secularism, because it prevented Christian teachers, children and public servants from practising their religion in their private capacity.

Another question which arises is, how would it be possible both to uphold religious freedom and to enact gender-just secular family laws for people of all religions? An example will illustrate. In 2013, the British parliament passed a law legalising same-sex marriage, which came into force in 2014. At the time, the Church of England was opposed to same-sex marriage, but several gay Christian couples promptly went to get their relationships registered as marriages. This seems to be an eminently secular relationship between religion and the state (which is an irony, because Britain has an established church and is therefore not a secular state): the state cannot force the church to recognise gay marriage, but neither can the church prevent the state from registering marriages of gay Christians who believe it is compatible with their faith. Most democracies, in fact, have family laws which apply to people of all religions, but which do not interfere with the right to conduct religious marriages according to the religious affiliations of the couple getting married.

India too has similar legislation. The Protection of Women from Domestic Violence Act is accessible to all women, regardless of whether or not their religions endorse the right of men to beat their wives. Similarly, a provision in the Juvenile Justice Act allows for people of all faiths to adopt, even though adoption is prohibited in

Muslim Personal Law. This allows Muslims who believe that adoption is compatible with their faith to go ahead with legal adoption of children even while the AIMPLB continues to oppose it. There seems to be no valid reason why secular gender-just laws covering marriage, divorce and inheritance cannot similarly be enacted, covering people of all religions, but presumably being used against religious laws only when someone who is denied justice under religious laws seeks to obtain it from the secular courts.

Defending secularism in India necessarily involves a critique of the prevailing model of the secular state, and admitting that a state which does not consistently enforce the principle of equality before the law is neither genuinely secular nor consistently democratic. The dominant version of most religions involves some degree of violation of the rights of women and girls, ranging from exclusion, discrimination and patriarchal control to sadistic violence. Such interpretations also often include hostility towards those who belong to other communities. Why should anyone respect such beliefs? On the contrary, violent and destructive practices arising from them should be opposed and condemned and, if possible, punished. The spate of murders of rationalists in India and Bangladesh from 2013 onwards proves beyond reasonable doubt the irrationality and barbarism at the heart of these versions of religion.

Where innocuous beliefs and practices are concerned, toleration is certainly desirable, but not necessarily respect. If certain religious beliefs or practices appear to someone as superstitious or irrational, that person is entitled to hold and express such an opinion, even if it offends someone else's religious sensibilities. Where religious beliefs and practices do not harm anyone, freedom of expression requires both that they can be engaged in freely, *and* that they can be criticised freely. The basic principle here is not equal respect for all religions, but equal respect for all *persons* regardless of their religion.

However, a secular state cannot survive, much less prosper, unless the society supporting it is also secular; after all, the personnel who run the state, from bureaucrats to politicians and policemen to the judiciary, are all drawn from civil society, and unless they are secular, the state will not be secular either. But is this possible in a country like India, where the vast majority of people are religious? What would it mean?

Just as a secular state is one which does not discriminate between people on the basis of religion or caste, a truly secular person too would not discriminate between people on the basis of religion or caste. Individuals can be secular and religious at the same time, provided they do not choose their associates, friends and family connections according to religion and caste. If a white person says, 'I have nothing against blacks, but I wouldn't want my son or daughter to marry one,' we would certainly think of that person as racist. Similarly, someone who claims to be secular, but cannot tolerate the idea of a son or daughter marrying someone from another community, is essentially communal; not necessarily in the same vicious way as those who spread anti-Muslim propaganda or organise pogroms, and yet sharing something in common with them: the feeling that 'they' are in some fundamental way different from 'us'.

Seen from this angle, it is clear that Indian society has a long way to go before it is genuinely secular. Tackling this problem is also an essential part of the struggle against communalism, and it requires an examination of conceptions of identity and community.

Identity

The question of identity can be posed in two ways: (1) who am I? (i.e. individual identity), and (2) with whom do I identify? (i.e. collective identity). These two meanings of identity are linked, to the extent that human beings do not develop a personal identity in isolation, and to a very great extent our image of ourselves is derived from what we see reflected in other people's eyes.

(1) A person's individual identity is shaped by everything which that person experiences and does from birth onwards. Experiences are of course affected by factors over which we have no control: our sex, our family, the class and religious and caste community into which we are born, our nationality, mother-tongue, and so on. All these elements influence our identity, and to reduce anyone's identity to just one of them – say religion – is a gross oversimplification. This does not mean that we have 'multiple identities' (unless we suffer from multiple personality disorder!), but, rather, that anyone's personal or individual identity is extremely complex, shaped as it is by a multiplicity of influences yet irreducible to any of them. Indeed, in addition to the influences already mentioned, there are a plethora of others: our relationships with those who care for us as children

and with our family, teachers, colleagues and friends, as well as the things we do (or don't do), the decisions we make (or allow others to make for us) such as our work, the partner we live with, the way we spend our leisure, etc. The list is potentially endless, and when all these influences are taken into account, it becomes clear why each person's identity is unique. We can say that we create our own identities, but out of material which is not entirely of our own choosing.

Given the uniqueness of each person's identity, the attempt to impose a uniform identity on everyone following a particular religion is an inherently totalitarian exercise, aimed at the elimination of real diversity and denial of the freedom to act autonomously. Such an attempt is most likely to succeed if begun when the victims are in their early childhood. Where the attempt is successful, the vacuum left by the underdevelopment of an individual identity can quite easily be filled by a communal one.

In Western societies there is a strong emphasis on individuality, but the context of competitive individualism deprives many people of a caring community in which this personal identity can be nurtured, leaving them with a sense of loneliness and isolation. In Indian society, on the other hand, there is very little respect for individual freedom. In education there is usually an emphasis on rote-learning at the expense of encouraging critical and creative thinking, and most young people are pushed into occupations (including, for many women, the 'career' of being a full-time housewife and mother) which hardly take into account their talents and abilities. Often, even the choice of a marriage partner is not free, but is undertaken by others in the family without much consideration for the young person's chances of emotional fulfilment. From a very early age, there is pressure to submit to caste and community norms, regardless of whether these are beneficial or harmful. In such circumstances, the growth of individual identity is often stifled; hence the heavy dependence on communal identities, completing the vicious circle of forced communal identities leading to stunted personal identities, leading in turn to reinforced communal identities.

Paradoxical though it may seem, a strong and stable sense of personal identity and the acknowledgement of individuality in others are necessary conditions for the recognition of universal human rights. A negative consequence of having a communal identity is that others too are identified primarily in communal terms rather than as individuals, and this results in the barbaric doctrine of collective guilt and collective punishment, whereby it becomes quite acceptable to 'punish' perfectly innocent people of a certain community in the most cruel manner for crimes committed (or supposedly committed) by others of the same community, sometimes centuries or millennia ago. Lacking a conception of individual responsibility for actions, which would lead to an understanding that the people being attacked are innocent while those attacking them are criminals, a communal consciousness has the essential characteristics which allow its owner to be used as a stormtrooper.

(2) On what basis do we identify with other people, especially people we don't know? Obviously, it is on the basis of what we have in common with them, but that 'something' is what is in question here. If we identify with a co-religionist regardless of what that person is doing and cannot identify with people of other religions in the same way, then that is a communal identification. It creates the basis for communal violence by enabling us to identify with perpatrators of atrocities in our own religious community while preventing us from identifying with victims of violence who follow another religion. We cannot approve of this kind of identification if we are opposed to communalism, but what is the alternative?

For many people, the alternative is a national identity based on citizenship. Such an identity would, it is argued, cut across religious, ethnic and linguistic differences and unite people on the basis of a common nation. However, a national identity suffers from similar drawbacks to a communal one. It excludes people who are seen as aliens in one's own country, and is therefore compatible with the persecution of migrant workers and other foreign nationals (especially, in India, Pakistanis and Bangladeshis). Moreover, anyone beyond the national boundaries could be seen as fair game for exploitation, oppression, and even extermination. A strong sense of national identity, even if it is not linked to religion, is quite compatible with aggression, imperialism and genocide directed against the populations of other countries, and even people who do not participate actively in such behaviour may consent to it passively because of indifference to injustices perpetrated against 'foreigners' and 'aliens'.

In fact, the drawbacks associated with communalism can be traced to all forms of identification unless our primary identification is based on our shared humanity. This means that in any situation of oppression, we identify with those whose humanity is being violated in one way or another. We might identify with a male worker against an oppressive employer, but with his wife against him if he oppresses her at home; with a woman from a minority community against communalists or racists who are persecuting her, but with her child or domestic worker against her if she ill-treats them; with our fellow-citizens against a foreign aggressor if our country is being invaded, but with the foreigner against our own nation-state if it is pursuing a policy of persecution or aggression against foreign nationals.

This is neither simple nor straightforward, because it involves identifying with different people at different times, and thinking about each situation. By contrast, with a communal or national identity, you can unthinkingly identify with the same people all the time, no matter what they happen to be doing. But identifying with people first and foremost on the basis of our shared humanity is the only way to avoid the danger of identifying on some occasions with people who in one way or another are oppressing others. A major element in the struggle against communalism has to be helping children to develop a strong and stable individual identity, and enabling them to identify with others on the basis of their shared humanity.

However, most of us need to feel we belong to a collective that is smaller than the whole of humanity, and this is why people have always created communities of various types.

Communities

We can say that a community is a collective based on a shared culture and traditions, but this is true only if we accept that community, culture and tradition are all constantly being redefined and recreated. It is strange that it should be so widely accepted that 'community,' 'culture' and 'tradition' are entities which are somehow given to us, as though there is some fundamental difference between us and our ancestors: they had the privilege of actually creating communities, cultures and traditions, whereas we are only given the option of accepting or rejecting them. According to this view, if we wish to break with the authoritarian, sexist norms of one or the other community, we are threatened with being left without any community at all, victims of Western atomised individualism; and if we refuse to use established religious symbolism, we are threatened with being cut off from our culture!

In fact, even values and practices which existed in the past can become a part of present-day culture and tradition only if they are reaffirmed in the present, and every generation has to do this anew. There is always a process of choice and selection when this takes place: some values and practices are ignored, while others are highlighted, reinterpreted, and combined with completely new ones to produce a culture and tradition which is essentially modern, whatever its claims may be. This has been done with spectacular success by the Islamic State, for example, whose use of modern weapons and social media stamp it clearly as a twenty-first century totalitarian state although it claims to be recreating a society which existed centuries earlier. Similarly, Hindutva certainly doesn't date back to Vedic times; it is a modern phenomenon using modern technology to propagate a modern form of ruthless authoritarianism. It presupposes a community based on multiple hierarchies: the domination and oppression of children by parents, women by men, lower castes by upper castes, workers by employers. Participating in the system of domination and subordination is degrading for everyone. The same kinds of relationships prevail in communities linked to the reactionary versions of other religions.

In spite of these disadvantages, most people still choose to be part of one or the other of these 'traditional' communities because they have grown up in them, become dependent on them, and see them as the only alternative to Western individualism, with its selfishness on one side and loneliness on the other. In other words, faced with the choice between a patriarchal, authoritarian community and no community at all, they choose the former. Paradoxically, belonging to these communities is also seen as helping them in the competitive struggle inseparable from modern capitalism, as in the case of different tribes in the Northeast fighting over land and different castes fighting over reservations.

But why should these be the only alternatives? In many parts of India, as in other parts of the world, friends, neighbours, workmates, and even family members include people from diverse ethnicities and faiths, including atheists and agnostics. This shows that it is not only possible but quite natural for such communities to develop, cutting across ethnic, linguistic, religious and caste divisions, in which relationships are egalitarian and caring rather than hierarchical and authoritarian, and membership is by choice rather than by birth. They can take multiple forms – workers' unions, student organisations, feminist, Dalit, tribal rights, environmentalist, anti-nuclear, LGBT, disability rights and other activist groups, neighbourhood associations, sports clubs, reading groups, and so on and so forth – and one person can belong to more than one. While no one can belong to all of them, they should share the same ethos and extend solidarity to each other when required. This is important, especially in the case of activist groups. A careful appraisal shows that communalism, caste oppression and patriarchy are closely connected; control over women and young people is essential to maintain caste and communal divisions.

At the same time, unemployment, economic crisis and lack of a social safety net often drives people into dependence on oppressive families and communities or prevents them from escaping from them. The reference to 'socialism' in the constitution can be seen to refer to ensuring that everyone has access to a home and livelihood, which in turn would mean ensuring that Adivasis, peasants and rural workers are not forcibly evicted from their forests, land and livelihoods, workers have decent jobs with trade union rights, there are attempts to create employment for all through employment guarantee schemes and cooperatives, there is social security to provide for the needs of those who are unable to work or cannot find jobs, and a welfare state will provide free healthcare and education of a high quality. A goal that has arisen since the Constitution was penned is care of the environment instead of plundering and destroying it, and this is linked to the sustainability of livelihoods. Mutual support and solidarity between groups fighting on these issues would strengthen all of them, and combat the violence resulting from competitive struggles for limited resources.

Creating alternative communities which are non-patriarchal, egalitarian, and cut across existing ethnic, linguistic, religious, caste, and even national divisions is a necessity if we are to combat the attraction that communal organisations exert on people who do not necessarily endorse their violent, genocidal agenda. This is not a completely utopian exercise: the beginnings of such communities do exist already, but it requires a sustained effort to ensure that they spread and grow. In reality there is nothing (other than our own inhibitions and lack of imagination) that prevents us from creating our own inclusive, egalitarian, democratic, humane communities and cultures which would attract millions of people suffering bondage to oppressive traditions. Standing up for just one item in this agenda – the right to love and live with the person of one's choice, regardless of caste, creed or gender – would by itself attract a large swathe of young people, who today face persecution and even so-called 'honour killings' simply for pursuing this most basic of rights.

Conclusion

The first requirement in the struggle against communalism is clarity in our use of terms. Progressive versions of all religions are perfectly compatible with secularism, but reactionary versions are not; the only version of secularism that is compatible with constitutional democracy is the one which separates the state from religion; and right-wing religious majoritarian 'democracy' does not uphold either equality or the freedom of religion. Working for a secular, democratic state requires us also to promote complex, stable personal identities as opposed to narrow communal ones, and egalitarian, democratic, inclusive communities as opposed to hierarchical, authoritarian, exclusive ones.

This is not a matter of being pedantic, but of being clear about what we are trying to achieve in practice. We already suffer a serious disadvantage vis-à-vis the far Right, since they appeal to sentiments which are fostered on a mass scale by the deeply authoritarian character of present society, whereas mass proliferation of the secular, democratic humanism to which we appeal would require nothing less than a cultural revolution: a movement to eradicate patriarchal family and community relationships, encourage students to be critical and think for themselves rather than unquestioningly accepting their teachers' authority, build workers' unions that are free of crippling dependence on 'leaders', introduce industrial democracy whereby workers have information and consultation rights in the running of their workplaces, create genuine local democracy giving residents control over the administration of their neighbourhoods, and so on and so forth. All the more reason, therefore, why our vision needs to be clear, and our articulation of it unambiguous.

Creating a movement which puts forward a positive alternative to communalism also implies a critique of the sectionalism of most of the existing progressive movements, which oppose one form of oppression and authoritarianism but not others. Thus, the trade union movement is compromised by being seriously contaminated with communal elements, feminists have raised slogans amenable to a communal interpretation, and even Dalits have not proved immune to the false promises of Hindutva. On the other hand, anti-communal groups suffer from the same kind of narrowness, often indifferent to class, caste and gender oppression. The alternative is not that each individual has to participate in every struggle, but rather that all the diverse struggles should be linked together into a movement by shared principles and practical solidarity.

Internal relationships within this movement too have to be radically different from what we find in many movements today. If these relationships are hierarchical, authoritarian or sectarian, the attractive power of the movement will be greatly diminished. Given the magnitude of the task, we need to attract as many people as possible to join in undertaking it, and this implies the ability to debate differences creatively while working together on the basis of shared principles. Unless we are capable of functioning in a truly democratic manner, our arguments for democracy will hardly be credible, and unless we can establish and maintain mutually caring relationships, we cannot attract people desperately seeking the security of belonging to a community. To this extent, means and ends are inseparable: the movement itself has to prefigure the kind of society we are advocating.

References

Ashraf, Ajaz, 2015: 'Irfan Habib: The Indian variant of secularism opens the door to majority communalism,' *Scroll.in*, 15 August, http://scroll.in/article/748241/irfan-habib-the-indian-variant-of-secularism-opens-the-door-to-majority-communalism.

Gandhi, Gopalkrishna, 2015: 'The sham and dangerous "secular debate",' *Economic Times*, 29 January. http://articles.economictimes. indiatimes.com/2015-01-29/news/58586380_1_preamble-best-comments-republic-day

Hensman, Rohini, 2010: 'Politics, Religion, History and the Law: The Ayodhya Verdict,' http://www.sacw.net/article1609.html

India Today, 'Govt's Republic Day ad removes Secular, Socialist from Constitution's preamble', 27 January, http://indiatoday.intoday.in/story/republic-day-ad-faux-pas-secular-socialist-preamble-of-constitution-narendra-modi-government/1/415614.html

Indo-Asian News Service, 2014: 'Narendra Modi announces Atal Bihari Vajpayee's birthday as "Good Governance Day",' 2 December, http://www.india.com/news/india/narendra-modi-announces-atal-bihari-vajpayees-birthday-as-good-governance-day-209864/

Nandy, Ashish, 1998: 'The Politics of Secularism and the Recovery of Religious Tolerance,' in *Secularism and its Critics* (ed. Rajiv Bhargava), pp. 321-344) http://notesonscholarlybooks.blogspot.in/2009/03/ashis-nandy-politics-of-secularism-and.html

Shankar, Aranya, 2015: 'Indian definition of secularism is incomplete, says Romila Thapar, *Indian Express*, 20 August, http://indian-express.com/article/cities/delhi/indian-definition-of-secularism-is-incomplete-says-romila-thapar/

The Hindu, 2015: 'Let nation debate preamble: Ravi Shankar', 29 January. http://www.thehindu.com/news/national/let-nation-debate-the-preamble-ravi-shankar/article6831215.ece

Visvanathan, Shiv, 2014: 'How Modi defeated liberals like me,' *The Hindu*, 26 May, http://www.thehindu.com/opinion/lead/how-modi-defeated-liberals-like-me/article6034057.ece?homepage=true

15

Towards Secular Society

—*Ram Puniyani*

The rise of sangh parivar, communalisation of society and increase in the suppression of Rights exploited sections of society during last two decades have been accompanied by the opposition to liberal ethos, attack on the concept of secularism and subjugation of the interests of oppressed sections of society. The social forces strengthening this onslaught have vitiated the 'Social Space' in the direction of constructed anti-minority, anti-dalit and anti-women myths, and projected their own interests under the umbrella of 'Hindu Rashtra'. Their politics at social and political level manifests through the 'Hindutva Onslaught' which basing itself on Brahmonical Hinduism, appropriates for itself a Nationalism of the religious brand.

Secularism Under Attack-Hindutva:Characterisation

Hindutva shares many a features with fundamentalism like, targeting against liberal ethos of society, imposition of retograde social values, selectively culled out from the past, built around holy book, holy diety and clergy, harping on traditional orthodox religious beliefs, projecting women primarily as mothers, projecting a golden past of religious rule, demanding a homogeneous culture, creating hysteria against internal enemy and is built on emotive appeal of religion. Some of these features like projection of golden past, creation of internal and external enemy, women primarily as mothers are also manifest in the fascist movements as well. There are certain other commonalities with fascism, like its getting strengthened in the face of assertion of exploited sections, precedence of national interests over the interests of the people, expansionism and being oppressive to workers, women and minorities. Social scientists are divided on the characterisation of this phenomenon, some calling it fundamentalist (Vanaik, 1994), while some others calling it clerical fascism, or fascism or Neo Fascism (Ram, 1996). Whatever be the outcome of debate on the issue, Hindutva aims to suppress and suspend the rights of oppressed. It is a social agenda of shaken threatened middle class in the service of big bourgeosie. It is a mass movement; it is the political agenda of petty industrialists, sections of middle classes and rich peasantry blessed by capital (Ram, 1996).

Hindutva's Projections : Hindutva projects itself as a religious nationalism, aiming at building a Hindu Rashtra, and attacks secularisation process and secularism at multiple levels. As per them secularism is anti-religion, unsuited for Indian conditions as it originated in the Christian West, and that it has been smuggled into Indian Constitution taking advantage of the dreadful emergency. They also go on to assert that secularism is insensitive to the religiosity of people by making religion as a private matter and that it delinks people from the community resulting in the loss of their identity. Taking a severe dig at Islam they are propagating that since fundamentalism is prevalent in Iran etc., the Muslim dominated country, and 'India's Secularism' is pampering Muslims so 'secularism is a new mask of fundamentalism'. The Sangh Parivar (SP) can not swallow the fact that democratic states implement affirmative action for the disadvantaged sections of society, so it comes up with another concoction that 'secular state pretends to be neutral but is partial to minorities'. And their breast beating reaches its peak with the cry that because of secularism a 'Hindu society' is saddled with anti-Hindu state. And finally SP shamelessly propagates that a party committed to 'Hindu Rashtra' (BJP) is the party of 'positive secularism', and not content with this it goes on to elevate religion (Hinduism) itself as a 'secular religion'. Many of these 'constructs' and 'concoctions' have rapidly been percolated through SP's vaste network in media, schools and various levels of bureaucracy and thus these propaganda materials are the dominant accompaniment of the onslaught of Hindutva.

Anti Secularists: The attack on secular concepts has been joined by scattered scholars, who though not a part of Hindutva bandwagon have joined the 'damn secularism' chorus. The term 'anti-secularists' is roughly used for some sociologists who neither support communal politics of Hindutva nor the secularists who are opposing the fundamentalist forces. They have some support amongst few academicians and some activist' Non Government Organisations (NGOs). "They propose an 'authentic' indigenism which seeks to oppose communalism and the various forms of perversion of religion through endorsement and utilisation of the resources in the India's religious traditions...they do endorse the view that if a notion of secular state in India is to be meaningful, then it must break away from enlightenment inspired notion of impartial religious abstinence to a more authentically indigeneous notion of active organisation of religious toleration" (Vanaik, 97, 153), further Vanaik adds, this group of anti-secularists, "is still united more by what it is against than what it is for. But in this discourse ranging over six general themes, there are common points of reference. These six general themes are: the issue of modernity; understanding of culture; civilisation; religion; Hinduism, in regard to Indian society's past and present; secularism and secularisation; particularism and universalism; individualism and communitarianism; neo-Gandhism' (Vanaik, 97, 153). The main exponent of these overlapping themes are Ashish Nandy, T.N. Madan, M.N. Shrinivas and Bhikhu Parekh. Nandy proclaims himself to be 'anti-secularist' and says that secularism and modernity are the source of violence in Indian Society. For Nandy secularism is 'A gift of Christianity' and "a child of modernity and colonialism, a product of western science and rationality and today functions as the ideology of modren state....which is the source of most contemporary problems." (Theramangalam, 1995). To overcome the problem Nandy advices that Indian secular state should learn about morality from Hinduism, Islam and Sikhism. While for Madan, "in the prevailing circumstances secularism in South Asia as a generally shared credo of life is impossible, as a basis for state action impracticable, and as a blueprint in foreseeable future impotent". (Madan, 1987: 748). 'As per him South Asian religions are incompatible with the ideology of secularism. As per Madan "One of the major reasons for the rise of religious fundamentalism all over the world today is the excess of ideological secularism all over the world and its emergence as a dogma or a religion" (Mehta, 1997: 86). M.N. Srinivas feels that India needs anew philosophy to solve the present grave cultural and spiritual crisis and "that philosophy cannot be secular humanism. It has to be firmly rooted in God as creator and protector" (Srinivas, 1993).

Though none of these 'anti-secularists' overtly identify with the Sangh Parivar's political project of Hindu Rashtra, there is a vague resemblence and overlap in the arguments which they proffer. Most of the anti-secularists gloss over the change in society brought in due to introduction of industrialisation. They cannot connect up the changes brought in the role of religion, changes in culture, human relationships, due to the change in the production techniques, which in a sense shakes up the totality of social milieu and hierarchical relationships. While SP wants to impose premodern, structural hierarchies on society, the sociologists are unable to see the totality of social change. The process of secularisation which is the kernal of modernisation process is conspicuously absent in their discources and thereby its no surprise that many a conclusions which they reach and prescriptions they suggest have a great similarity to those put forward by the SP.

Liberal - Left Response : The demolition of Babri Masjid came as a thunderbolt waking up many a left-liberal activists and ideologues. Secularisation process in India has not been the subject of intense study amongst this group of scholars. Unfortunately here the two main social groups contributing to secularisation process, the dalits (Ambedkarite and allied), and worker-peasant (Communist party, followed by Communist parties) had been spearheading their movements, unconnected to the movements of the other. Left scholarship contributed heavily to different facets of land reforms, workers, issues etc. Dalit literature presented the cry of the community in a intense and moving way. But the attempt to present the canvass was not as sizeable as needed in this vast and complex society.

Some of the scholars, activists sensed the communalisation of society, ascendence of Hindu right from early eighties and few studies and contributions started coming out from late eighties. But Babri Masjid demolition and the vehemence of Sangh Parivar and its stranglehold on society shook up a sizeable section of left intellectuals, resulting in substantial contributions to understanding the process of Secularisation and the concept of secularism. Also it forced the leaders of communist parties to revise their political strategies as a fire fighting measure to ward off the coming into power of Bhartiya Janta Party (BJP), the political wing of SP.

The confusion of the role of religion in human life had been a subject of many a debates. The offensive of Hindu right has been proclaiming that religion cannot be separated from public life and more so our 'Dharma' (religious duty) the core of our social life from political life. Most of the progressive commentators have by and large posited the necessity of separation between politics and religion. The major misunderstanding is caused due to conflating different of facets of religion. Secularisation and modernity are accompanied by the rise of nation status and decline in the clout of clergy in particular. With this transition religion comes to occupy a different place in industrialised, modern, secularised societies, while in the societies where these processes are going on at snails pace the grip of 'clergy' on society remains strong and in due course the 'clergy' and the declining social classes come up with different political movements which aim to halt the process of 'secularisation' in the face of 'industrialisation' process. This schizophrenic situation, where industrialisation and technology are welcomed and their accompaniments, i.e., relations of 'Liberty, Equality, Fraternity,' and 'Scientific temper' are ignored and positively curbed, is the 'gift' of offensives like those led by Ayatollah Khoemini and the RSS.

Rajeev Bhargava argues this on the grounds of democracy: "democracy requires that there be no concentration of power in any one institution or in any one group. If people with authority in religious affairs begin to exercise power in political matters, then this inevitably undermines democratic values. For the sake "of democracy, therefore, religious and political institutions must be separated. Separation is required to curb political absolution" Bhargava, 1994), and further goes on to add, "Religion and politics form distinct spheres with their own respective areas of jurisdiction. Each is valuable in its own right. Religion and politics respect each other as well as their own limits. The world of worship and congregation, of prayer and conscience, must not be intruded upon by politicians and bureaucrats. Likewise deeply religious people, in particular leaders of religious communities must not tread on the toes of politicians". (Bhargava, 1994: 1786).

Some of the scholars have tended to take the problem in the arena of the introduction of the concept of secularism in Indian Constitution due to the efforts of Jawaharlal Nehru (Bilgrami, 1995), summing up the arguments of Nehru's critics Bilgrami point out "the Hindu Brigade and ideologues on similar wavelength assert that, Nehruvian Secularism...is an alien imposition upon a people who have never wished to separate religion from politics in their everyday life and thinking, and therefore, leaves the people no choice but to turn to the only religious politics allowed by modernity's stranglehold i.e., Hindu nationalism. Thus, secular tyranny breeds Hindu nationalist resistance, which threatens with the promise of its own form of tyranny". (Bilgrami, 1994: 6). Bilgrami while refuting the charges of people like Nandy states that, "Secularism thus never got the chance to emerge out of the creative dialogue between these different communities. It was *sui generis.* This archimedean existence gave secularism procedural priority but in doing so it gave no abiding substantive authority. As a result it could be nothing more than a holding process, already under strain in the time of its charismatic architect and increasingly ineffective after his death". (Bilgrami, 1994: 20). This type of exposition betrays the chinks in the armour of left secularists, their lack of emphasis on the secularisation process, their approach which cannot relate the secularism's place in the Constitution to the struggles of dalits and workers and also of the secular aspirations of the rising industrialists and their paraphernelia.

Similarly SP has been gradually working at a deeper level to change the meaning of secularism from the Dharma Nirpekshta (aloofness from religions) to Sarva Dharma Sambhav (equal respect for all religions). While the former is the Hindi translation given in the Constitution and so far accepted, the latter is being projected as the 'real' meaning of secularism in Indian context. Cossmen and Kapur summarise the SP's stand on this very well (Cossman and Kapur, 1993, W-37), "Hindu fundamentalists explicitly argue in favour of Sarva Dharma Samabhava and positive secularism. There is a perverse logic to this RSS argument, based on its ability to define the terms of the debate. Secularism is defined as toleration of all religions; Hinduism is defined as the only religion with a true tolerance for all other religions, thus according to these terms, only a country based on Hinduism can be truely secular. Within this vision secularism collapses into its antithesis—a theocratic state".

Dealing with the issue of seperation of religion and politics is not easy. Rajeev Bhargava (EPW, 1994 : 1786) tries to grapple with this vexed issue by dividing the concept of secularism into political secularism and ethical secularism, and based on this comes up with four versions of secularism *per se:* "(a) ethical secularism that excludes all religions from the affairs of the state; (b) ethical secularism that requires that state keep a principled distance from all religions; (c) political secularism that excludes all ultimate ideals including religions from the affairs of the state ; and finally (d) political secularism that demands that the state be principally distanced from all religious and non-religious ultimate ideals", and concludes (Bhargava, 1996 : 72), "Political secularism has little or no conception of community. It is non-communitarian. From this, it does not follow that there are no secular communitarians and that to live together well, we must prepare a gingerly mix of political secularism and non-secular communitarianism. The pluralist version of ethical secularism which is both secular and commmunitarian is worth exploring and enriching. It is superior to political secularism though the level and quality of motivation that it requires is not always easy to obtain. Ethical secularism is better but difficult, political secularism somewhat less attractive but well within our reach. Both insist upon the separation of religion and politics without undermining either. Both should be invoked to justify a secular state. But, in the short run and in some contexts, political secularism may not only be good fallback strategy but the only way to prevent a community from falling apart". In all this analysis the role of clergy is missing and that probably makes it look a bit more complicated. Secularism has no problems with religious practices and beliefs going on, on there own, but clergy dictated social and political norms cannot have a place in secular state policies.

K.N. Panikkar takes the debate on cultural and political level (Panikkar, 1997: 50), "that India consciously opted for secular polity, despite occasional spasms of sectarian violence, communal politics and partition, is no historical accident, no conjuring trick of Westernized intelligentsia. It is rooted in the historical experience and cultural dynamics of Indian Society". One can add that this historical experience and cultural dynamics is in the context of a series of anti-caste struggles led by Phule, Ambedkar and Periyar. The struggles which challenged the existing hierarchy of caste system, the struggles which stood to change the *status quo* of society, paving the way for the breaking of the pre-modern patriarchal relationships. These struggles met there supplement in the struggles of workers whose endeavours brought into being a new 'Contractual' 'wage labour' relationships. On the other side the modern intelligentsia and section of modern industrialists and intellectuals articulated the secular aspirations of the emerging Indian Nation State, ensuring the incorporation of secular ethos in Indian Constitution.

Secularisation: As such secularism is the flag of a deeper secularisation process. Not much literature has come out on this deeper process of our society. As such there is no universal model of secularisation process. Indian secularisation process is peculiar in the sense of its being an extremely slow one, also giving rise to the reaction to itself in the form of rise of communal politics, both Hindu and Muslim.

K.N. Panikkar (Panikkar, 1997 : 16) makes a brilliant attempt to locate the reflection of this process in the rationalist and humanist ideas which were struggling to make their advent on the social scene. Panikkar lays a big stress on the ideas of Raja Ram Mohan Roy in whose writings, "religion was looked upon as a mechanism to preserve the existing property relations and to regulate social intercourse...social explanation of religion inevitably led Ram Mohan to question and reject dogmas of faith and miracles which were not integral to the original character of religion, they saw them as part of an accretionary process brought into play by religious leaders purely for their selfish interests and which they realised by misleading their unsuspecting followers. Supernaturalism and monopoly of scriptural knowledge were the effective instruments used to achieve this end. The religious systems, beliefs and practices, therefore assumed the character of deception. All religious systems, Ram Mohan Roy argued, were systems of human deception".

Panikkar's analysis of weakness of Indian secularisation process, as reflected in the ideological battles of nineteenth century is very apt, (Panikkar, 1996 : 19), "Our experience of the nineteenth century is sufficient proof that neither respect for all religions nor the idea of the unity of Godhead in themselves could create secularism. Instead they circumscribed social consciousness within religious parameters, thereby keeping the possibility open for particularistic and antagonistic tendencies to re-emerge at appropriate moments. This is precisely the weakness of the Indian notion of secularism. It keeps religion in play and in turn enhances religiosity, it preserves and projects religious idenities and thus increases the social distance between different religious communities". Panikkar's solution to this impasse, "The only way out of this impasse appears to be a frontal confrontation with religion: an all out critique of religion, with a view to its eventual negation..." (Panikkar, 1987: 20), though essentially true can be easily misinterpreted as like most of the other progressive intellectuals he too glosses over the different subsets of religion. The focus has to be to oppose and fight against the stranglehold of clergy represented by Church, Mullahs or Pandits, and not to oppose religion as such.

Though there are some theoretical elaborations of the secularisation process (Heredia and Mathais, 1995) a lot needs to be done to unravel the dynamics of secularisation process in our society. Apart from Panikkar the other contribution on similar lines is that of Achin Vanaik. Vanaik delves in depth on the process of secularisation albeit slightly abstractly and again in the framework of 'Marxist Perspective'. Though this work is full of good insights, again the contribution of movements of dalits in the process of secularisation is conspicuous by its absence. Vanaik point out that, "the term 'secularisation' emerged after the peace of Westphalia in 1648 and originally referred to the transfer of ecclestical lands to civic control. By the nineteenth century and in still powerful flush of Enlightenment values, G.L. Holyoake of Britain coined the term 'secularism' to define an ideology and movement, wherein social morality, hitherto determined by the transcending principles of religion, were now to be determined by reason, and anchored to the good man or woman in this life." (Vanaik, 1996 : 65).

Vanaik further states "Capitalist industrialisation, the rise of science and of enlightenment, the emergence and consolidation of civil society, in short modernity, posed the question of religion anew. How did religion, specifically Christianity, relate to modernity's emergence? Broadly speaking to this day three notions of secularisation have vied, singly or in combination, for controlling emphasis. There is the concept of secularisation as decline of religious institutions, beliefs, practices and consciousness losing social significance. There is the concept of relative separation. Here there is a shrinkage in the social space occupied or influenced by religion, also an implied reallocation of religious functions in polity, society and culture. The third notion is intimately connected to the growing importance of rational thought and activity. This dynamic implies newer claimants to intellectual and moral authority other than traditional religious systems". This is an excellent summary of the dynamics of the process occuring in the West. Vanaik supplements in the similar vein, "the emergence of secular State in Western democracies was more a practical consequence of a specific historical experience than an institutionalisation of an abstract secular ideal". And finally Vanaik describes a fourth notion of secularisation, "This Indian contribution is product of its specific history. In the context where the values associated with liberal democracy and nationalism were imported, secularism was conceived as the unifying principle mediating between different communities in order to forge a common struggle for national liberation....Like Western democratic counterpart the Indian secular state would be religiously impartial. But this impartiality would be ensured not by abstinence from religious affairs but by its 'fair' involvement on India's multireligious terrain...such a notion meant that Indian State did not represent that sharp contrast from broad Western model", this proposition is open to debate as more enlightening work needs to be put in before Indian secularisation process can be properly grappled. We will shortly look at the constributions of S. Anandhi and G. Omvedt who partly try to present a deeper view of the Indian secularisation process.

The core process of Indian secularisation process differed from the Western model because here the bigger impetus for the process came from the exploited and oppressed of society. The slower pace of industrialisation in the colonial society threw up a section of industrialists whose social and political will to overthrow the colonialism-Landlord-Priests nexus was not as sharp as in the Western countries. The turmoil created by industrialisation's impact on the subalterns, shudras, women and other exploited sections, who were tied by the priestly dictates and landlord exploitation was immense and got reflected in the movements represented and led by Phule, Ambedkar and Periyar. Gail Omvedt (Omvedt, 1995: 23) states, "Phule's argument that knowledge, education and science were weapons of advance for the exploited masses, was in contrast to all elitist theories that sought to link Western science and Eastern morale and argues that Indians could maintain their (Brahmonical) traditions, while adopting science and technology from the West for material development. For Phule, rather, *vidya* or knowlege was in direct contrast with the brahmanic, ritualistic *shastra* and was a weapon for equality and human freedom as well as the economic advance". Omvedt demonstrates the role of various radical dalit thinkers of the 1920s like Bansode (Nagpur), Bhagyareddy Varma (Hyderabad) and Mangoo Ram (Punjab). Omvedt is not blind to the deficiencies of the movements of the oppressed, despite their contribution in shaking up the existing hierarchical relationships. "Thus, two opposing ideologies prevailed among the toiling masses, one arguing from the standpoint of being original inhabitants or non-Aryans, and the other basing itself on the theory of class struggle. With the failure, in particular, of more all-encompassing Marxist theory to incorporate the problems of caste in India, the broad movement of the oppressed was split into class movement and a caste movement. There was no synthesis, no development of an integrated ideology and, as a result, those lower castes/classes who did get drawn into the national struggle or left-led working class movement, gave up the sharpness of their anti-caste fight" (Omvedt, 1995: 42).

Ambedkar emerged as the most significant dalit leader. His mammoth contributions included anti-caste struggles in the form of agitations like Chavdar Talab (for access of dalits to public drinking water), Kalaram Mandir (right to enter Hindu Temples), Manusmriti Dahan (Burning Manusmriti, the book codifying Hindu Dharma : rules, and consolidating the slavery of shudras and women and conversion to Buddhism and his laying the foundation of organisations/movements represented in Bahishkrit Hitakarinisabha, Indian Labour Party, Scheduled Caste Federation and the Republican Party of India. He supplemented this by his fundamental contributions in the form of Annihilation of Caste, Riddles of Rama and Krishna, and Buddha and His Dhamma. To cap this all he presided over the drafting of Indian Constitution which aimed to base itself on Liberty, Equality and Fraternity, the principles defining the 'core' of teachings of Ambedkar. As per Omvedt, "The way to liberation, then involved economic and ideological struggle and Ambedkar never gave up the former. But his stress was on ideological, cultural struggle, and though he could not succeed in fully integrating it with an economic alternative, he gave it a sharpness that would remain challenging before socialists to deal with the 'monster that would always cross their path', the issue of caste and its religious justification". (Omvedt, p. 55).

Periyar's contribution in contrast took a regional Tamil touch though essentially attacking the Brahmanical (upper caste domination). Periyar spearheaded a movement whose, "focus was similar to that of Phule's Satyashodhak Samaj, opposing Brahman Priesthood, calling for abolition of caste and supporting the liberation of women. He attacked all religions more than Phule did, taking an atheistic stance that contrasted with the modified stance of the non-Brahman elite" (Omvedt, p. 56).

Anadhi S. (Anadhi, 1995) has thrown significant light on the process of secularisation while studying the Dalits and secular politics in Madras slum. As per her (P. 9), "While the rest of the country has witnessed worst forms of Hindu communal mobilisation and violence against the Muslims, Tamil Nadu has remained an exception with remarkable communal harmony ; and this has been attributed to the Dravidian movement. We may note here that while the self-respect movement phase of Dravidian Movement problematised Hinduism by means of Sudra/Adi Dravida identity and gender inequality, its later incarnations subsumed religious and other identities under a pan-dalit identity".

Pariyar founded the self-respect movement and "his politics was by and large framed by a search for free and equal citizenship for different subordinate social groups such as shudras, the Adi Dravids and Women'. (Anadhi, S., p. 22) and further he argued that "Hinduism not only gave its adherents a religious identity, but also invested them with a range of other identities which, for him, were demeasuring, disempowering and oppressive. The most obvious of these subordinated identities were that of Adi-Dravids and the Shudras, which in practice forced the bulk of Hindus to a situation of wretchedness". (Anadhi, p. 23).

The Hindutva offensive cannot be properly placed in its socio-political and historical perspective without understanding the post-Mandal assertion of the dalits and other exploited sections of society. Hindutva's political baby, the BJPs success in rampaging the electoral battlefield, though highly disturbing in itself, cannot be negated without upholding and supporting the struggles of these groups who bear the brunt of Hindutva's onslaught at a deeper level.

Political Responses : The rise of petty industrialist, rich peasants and other middle layers of society along with a geometric increase in communalisation of society has brought to fore the electoral strength of the BJP. The party which began with a slogan of 'Gandhian Socialism', which was a mere attractive packaging material to be thrown away as soon as the contents are unpacked. The decade of 80s saw Congress taking advantage of this communalised common sense, but soon the 'communal dividends' were taken over by its 'rightful claimant' the BJP, which emboldened by its initial success in using 'religious emotive' appeals for political purposes, went all out to use the 'chariot of religion' in an attempt to trample the liberal democratic ethos under the wheels of its frightful armada of religion.

The implementation of Mandal by V.P. Singh government put the rising tide of BJP in a fix. On one hand seeing the contingencies of electoral politics it had to pay 'Lip support' to Mandal Commission, on the other it had also to please its own support base of 'rising middle classes'. By a 'shrewd and clever' manoeuvre it 'made best of both the worlds' by deflecting the issues related to social justice and rights of oppressed into religious issues and Ramjanmbhoomi issue came in as an apt battering ram to propel its communal political agenda. The progressive, secular and potential secular political formations kept watching the rise of communal political power and the demolition of Babri Masjid with a mixed sense of disbelief, awe and terror. The rubbles of Babri Masjid and rivers of blood flowing from the communal carnage unleashed by the campaigns of Sangh Parivar finally woke up the secular and potential secular formations into a sort of soul searching.

On one hand one is witnessing the apparently unstoppable march of BJP, duly supported by other wings of SP which are deftly using the 'communalisation of social space' to win over average middle class voter and by applying the 'social engineering' precisely to electorally win over those social groups whose social and political rights BJP wants to crush, i.e., dalits, women, workers and minorities. After the Babri demolition the SP has come to a 'fairly stable' phase and is pursuing its communal agenda with definite goals. The response of other electoral outfits from Congress to the Communists had been a 'knee jerk', one, of coming together to halt the march of BJP to power. The 1996 elections were an enough eye opener and a warning of the state of things to come. The coalition of parties, united front, supported from outside by the Congress and CPM was the outcome of this attempt to keep the BJP off from power. While coming towards this gravitation different parties were forced by what they had witnessed in the preceding years, as they could perceive that the communal forces "will always try to wade through rivers of blood of minorities to get to power, but a carnage that involves the 'Hindu Nation' itself is more than what they can muster;

that will be the surest way to destroy themselves" (Ahmed, 1996 : 1342). The expectation from this coalition was that it will not pose a threat to minorities, try to walk on the secular path, try to be representative of regional pluralism and try to take the political course away from Brahmin-Bania nexus.

At the moment there is no 'electoral vision' for keeping the communal BJP at bay. Things are just drifting and the unpreparedness of non-BJP parties are feeding into BJP's strength. Though BJP's major problems at the moment are equally from inside as from outside. The breakaway of Shankar Singh Waghela in Gujarat and many a dissident satraps of the states are an indicator of the party's inner contradictions overturning its applecart. Though BJP is projecting itself as the 'party with a difference', it betrays its weaknesses many of which are similar to the ones shown by other parties, "the reality proving not to be different from the practice of other parties, in relation to power and patronage. There is hardly any state unit of the party which is not riven with factionalism and infighting. What happened in Gujarat holds a mirror to the future" (Panikkar, 1996 : vii). Though this may be true when the BJP is not in absolute power, with grabbing of a 'absolute power' one imagines the real controller of BJP, the R.S.S. will be ruling the roost and crushing the dissident elements with 'Lathi blows'. So though one can register the inner contradictions within BJP, one has to be a bit cautious in reading too much into them once the BJP is in total command, when all the wings of SP will come forward to ruthlessly execute the Hindutva agenda.

The coming together of Non-BJP parties cannot be seen as the total answer to the threat of SP. Vanaik, (Vanaik, 1996 : 333) makes a pertinent point, "Electoral politics bases itself on existing levels of consciousness and prejudices. A left wing politics which wants to retain its distinctiveness and operates in a context where centrist populism is already strong cannot hope to expand (beyond a point) by shifting its politics forwards to take the electoral risks of more frequently and determinedly going 'against the grain' of popular consciousness in order to change such 'normal' consciousness".

The need for initiating the extra electoral campaigns to take on the threat of communal politics is very clear from this.

Platform for Secular Democracy

The problem posed by the ascendence of Hindu Right is multipronged. On one hand it is a sociopolitical agenda of the middle layers of society out to undo their social insecurity by asserting the pre-modern patriarchal values which cater to their ambitions, on the other they manifest in the form of a onslaught which utilises multiple forms of programmes to appeal to broad sections of society. This peculiar problem of post-colonial societies is manifesting the features of 'clerical fascism', i.e., having the features both from fascist and fundamentalist offensives. Unlike the fascism of Europe, this onslaught grows slowly, infects the social ethos in a chronic fashion and strangles the liberal ethos of society in due course of time. It has some added features like restoring the pre-modern patriarchal values at a deeper level, i.e., at the level of culture. "That Hindu communalism is bidding for political power is too obvious to be stated. Its perspective of power, however, is not confined to electoral success. Electoral success is envisaged as the end-product of social acceptance of its cultural and ideological hegemony" (Panikker : 1997 : 91). Hindu communalism has experimented with various religious cultural symbols and finally has succeeded in getting some of its symbols popularly accepted and also sinking them in the emotive psyche of the society.

The response to the communalisation of society has come up in the form of coming up of various groups with secular programmes aimed at the level of a dessimination of secular ideas aimed at combating communal ideology. Ekta Samiti is a good example of this which since 1987 has been engaged in meaningful symbolic activities. Also Non-Government Organisations like Centre for study of society and secularism and INSAF (Indian National Social Action Forum) have been engaged in publication work and have been organising multiple seminars regularly to deepen the anti-communal ideas at a deeper level. Also another significant activity has been the publication of Communalism Combat (popular level) and Indian Journal of Secularism (scholarly, aimed at intellectuals). There have been many other projects like KHOJ, interacting with school children to remove their communal biases, and initiatives like Pakistan-India Peoples' Forum targetted to remove the mutual misconceptions and hatred amongst the sections of two countries.

Where does one go from here ? Is this response adequate enough to fight a cultural, social, political force which is knocking at the door of power and, once in power its semi-concealed poisonous fangs will be capable enough to strangle-hold the democracy and liberalism for a long time to come.

More needs to be done to be able to take on the might of this monster of 'Religious Nationalism'. The measures described earlier are a very good beginning, but surely they are just the beginning. A long term political-cultural-social programme of agitational movement is to be thought of to be able to overcome the dark clouds of communal politics.

How can this agitational movement be built up? Which social groups will feel the need to make this as their short-term and long-term goal ? If more than one, why should these groups come together? This struggle of taking on the 'clerical fascism', is also going to be the struggle to secularise the Indian Society. "Any struggle for secularising Indian life has two objectives : the struggle to defend and deepen the secular character of Indian state today under seige ; the struggle to secularise civil society. The first struggle requires aggressive propoganda on the need to sustain a basic separation of religious influence from governance to preserve and deepen democracy. It requires aggressive extra-parliamentry mobilisation against specific campaigns launched by Hindu communalists and if need be, extra-legal defence against the perpetrators of communal violence and bullying" (Vanaik : 1996 : 335).

The main victims of SP onslaught are the minorities (Muslims in particular), dalits, women and workers. But from distance these don't appear to be that obvious as SP is 'clever' enough to conceal its hard punch under the velvet gloves. It is clever enough to try to coop them, win over a section of them by different mechanisms.

At superficial level there does not seem to be anything common between these diverse groups. So how can they come together to form a 'Secular democratic' platform which gives them enough space to struggle for their rights ? Rohini P.H. (Mimiographed: 1996) perceives the question in its depth, "The saffron parties have exploited this complexity with a great deal of skill and sophistication. For millions of people with insecure jobs in the unorganised sector, or no employment at all, the promise of self-employment through ownership of an autorickshaw or a paan stall could be enough reason to be committed supporters of Hindu communal party. For dalits the lure of political power or elevation of status could lead to compromises. For women subordination in a male dominated movement could be accompanied by the possibility of engaging in activities which widen their scope of influence outside the family. All of these workers, dalit and women could gain ephemeral 'empowerment' from participations, actively or passively, in communal violence, and more stable satisfaction from feeling of superiority over a persecuted minority... minorities are themselves divided into different religious groups who do not necessarily identify with one another... Internal stratification (amongst these groups) means that those who are in a privileged position within-these communities are more anxious to cling to those privileges than to fight against the oppression of the communities as a whole". Rohini goes on to opine, "the only way to build a common platform which will accommodate these diverse groups is to work for a consensus which is opposed to oppression in all its multiple form".

It is undoubtedly true that these movements of minorities; dalits, informal sector workers and women are scattered and isolated from each other. These movement's combined assertion is the only force which can confront the communal attack on the society. Time is over try to explore the possibilities of drawing out the common issues across these movements which can bring them together on the basis of issues. This process is a process of a 'Social experimentation', a process of learning through social struggles, a process of bringing out the common threat of communal politics which affects them in common irrespective of their social location. Thus, secular movement has to grapple with forms of activity like community work, organising the informal sector, giving economic content to caste struggles and defining and developing the movements against gender injustice.

The social struggles cannot go on in a void. They are necessarily to be accompanied by disseminations of secular values and cultural ethos. "What is immediately required is an all-out effort to expand the secular cultural space. This can be achieved only through a vigorous movement striving for secular ethos through cultural endeavour, contending with seeking to replace the fast advancing communal ethos. The movement should aim to organise, on a large scale, an institutional infrastructure of newspapers, audiovisual production centres, theatre groups, music societies, local history associations, publishing houses, environmental groups, literacy activity and so on"(Panikkar, 1997 : 100).

Conclusion

The communal threat has awakened the progressive, liberal and left movement of the country to adopt newer strategies to take on this monster. Since the political movement did not anticipate the vicious intensity of communalisation of society and the consequent increase in the electoral strength of BJP and social impact of Sangh Parivar, in a way it has been caught napping. The 'first aid' measures of temporary coalitions can not confront the aggression of communal politics for long time. A series of steps leading to emergence of secular Democratic platform which draws out the common programme leading to egalitarian society respecting the democratic rights of oppressed sections of society and practising the secular ethos needs to be undertaken. The struggles and campaigns have to be aided by number of cultural initiatives in different arenas of life to de-weed the society from the influx of poisonous seed sowed by religious nationalism, in Indian context, the Hindu Nationalism. The venom of Hindu Rashtra agenda from popular psyche needs to be eliminated and the humane values of mutual respect for 'others' life and culture, secular ethos and liberal space has to be brought in by engaging in struggles at different levels of social and political life.

References

1. Achin Vanaik, 'Situating the threat of Hindu Nationalism', EPW, July 9, 1994, pp. 1729-1748.
2. P.R. Ram, 'Hindutva offensive : Social Roots and characterisation', Towards Secular India, No. 4, 1996, pp. 18-42.
3. Achin Vanaik, 'Contesting Communalism', Sage, New Delhi, 1997, p. 153.
4. Thararnangalam Joseph, 'Indian Social Scientists and Critique of Secularism, EPW, March 4, 1995, pp. 457-459.
5. Madan, T.N. (1987) 'Secularism in its Place', 'Journal of Asian Studies, Vol. 46, No. 4.
6. Uday Mehta (1997), 'Problem of Crisis of Indian Secularism', Indian Journal of Secularism, CSSS, Vol. 1, No. 1, p. 86.
7. M.N. Srinivas, 'The Times of India, Bangalore', July 9, 1993.
8. Rajeev Bhargava, 'Giving Secularism its Due', EPW, July 9, 1994, p. 1785.
9. Bilgrami, Akeel, 'Secularism, Nationalism and Modernity', RGICS, 1995, p. 6.
10. Rajeev Bhargava, 'How not to defend secularism', in "Religion, Religiosity and State" (Eds. Bidwai, Mukhia and Vanaik), Manohar, 1996.)
11. K.N. Panikkar, 'Communal Threat : Secular Challenge', Earthworm, Madras, 1997.

12. Rudolf C. Heredia, Edward Mathais, 'Secularism and liberation', Indian Social Institute, New Delhi, 1995.
13. Achin Vanaik, 'Contesting Communalism', Sage, New Delhi, 1996.
14. Gail Omvedt, 'Dalit Visions', Orient Longman, New Delhi, 1995.
15. Anadhi, S., 'Contending Identities', Indian Social Institute, New Delhi, 1985.
16. Aijaz Ahmed, 'In the Eye of the Storm', EPW, June 1, 1996.
17. K.N. Panikkar, 'Communal Threat : Secular Challenge', Earthworm, Madras, 1997.
18. Rohini, P.H., 'Overcoming the Fragmentation of Secular Forces', Mimiographed, 1996.

Index

D

E

F

G

M